LIGHT-HORSE HARRY

By Noel B. Gerson

Nonfiction

Fiction

Light-Horse Harry

A Biography of Washington's Great Cavalryman,
GENERAL HENRY LEE

By NOEL B. GERSON

DOUBLEDAY & COMPANY, INC.
GARDEN CITY, NEW YORK
1966

FRONTISPIECE: Major General Henry Lee ("Light-Horse Harry")
From the painting by C. W. Peale
(INDEPENDENCE NATIONAL HISTORICAL PARK COLLECTION)

Library of Congress Catalog Card Number 66–17424
Copyright © 1966 by Noel B. Gerson
All Rights Reserved
Printed in the United States of America

For
George Shively

TABLE OF CONTENTS

If you ride a horse, sit close and tight,
If you ride a man, sit easy and light.
BENJAMIN FRANKLIN

I

THE PRINCELING

The rumor was baseless, totally without foundation and slightly absurd. Nevertheless, many of Henry Lee's contemporaries believed it, and he himself frequently behaved as though he, too, accepted it as Gospel truth.

It was said that he came into the world booted and spurred, his spurs made of the purest hand-hammered silver, twirling his saber over his head and shouting, "Charge the bastards! Ride them down, boys!"

Fact is less romantic than fiction. On January 29, 1756, during a hailstorm, Lucy Grymes Lee, the most celebrated beauty in the colony of Virginia and once the unrequited object of George Washington's love, presented her husband with their second child and first son. The place was an imposing brick house, Leesylvania, the principal building on an estate of thirty-five hundred acres in Prince William County a few miles from the little town of Dumfries.

The exhausted Mrs. Lee, who had undergone a brief but painful labor, wept when her clergyman, the Reverend William Preston, informed her that the baby would live and was a remarkably healthy specimen. Her ten-month-old daughter, a sickly infant, had died only a few weeks earlier.

The child's enigmatic father, Henry Lee, Jr., who had spent his entire life in the shadow of his two energetic brothers and his dashing father, "Dragoon Harry," reacted in characteristic fashion. He announced the news to the household staff of twenty to thirty servants, directed that each be given two pounds of boiled bacon, and then retired to his library, where he recorded the event in the family Bible while drinking a stiff tankard of mulled rum.

Not until the afternoon of the following day did he pay a brief visit to his wife, but he compensated for his tardiness, or so he thought, by presenting her with a half-bolt of linen imported from England that she had admired. In the meantime he had written three letters of inquiry regarding a suitable tutor for his son, painstakingly drawn a sketch of a saddle he wanted made for the boy and paid a visit to his extensive stables, where he selected a foal which, he informed his chief groom, he intended to train himself as a mount for the child.

Before the day ended he sent short notes to his brothers, telling them of the birth of "Mrs. Lee's son, Henry." Aside from these few distractions he refused to alter his daily routines, and although he offered the hospitality of his manor to relatives and friends in a manner befitting a colonial squire, he left their entertainment to his wife, preferring to ride alone across his acres or barricade himself behind a copy of Aristotle's *Politics* in his library.

Charming ladies and handsomely attired gentlemen came to Leesylvania in a steady, daily stream, of course, as both husband and wife were related to the most distinguished families of northern Virginia. The Fairfaxes and Blands and Tyloes came to pay their respects to the proud mother and retiring father, and so did the Wormeleys, Corbins, Turbervilles, and Ludwells, not to mention all the Lees. Almost all were great landowners, and together they comprised the nearest thing to an aristocracy in the Virginia that swore allegiance to His Britannic Majesty, George II.

The excitement soon subsided, childbirth being commonplace in the Lee family. Lucy bought two competent slaves at the market in Alexandria to take care of the hour-by-hour rearing of her son, and busied herself with the supervision of her household. Her task was formidable, as her staff included a cobbler, tailor, and dressmaker, a part-time herb mixer who also painted rooms when otherwise unoccupied and a carpenter whose chests of oak, chestnut, and cherry were the envy of the county. She made frequent trips to Alexandria and Dumfries to buy foods that weren't grown on the estate, and habitually spent several hours in the kitchen outbuildings every day supervising the smoking of meats and fish and the preserving of boiled vegetables and fruits.

Henry Lee, Jr. led an even busier life. His tobacco and corn fields were among the most productive in the colony, thanks to the personal care he lavished on his crops. He was required to make frequent journeys to the capital, Williamsburg, too, as he was one of Prince William County's two representatives in the colonial legislature, the House of Burgesses, where he served faithfully, doggedly, and without distinction for many terms. He considered it his duty to sit there, and apparently it did not occur to his constituents to elect someone more vigorous and incisive in his place. Electors and elected knew what was expected of them, and acted accordingly.

It was natural that Henry, Jr. should also serve as a justice of the peace and Royal Lieutenant for the county. A Lee accepted such obligations as part of his heritage. Within the family, however, it was freely if discreetly admitted that he was not the most brilliant of men. Although he enjoyed reading, he confined himself to the classics, and seldom joined in literary discussions. Like so many others, he resented the Crown's refusal to grant greater rights of self-government to England's North American colonies, but rarely contributed more than a hearty, "I agree!" when the subject of politics was raised at social gatherings.

Lucy Lee had no intellectual pretensions whatever, and even if she had wanted to exercise her mind, it was doubtful that she could have found the time. Annually, for six years after the birth of her first son, she brought another little Lee into the world. But she remained pretty, sweet, and so cheerful that she unfailingly amazed her closest friend, the childless Martha Washington, with whose husband Henry, Jr. frequently went riding after a late and leisurely breakfast.

No one expected much of young Henry, who was overshadowed by brilliant, older cousins who were already making colony-wide reputations for themselves when he was a small boy. There was Richard Henry Lee, already a renowned orator and statesman at the time of young Henry's birth. Richard Henry's brother, William, who also loved Virginia, had temporarily settled in London, where he was becoming wealthy as a merchant. Another of Richard Henry's brothers, Arthur, had been unable to decide whether he wanted to be a lawyer or a physician, and had shown so much promise in both fields that, after studying in England, he came home to practice both medicine and law.

Henry, the quiet son of a quiet father, attracted little notice in his childhood. Relatives agreed that the boy had a natural talent for handling a horse, to be sure. He had learned to ride at the age of three or four, perhaps earlier, and when he was only eight he alarmed his father's good friend, Colonel Washington, by leaping onto the back of a stallion one morning and cantering off gaily.

He showed an unexpected aptitude for letters, too. The first to realize it was the Reverend Preston, the Anglican clergyman who had married his parents. Paying a visit to Leesylvania in 1762, Preston was startled when the six-year-old boy greeted him in faultless Latin. The following year the child expressed a desire to learn French, but his request was considered unpatriotic, as Virginia was unable to forget the humiliating and costly raids made on the colony's western outposts during the earlier days of the devastating French and Indian War.

Certainly Henry Lee became accustomed to luxury from earliest childhood. On cold mornings a slave lighted a fire in his chamber before he climbed out of his feather bed, another brought him a mug of hot tea and a third helped him dress. He ate off fine plate with knives and forks of heavy silver, wore shirts of superbly woven lawn, and accepted the homage of tradesmen as his due. A tutor, two cousins, and an uncle taught him to fence, his father made him familiar with both pistols and the long frontier rifles that were so much more popular in the colonies than cumbersome English muskets, and when he was ten he owned three horses, two geldings and a mare. At twelve he had acquired a library of his own, consisting of more than sixty books, at least ten of them in Latin.

By the time he was fourteen years old, the daughters of neighbors thought Henry strikingly handsome. He was tall, and still growing, eventually reaching a height of five feet nine, which was considerable in the eighteenth century. He had inherited his mother's fair hair, which he wore long, fastening it at the nape of his neck with an eelskin. His eyes were blue, rather piercing and alert, and he seemed to be the only member of his immediate family endowed with an ironic sense of humor. Already husky, he was growing still more muscular, and a quick, sometimes uncontrollable temper, his worst character trait, caused other boys to weigh their words in his presence.

At fourteen Henry embarked on the first independent venture of his life. Accompanied by the son of family friends, James Madison of Orange, and his own brother, Charles, who was only thirteen, he set out for the College of New Jersey, an institution of higher learning located in the town of Princeton that members of the Virginia aristocracy considered the equal of Harvard and Yale. The three boys, traveling on horseback by slow stages, made the journey in ten days, and found themselves in a strange, Spartan, and awe-inspiring world.

The college had one building, Nassau Hall, where one hundred students from the thirteen colonies slept and ate, studied and worshiped. Only the sons of the wealthy could afford the education offered at Princeton, for the total annual fee, which included the washing of clothes and bedlinen, wood for fires and assistance rendered young gentlemen by servants, as well as tuition, room, and board, was a stunning twenty-five pounds and six shillings.

Henry and his colleagues were fortunate youths. The Reverend Dr. John Witherspoon was the president of the College of New Jersey, and no eighteenth-century educator in the colonies—or in England, for that matter—was more ambitious or enlightened. A strict disciplinarian, a Scotsman who loved Edinburgh only a shade less passionately than he did the New World, Witherspoon was a farsighted, dedicated man. Believing college curriculums too limited in scope, he had added courses in debating, literature, and science to the school's program in 1768. Courses in Hebrew and Greek were obligatory, and in 1770 a course in French was also added.

Aware of the tendency of young men to band together, he encouraged the formation of undergraduate societies, to which he granted special privileges. When a student broke one of his many rules, however, he was swift in inflicting punishment. A rebellious undergraduate received only one warning; when he erred a second time, he was expelled, and sent home in permanent disgrace.

Daily life at the school was rigorous. Dr. Witherspoon himself walked through the corridors at five o'clock every morning, clanging a large bell, and was followed by a corps of servants who

literally threw out of bed those undergraduates too sleepy to respond to the president's summons.

At 5:30 A.M. faculty and students gathered in the chapel for
a half-hour of prayer and a crisp sermon. At six o'clock, spiritually
refreshed, the students marched in order of seniority into the
library for two hours of reading in philosophy, history, meta-
physical science, the principles of public law and the "canons of
criticism and taste." More often than not, there were also original
literary compositions to write.

The doors of the dining hall were opened at eight, and the
ravenous young men broke their fast with a light breakfast of
either grilled meat or fish, washed down with coffee or tea. Food
and drink were secondary, however, as tutors spent an hour cross-
examining the undergraduates on their previous day's labors.

Formal classes began at nine, and for the next four hours the
students took notes at formal lectures. Attendance was compulsory,
and sleeping in class was strictly forbidden. The undergraduates
were required to maintain a respectful silence at all times, and
only seniors were granted the privileges of wearing hats and taking snuff in class.

At one o'clock Dr. Witherspoon again rang a bell that signaled
the most welcome respite of the day. The students trooped back
into the dining hall for a hearty meal of soup, fish, meat, vegetables, and the sour fruit tarts which Witherspoon enjoyed more
than all other food. "To this day," Madison wrote during his
second term as President of the United States, "the mere sight of
a fruit cutlet sends a shudder up my spine."

No one dared to question Dr. Witherspoon's personally dictated
menus, and teen-aged boys were usually so hungry they ate anything placed before them. "I found dinner tolerably good," Henry
Lee wrote in later years. "Breads, gravies, and potatoes were always in plentiful supply, and only rarely were we unable to obtain
a third helping of meat."

Small beer and hard cider were available in pewter pitchers
on every table at dinner, and the lordly seniors, who sat a table
of their own, were allowed to drink ale and mead, too, if they
paid for it out of their own pockets.

All classes were allowed the luxury of free time until three in
the afternoon. The diligent studied or discussed their current work,
and the lazy who retired to their own rooms for naps were soon

chagrined to discover that if they did not mend their ways they would fail. Witherspoon was a perfectionist who allowed the slimmest margins of error.

Lectures were resumed for two hours at three o'clock, when there was another pause for prayers and a light snack of buttered bread and hot chocolate. Princeton students were expected to be young gentlemen, and at six everyone retired to his room to dress for the evening in tailcoat and silk stock, satin breeches, white stockings, and silver-buckled shoes. The wearing of powdered wigs was not mandatory, but no self-respecting undergraduate thought of appearing without one. Those old enough to need a razor also shaved, and at six-thirty the entire undergraduate body convened in the assembly hall to hear another sermon.

At seven the students went to their rooms, and thereafter the tutors constantly roamed the corridors to make certain that every undergraduate was studying at his work desk. At eleven o'clock the indefatigable Witherspoon rang his bell for the last time, and all candles were extinguished, the young men undressing in the dark.

The routines were relaxed on Saturday afternoons, when students went for rides or walks in the countryside. On Sundays chapel services were held at eleven in the morning, and at six on Sunday evenings the undergraduate societies held their own meetings, which featured the singing of psalms, the recitation of prayers and the delivery of sermons by students themselves. Only illness, certified by a physician and approved by Witherspoon himself, excused a student from any day's routine.

The moral tone of the undergraduate body was remarkably high, and the standards were those of a theological seminary. Under no circumstances were females admitted to Nassau Hall, and it was considered bad form for anyone who had an affair with a girl in the town of Princeton or elsewhere to boast of his amatory exploits. Gaming, cock fighting, and the drinking of distilled liquor were forbidden on penalty of instant expulsion. Anyone who cursed or used "foul, vulgar, and impure language" was subjected to a private lecture in Dr. Witherspoon's office. Students who engaged in fist fights with each other or outsiders were caned by the president in a public ceremony before being placed on suspension, and those who committed "moral wrongs" were expected to stand up before the entire student body at special meetings held at three o'clock every Sunday afternoon and confess their sins.

Healthy young men needed outlets for their energies, however, and Saturday evenings were devoted to convivial gatherings at which popular songs were sung and the musically talented played flutes and guitars. Practical joking was common, too. On cold winter nights Dr. Witherspoon's hated bell frequently disappeared, and when he found it at dawn, its clapper was frozen in a solid block of ice. New students were awakened by explosions of gunpowder in their rooms, and the undergraduate outhouse was burned to the ground with monotonous regularity. Raids on the brothels of Princeton were common, and any student who stole a bawd's corset, stockings, or shift was considered the hero of the hour by his peers.

The good citizens of Princeton complained that their chickens, ducks, and geese frequently disappeared, but their charges were never proved, even though the scent of roasted fowl was often strong in the hearths of the students' rooms. Underpaid tutors, some of them recent graduates, were happy to close their eyes and accept a succulent bribe. Feathers from the same mysterious sources were also put to use. Dripping with grease, they were hurled by the bucketload into the rooms of unpopular students.

Late in Henry's freshman year a major scandal erupted when Dr. Witherspoon discovered several ingeniously contrived telescopes in sleeping quarters located on the top floor of Nassau Hall. Looking through them, he was shocked to discover they were trained on the bedchamber of an attractive young woman in the neighborhood. The penalty was a particularly long and depressing sermon, but no one was expelled because, as Henry wrote to a friend in Prince William County, "nearly the whole of my class, which is housed on that floor, is involved."

The student body during Henry's undergraduate days was a remarkable group. Madison, a prodigious worker, saw little of his fellows, but he and Henry were on friendly terms. Mercurial Aaron Burr and Henry were close, and another friend was Philip Freneau, who later became known as the "Poet of the American Revolution" and one of America's first distinguished men of letters. Oddly, still another colleague, Hugh H. Brackenridge, was destined to become a leader of the Whisky Rebellion a quarter of a century later, an insurrection that General Harry Lee would smash on President Washington's orders.

Until young Lee went to the College of New Jersey, he was always known as Henry, but his classmates soon dubbed him Harry, and from that time until the end of his days his formal Christian name appeared only on legal documents. The newcomer threw himself into the school's many activities with unprecedented zeal. It was customary for freshman to apply for admission to either the debating or literary society, and inasmuch as each took up a great deal of precious time, virtually no one wanted to be a member of both. Harry Lee was one of a tiny handful of students in the entire history of the college who applied to both, and was promptly granted membership in both.

His social society, which he also joined in his first year, was the Cliosophic, a group interested in legal philosophy. Encouraged by the large Lee clan, he mistakenly believed he would become an attorney. The following year, however, his real interests became evident when he transferred his allegiance to a new organization founded by Madison and Freneau. This group, known initially as the Plain Dealers, wrote political satire for its own amusement and, at a time when the political and economic conflict between Great Britain and her North American colonies was becoming sharper, it was inevitable that the Plain Dealers should devote their thought and energies to that dispute.

The issues were so clearly drawn within the next twelve months that the society changed its name to the American Whigs, and its members boldly advocated complete independence for the colonies, echoing Sam Adams of Boston and, technically, branding themselves as traitors to the Crown. The rules of the school required them to renew their oath of allegiance to His Majesty every morning, and they paid their lip service glibly, their real attitude encouraged by the silence of Dr. Witherspoon, who was himself becoming increasingly sympathetic to the cause of American freedom.

Charles Lee found it difficult to adjust to the environment and regimen of the school, but Harry was in his element from the day he first arrived at Princeton. He roared with laughter when a charge of gunpowder was exploded in the room he shared with Charles, and was scornful when his brother was reduced to tears. Calmly rounding up other victims of the practical joke,

Harry and his new friends returned the compliment twenty-four hours later, placing still larger charges in the rooms of the perpetrators.

Freshmen were expected to behave meekly, and several upper classmen threw him and two other freshmen into Stony Brook in order to teach them their proper place. Refusing to be cowed, Harry and his cohorts bound and gagged two of the ringleaders, then dumped them in the undergraduate outhouse, where they were found some hours later. The prank could have caused serious trouble for Harry and his friends, but the older boys grudgingly admired their courage and said nothing of the incident to the authorities.

Dr. Witherspoon's charges had few opportunities for such rough games, however. A student worked hard or was dropped, and Harry soon proved himself an able scholar. Latin was still his first love, and he developed a passion for legal and military history. He wrote long essays on Solon and Lycurgus during his second year at the college.

Significantly, he studied the strategy and tactics of various great generals for his own amusement and edification. Hannibal, he wrote in his notebooks, was the greatest general in all history, and he drew countless sketches of the evasive tactics that had enabled the Carthaginian to fool the leaders of the formidable Roman legions he defeated.

Harry also developed an admiration for Epaminondas of Thebes, a Greek general who had developed new methods of deploying cavalry on his flanks in battle and, subsequently, proved his theories so effectively that he changed the whole nature of warfare. Aristides of Athens, another ancient Greek, a firm believer in democracy who used cavalry in unorthodox ways to support infantry, was one of Harry's idols, too, and a treatise he wrote on the subject won him a rare "Well done" from Dr. Witherspoon before the entire student body.

Anti-British feeling flared higher during Harry Lee's sophomore year, and he became a leader of a patriotic movement of a somewhat questionable and thoroughly undemocratic nature. Merchants in every colony were being urged to boycott England and refuse to buy British-made goods, but the storekeepers, reluctant to lose their profits, were slow to respond to the demands made on them. There were only a few merchants in the little town of

Princeton, but they, like their colleagues elsewhere, couldn't understand why they alone should take a financial beating.

Forty students, parading to the rhythms of a fife and drum corps, marched through the streets of the town, halted in front of each store and shouted anti-British slogans in unison. The merchants, afraid that their shops might be burned and sacked by unruly undergraduates, were duly intimidated and stopped buying English wares.

"I can recall no other incident in my past," Harry wrote many years later, "that fills me with such shame. I preached the virtues of law and order and sang the praises of democratic government, but I was guilty of the grossest violation of the principles I claimed I loved. Terror and the threat of force are inexcusable, regardless of whether the majority make its will obeyed by a minority, or a minority impose its dictum on the majority. Would that I could hide behind the façade of callowness, but I cannot. Alas, although I was but fifteen, I knew better."

Studies continued to claim the better part of Harry Lee's time, and when his sophomore year ended after a week of back-breaking written examinations, he won third prize in Greek and in Latin, and first in translating English into Latin. His record, for a sophomore, was remarkable, and Aaron Burr, who stood one class ahead of him and won still higher honors, predicted a brilliant future for his friend.

Harry and Charles went home for their first vacation in two years, and although the growing threat of war between England and her colonies had cast a pall over Virginia, the mansion in Prince William County was the scene of several lively parties during the six weeks that the two brothers were on holiday. Harry proved himself a sophisticate worthy of the Lee name, dazzling girls with his courtly manners and smile, and cutting a dashing figure in his powdered wig and superbly tailored suits of pure silk.

But, unlike most college undergraduates on vacation, he had more on his mind than girls. He broke in a new stallion that no one else had been able to ride, he spent hours in the saddle every day, and he alarmed his bewildered family by retiring to his own room most evenings to read the works of Alexander Pope. One goal he set for himself was a line-by-line comparison of Pope's translation of the *Iliad* with Homer's original, and he completed the task handily, boring the other Lees by talking of nothing else at the dinner table, where he ate prodigiously.

"*Our Henry,*" a troubled Lucy Lee confided in a note to Martha Washington, "*behaves in a manner so unpredictable that I know not from one day to the next what he will do. He seldom speaks of the law, but is firm in his intent to practice before the bar. Yet he speaks so much of English poets that I sometimes wonder if good Dr. Witherspoon will make him into a college president, no true vocation for a man of wit.*"

Harry paid a visit to the Washingtons at their Mount Vernon estate, and the colonel, although preoccupied with the angry Anglo-colonial quarrel that grew more intense each day, found time to take the youth on an inspection of his estate. The boy's father accompanied them, and Henry, Jr. later had good cause to boast, "The colonel tells me that no man sits a saddle more firmly or has a sounder leg and more delicate touch than our eldest. For this we give gratitude to the Almighty Lord, the lad otherwise caring little for the pursuits so dear to young bloods."

The principal cause of paternal concern, perhaps, was Harry's indifference to the brothels of Alexandria, which Charles sometimes visited with other gallants of the neighborhood. Harry, at sixteen, had not yet really sparked to the opposite sex.

In September 1772 the brothers returned to Princeton for their final terms at the college, the last eleven months being equally divided between the junior and senior classes, the entire process of obtaining a bachelor's degree taking three years, in accordance with the English system of education universally observed in the colonies.

Literature remained Harry's great passion during his junior term, and his enthusiasm for the works of Pope was undiminished. He wrote a long paper proving—to his own satisfaction—that Pope was far more talented than John Milton and Ben Jonson. He dismissed Shakespeare in a single, faintly contemptuous paragraph, calling him a "scribbler of verse who tries with little success to imitate the ancients; he lacks the grandeur of Sophocles and the power of Aeschylus."

Dr. Witherspoon, who considered Harry his brightest student in the upper classes, found nothing to criticize in the paper and invited the youth to attend his lectures on moral philosophy, the highest honor he could bestow on an undergraduate. As a senior

Harry also took courses in natural philosophy, natural science, and mathematics, and at the president's suggestion plunged into independent reading on the history of Anglo-Saxon law.

The future had been planned with care, and Harry thought he knew what was ahead. He would spend a month or two at home after his graduation, riding and resting. Then he would sail to England and take up residence with one of his many cousins in London, where he would spend one to two years as a law student and apprentice solicitor. For the sake of experience he might spend a year or two at the bar in London before returning home, but eventually he intended to take up practice in Virginia, where his family connections would assure him a substantial income.

But the continuing deterioration of relations between England and her colonies were making it increasingly unlikely that the youth of seventeen, who received his diploma from Dr. Witherspoon in August 1773, could carry out his scheme for the tidy future he had envisioned.

His kinsman, Richard Henry Lee, working with a bold and eccentric attorney named Patrick Henry, had been instrumental in forming Committees of Correspondence in each of the thirteen colonies. These groups exchanged letters in which ways and means of fighting the Mother Country's high-handed treatment of the colonies were discussed, refined and put into operation. Each new punitive measure designed by stubborn young King George III and his insensitive Prime Minister, Lord North, met with increasingly stiff and sullen resistance in America, where radicals like Sam Adams of Massachusetts exaggerated and fanned the flames of rebellion. Strained relations were being stretched toward a breaking point.

In Virginia the situation was unique. Elsewhere men of substance and social standing were doing their utmost to avoid an armed conflict, and only the wealthy merchant prince of Boston, John Hancock, was giving unqualified support to the radicals. In New York Town the rich were almost unanimous in their desire for a peaceful solution of the problem. Philadelphia, heeding the advice of America's most distinguished citizen, Benjamin Franklin, supported by banker Robert Morris, quietly insisted that armed conflict would be catastrophic.

The aristocrats of Virginia felt otherwise, and most of the great landowners and planters—many of them related to Harry—

were calmly but urgently insisting that the colonies should declare themselves free and independent. A tiny minority of wealthy lawyers and merchants remained fiercely loyal to the Crown, and virtually no one listened to moderates like Colonel Washington, who wanted to find some accommodation satisfactory to both sides.

Harry, already a prominent and active member of Jamie Madison's American Whigs at Princeton, needed no time for reflection. He admired Cousin Richard Henry, and agreed that if England refused to grant America's demands for greater self-government, the colonies would be compelled to go their own way, no matter what the cost.

The seventeen-year-old Bachelor of Arts expressed his views in no uncertain terms at the taverns of the neighborhood. One of his many cousins, George Lee, wrote that "No one proclaims his admiration for the Massachusetts Bay Sons of Liberty more loudly than does Harry. His arguments in their favor are based on literary and legal allusions which I find thin and unconvincing. It is enough that the Sons of Liberty exist and do what they must and should to further our cause. But Harry is already a lawyer by temperament. No step can be taken, no move made, no torch burned without ample precedent. If one listens long enough to Harry, Pope and Milton were writing of American freedom in their poems, which he recites in such solemn tones that I would laugh if I dared.

"No one laughs when Harry makes his recitations, for his temper is well known to all, and he has so perfected his skill with sword and pistol that I believe he would run through or shoot to death anyone who mocked him or the cause in which all of us believe.

"A Lee does not brawl with his fists in the gutter, but Harry creates in everyone the feeling that he would not hesitate to lower himself to such pastimes if in the mood. He is learned, but there is in him a wild and savage humor that neither the gracious living at Leesylvania nor his years at the College of New Jersey have tamed. M—— has said to me privately that she pities the girl Harry will some day marry, for he is certain to beat her if she disputes his word in any matter."

The unknown M—— was a poor judge of Harry's character. He displayed unflagging gallantry to the ladies throughout his life, and always treated them with consideration and gentle kindness. Cousin George was more perspicacious. There was a wild streak in Henry Lee, Jr.'s eldest son and heir that the growing war fever stirred to the boiling point.

For the first time in his life Harry confided in his father, confessing that he didn't know what to do. Parties at Leesylvania were pleasant affairs, and a young man could drift from one day to the next, waiting for events which he could not control to decide his future for him. But he already hated inactivity, and was unhappy, restless, and bored. On the other hand, he was less sure of his stand than his public remarks in the taverns of northern Virginia had indicated. The Lee family had always respected law and order, and open rebellion against the Crown was treason, justifiably punishable by hanging.

Arthur Lee was still in London, living as a prosperous and respected colonial, and so was William Lee. Harry had long looked forward to living with them while pursuing his studies. From a purely selfish standpoint, too, he could not obtain an education as a lawyer in Virginia on a level even remotely comparable with what he could learn in England.

The ever-cautious Henry, Jr. urged his son to do nothing for the present. With each passing month the inevitability of open revolt became greater, and the colony was thrilled as Patrick Henry, the leader of the Burgesses, edged closer and closer to a declaration of Virginia's independence.

Three times Harry engaged passage on a ship bound for London, and three times he canceled his reservation. He attended innumerable parties, played cards with other young men at supper parties and spent his days in the saddle, riding around his father's estate. Politics fascinated him, and he made several journeys to Williamsburg in order to watch the Burgesses in session from the visitors' gallery. He spoke vaguely of entering the political arena himself, but made no real attempt to seek office.

Events moved still more rapidly. Boston defied the Crown, and the port of Boston was closed. The Virginia Burgesses, prodded by Richard Henry Lee and Patrick Henry, defiantly passed a resolution sympathizing with the citizens of a sister colony. The authority of Lord Dunmore, Virginia's governor, had been challenged, and his lordship felt compelled to dissolve the Assembly. Young men began to drill in the towns and villages, and Lord

North, the British Prime Minister, was hanged in effigy in a dozen or more places.

It was beneath the dignity of a Lee to take part in such public spectacles, but Harry went off quietly to a patch of woods that stood on his father's property and practiced his marksmanship with both pistol and rifle. He wanted to brush up on his swordsmanship, too, but couldn't persuade Charles or Cousin George to cross blades with him. Left to his own devices, he was reduced to riding his stallion bareback, and spent hours each day slashing at targets suspended from the branches of trees.

The year 1775 was one of decision, and the nineteen-year-old youth knew now that he had to give up his dream of studying in London. His father was elected to the new House of Burgesses, but first sat as a member of the rump colonial parliament which solemnly threatened to break off all trade relations with England unless Virginia and her sisters were granted greater rights.

Cousin Richard Henry Lee had been a member of the First Continental Congress, sitting at Philadelphia, and had been prominent in the committee that had drawn up a list of grievances to be presented to the King, Prime Minister, and House of Commons. Patrick Henry made an international reputation for himself by demanding liberty or death in the most impassioned speech ever heard in the Burgesses. Even the levelheaded Colonel Washington, who frequently dined at Leesylvania with his lady, now believed that it might be necessary to fight for freedom.

Harry put up still more targets and, using a saber weighted with metal odds and ends in order to make the task more difficult, sliced and slashed and thrust while riding bareback at a full gallop. It is impossible to determine whether he sensed his destiny and deliberately, methodically made ready for it, or whether he was guided by blind instinct.

Several of his relatives commented in passing on his curious practice, making notations in their diaries or writing to other members of the clan. Harry himself made no mention of the subject in his *Memoirs* or elsewhere. Many years later his son, possibly the greatest of all geniuses in American military history, was also silent on the subject, even though he admired every phase of his father's career. Robert Edward Lee, like Light-Horse Harry, took it for granted that a fighting man made all necessary preparations when war became inevitable.

II

CAPTAIN OF CAVALRY

Skirmishes at Lexington and Concord in Massachusetts signaled the active outbreak of the American Revolution in the spring of 1775. Patriotic farmers and artisans by the thousands joined the new Regular Army, the Continentals, which the Congress authorized after electing Washington as commander-in-chief. Others enlisted in the militia of the different colonies, the majority cautiously agreeing to serve for no more than ninety days.

The British were determined to crush the insurrection, and a powerful fleet commanded by Admiral Lord Howe sailed for the New World to block the American coast and starve the rebels into submission. Meanwhile thousands of seasoned troops were sent south from Halifax, Nova Scotia, while other regiments were dispatched direct from England in troop transports. The War Office in London also hired some additional brigades of German mercenaries, considered by many to be the world's finest soldiers, and everyone except the beleaguered Americans considered the colonial cause hopeless.

Boston was already occupied by Redcoats, and New York, Philadelphia, and Charleston were threatened. But the Americans refused to admit they had no chance of winning. A column of ragged irregulars jointly commanded by the dashing Colonel Benedict Arnold of Connecticut and Colonel Ethan Allen of Massachusetts' Vermont District captured an important British post, Fort Ticonderoga, in New York. Continentals took Montreal, and Arnold led a corps against Quebec. The odds against him were enormous, and although his expedition was forced to retreat, he and his men—among them Harry's former college friend, Aaron Burr—demonstrated to the world that Americans could fight.

The odds against General Washington were overwhelming, and not the least of his problems was the inexperience of his senior officers. His chief of artillery was Henry Knox, a plump Boston bookseller who had studied war in the quiet of his library, but had enjoyed no significant field experience. General Nathanael Greene of Rhode Island was a member of the Society of Friends who gave up his religion because of his dedication to the American cause. Lord Stirling, one of America's few native-born peers, was a New Jersey man whose eagerness for battle was offset by a fondness for strong alcoholic spirits. General Philip Schuyler, a patrician New Yorker, was exceptionally able, but too old for active field service. The Congress placed its hopes in two British veterans, Horatio Gates and Charles Lee, but General Gates had too great a fondness for intrigue, and Lee, who was guilty of cowardice at best and treason at worst, never lived up to his promise.

Eventually Knox and Greene would establish enduring reputations, but most of the American leaders who would emerge from the war as major figures were inexperienced unknowns in 1775 and 1776. Certainly no one was more obscure than Harry Lee, whose lassitude in joining the colors seems inexplicable at first glance.

A firm believer in American liberty, a young man who had spent months arduously practicing for combat, he continued to loll in comfort at his parents' home. Why?

Paradoxically, in spite of his restless impatience, he was a Lee, and his own training at Princeton, combined with his family traditions, made it impossible for him to act until he believed it legally right for him to take up arms. The fledgling lawyer respected the proprieties, and insisted on observing them.

Early in 1776 it became obvious to everyone except a few lonely moderates on both sides of the Atlantic that a reconciliation could not be achieved. General Washington spoke openly of independence, and so did Richard Henry Lee.

The views of these middle-aged gentlemen, one a close family friend and the other a relative, convinced Harry that he should hesitate no longer, and he announced to his family that he intended to enlist in the Virginia militia as a private. His father, who had spent many weeks at Williamsburg and knew something of what was being planned, urged him to wait a few days longer.

Cousin Theodorick Bland came to Leesylvania for dinner, and quietly told twenty-year-old Harry that he intended to organize a regiment of cavalry to be known as the Virginia Light Dragoons. Harry enlisted on the spot, and became the first to join the unit. For the moment he was an ordinary trooper, holding the rank of private, but it was unthinkable that a Lee should be less than a commissioned officer. Harry may or may not have known that he would serve as a gentleman, but his father certainly had a private understanding with Cousin Theodorick and with Patrick Henry, who was the unanimous choice of the Burgesses for governor of the embryo state of Virginia.

Cousin Richard Henry Lee was an influential member of a Continental Congress committee that drew up a document called the Declaration of Independence. It was published in July 1776, and a new nation, the United States of America, came into being.

The last legal obstacle had been cleared away. Governor Patrick Henry created the Virginia Light Dragoons with the stroke of a quill pen, and appointed Theodorick Bland its colonel. Harry Lee, a total stranger to combat whose only knowledge of war came from his studies of the ancients, was immediately granted a commission as a captain and was given command of the Fifth Troop, which existed only on paper.

July and August were the most hectic months Harry had ever known. All militiamen enlisted as volunteers, and Colonel Bland felt confident that he could fill his ranks quickly. After all, there were thousands of Virginians who were accomplished horsemen. Captain Harry Lee of the Fifth Troop immediately requested— and received—permission to obtain his own men in his own way. From the moment he had been given his appointment, he had been determined to organize a band of cavalrymen that would be the equal of an elite regiment of infantry riflemen formed by a fellow Virginian, Colonel Dan Morgan.

Harry knew scores of people in the northern part of the state and everyone, of course, knew the Lee family. He rode from village to village and farm to farm, dazzling in his superb new uniform of blue-and-buff, the Continental colors, which he, a mere militiaman, actually had no right to wear. Unfortunately, the tailor on the Lee estate hadn't known any better, and there wasn't time for him to make another uniform.

Word spread from county to county that only the most accomplished and courageous horsemen would be accepted in the Fifth Troop, and Harry was inundated with applications. But he tested every potential member himself, leading the would-be cavalryman on a wild ride, and then turning suddenly to charge with drawn sword at his companion. Those unable to maintain his pace and those who flinched were politely told there was no vacancy in the Fifth Troop.

The formal but hastily drawn tables of organization specified that there would be four officers, twelve noncommissioned officers, and eighty-four men in each troop. But Harry soon discovered that military red tape was interfering with his ideal. He was unable to obtain the supplies he requisitioned from the overburdened regimental quartermaster, the ordnance officer gave him only a fraction of the gunpowder and bullets he needed and the regimental adjutant drove him to distraction with demands that he fill out forms in quadruplicate for each new recruit.

"*Hannibal,*" the irritated Harry wrote to his parents, "*would have been a miserable failure had he been hampered and badgered by so many incompetents who think themselves soldiers only if they imitate the pompous manners of the enemy.*"

The ranks of the Fifth Troop were closed when one lieutenant and two ensigns, nine noncommissioned officers, and seventy privates had been admitted. Harry had waited long enough for action, and the addition of each new recruit presented him with more paperwork headaches than he wanted.

General Washington's corps of Continentals and militia was mustering on Long Island to meet the British army commanded by General William Howe, who had replaced General Thomas Gage after the Redcoats had evacuated Boston. The young commander of Dragoons assumed that the regiment would ride north to join in the battle that was looming, but fresh disappointments and delays were in store. Only a few weeks earlier the enemy had been repulsed at Charleston, and a great many leaders of the Burgesses were afraid that the Royal Navy might try to stage a landing somewhere on the Virginia coast, too.

Inasmuch as few of the new units were yet ready for combat

outside the state, the Assemblymen persuaded Governor Henry to keep all regiments other than those specifically requested by General Washington within the state boundaries. The governor agreed, thinking it likely that some of the more powerful Indian nations, who were being encouraged by the British, might raid the settlements in the western portion of the state.

Harry was confident that he and his troop would be permitted to ride north, and his junior officers started preparing for the journey when he went off to apply for the privilege. He tasted military discipline for the first time when his request was brusquely rejected. Colonel Bland showed him the governor's order, told him there was nothing to discuss and dismissed him. The humiliated captain returned to his own bivouac, fuming.

While the hard-pressed Washington was losing the Battle of Long Island and, subsequently, abandoning New York to General Howe, who was knighted by a grateful monarch for his victory, the Fifth Troop of Virginia Light Dragoons rode out on daily practice forays and waited in ill-tempered disgust for a foe that never appeared.

By any standard, the little unit was extraordinary, but no one outside the organization quite realized it. The lieutenant was Harry's age, twenty, and the two ensigns were eighteen and seventeen, respectively. The oldest man in the troop was the sergeant major, a graybeard of twenty-four. Many of the troopers were still in their late teens, and the youngest were twins of sixteen.

Everyone was completely at home in the saddle, and could ride bareback if necessary. Every trooper spent hours each day riding at full tilt and cutting down targets dangling from the branks of oaks. No one had to be taught that the care of horses was more important than the welfare of mere men, and the troopers, all of whom owned their own mounts, developed the spirit that has always been so essential to the success of any military organization.

Harry himself did not know it, but he was already demonstrating qualities of leadership that would soon win him enduring fame as the American Revolution's greatest cavalryman.

His opportunity came when word reached Williamsburg that Washington's poorly equipped, untrained rabble had been forced to evacuate New York on September 14–15, and that only the commander-in-chief's genius had permitted him to escape from Billy Howe with the better part of his force still intact.

The new United States faced its first great military crisis, and Patrick Henry unhesitatingly countermanded his previous order, instructing all regiments to release subordinate units ready and able to assist the general, who was beginning a slow, dogged retreat south through New Jersey. The governor wisely refrained from telling anyone that militia units were deserting at an alarming rate, and that each morning Washington's personal aides were dismayed to find that hundreds more had silently departed for their homes.

Three troops of the Light Dragoons were ready for service, the Second, Third, and Fifth, and Colonel Bland sent them north together, under the designation of the 1st Battalion. Harry Lee's Fifth was so anxious to see action that it far outstripped the pace set by the other troops on the first day's ride, and a messenger was sent ahead to order Captain Lee to wait.

Lee saw the courier on the road, suspected his mission and ordered the troop to ride still harder. Contact with the other units was lost, and from that time Harry operated independently, never serving either with his regiment or with its 1st Battalion. Neither then nor later did he accept any cavalryman as his immediate superior. In a better-organized army he might well have been court-martialed for his impudence, but the Continentals knew little discipline in the early years of the American Revolution and the militia virtually none. No unit was better or worse than its own commander, and the morale of the Fifth Troop was superb. Harry Lee eagerly sought glory, and his men thirsted for it with him.

The little unit looked crisp and smart, almost spectacular, funds from the Lee fortune having been spent freely for uniforms. The men wore narrow-brimmed hats, tunics and breeches of blue wool and calf-high boots into which they had tucked long-handled knives, an affectation they had copied from the frontiersmen of Virginia's Kentucky District. The officers were even more magnificent in burnished helmets with white-dyed horsehair plumes and short blue capes lined in buff-colored silk.

The residents of Maryland and Delaware villages gathered in the streets to gape at the sartorial splendor of the young warriors, and occasionally a small boy cheered. Adults, who knew of the debacle at New York, realized there was little cause for optimism, and militiamen who had deserted and returned to their homes sneered openly. A fist fight was narrowly averted at the little town of Dover, Delaware, when several veterans of the Battle of Long Island called the troopers "toy soldiers."

One morning early in October, Harry, who was riding at the head of the column, saw the ragged Continental vanguard in the distance, and an hour later he reported to General Washington, who had paused for an early mid-day meal at a farmhouse. The commander-in-chief was pleased to see the young man he had known for so many years, but gave him no instructions and seemed lost in thought.

Staff officers took Harry to another room, and after offering him a little bread and cold meat, explained the ugly facts of life to him. There was virtually no food in the quartermasters' wagons, the corps had lost almost all of its artillery, and supplies of lead and powder were dangerously short. The army was shrinking every day, and even the most devout patriots were willing to concede that the American cause was on the verge of being lost.

A large force of General Sir William Howe's Redcoats and German mercenaries remained close on Washington's heels, capturing one town after another as the corps retreated. But Sir William, who personally believed that a policy of conciliation would pay dividends, had chosen not to attack and destroy the enemy. His policy appeared sound, as further bloodletting seemed unnecessary. Each day he took more ground, each day scores of American civilians hastily decided to renew their allegiance to the Crown and each day Washington grew more feeble.

"We are so weak," said a mournful Henry Knox, whose artillery consisted of only a few battered cannon that might explode if fired, "that we are incapable of fighting. Howe holds us in the palm of his hand as a tomcat holds a trembling mouse."

No one gave the dashing young commander of Virginia's Fifth Troop orders of any kind. Presumably he was invited to join the retreat, if he wished.

Fresh shocks were in store. The cavalrymen had carried food for themselves and forage for their mounts on their journey, but now their supplies were exhausted—and the quartermasters could give them nothing to eat. The Fifth Troop was hungry, and Harry decided to take matters into his own hands. His funds were limited, so he was unable to buy food from the New Jersey farmers who were hiding sacks of grain and barrels of pickled beef in their cellars and barns. Washington had given strict orders prohibiting the "requisitioning" of food from fellow Americans, a policy with which the young gentleman from Virginia heartily agreed.

Harry had excelled in logic in his studies at college, and logic dictated his next move. The British who were following the corps had ample supplies of everything the Americans needed. Therefore he would take what he needed from the enemy.

The troop set out immediately, riding north and making a wide swing to the west in order to avoid the Redcoat cavalry and light infantry. The tactics Harry devised for his raid were simple. He knew that the British supply wagons followed the heavy infantry, and that only the mounted rear guard threatened his security. So he carefully scouted the position of the British horsemen before striking, riding forward with only a few of his men to observe the precise situation for himself.

He was delighted to find that the Redcoats, careless of their own security and refusing to believe that the Americans were capable of mounting even a primitive assault, had allowed a gap of a half-mile to develop between the last of the supply wagons and the first troop of rear-guard cavalry. The fact that his small band was outnumbered by at least ten to one seemed to cause him no concern.

Timing his attack with an instinct that was to prove almost infallible in the years ahead, he waited until dusk. The growing dark and the weariness of the enemy after a day's march were factors that helped his bold maneuver. Suddenly he and his troop swept out of the woods, each squad having been given a specific assignment. In less than five minutes the young Virginians had captured more than twenty wagons, and by the time the startled British quartermasters notified the cavalry regiment bringing up the rear, the Americans had vanished.

At midnight a triumphant Harry Lee, still fresh in the saddle, rode through the American lines with twenty-one wagonloads of supplies, not to mention the mules hauling the carts. He was chagrined because two other wagons had broken down, but his troopers had piled sacks of flour and bags of jerked beef onto their saddles, so little of the precious food had been left behind.

Washington's aides awakened the general to tell him the good news, and he offered the son of his old friends the warmest congratulations his austere nature permitted. The Fifth Troop enjoyed a feast before retiring in the open for a well-deserved night's rest, and the next morning the whole corps enjoyed a hearty meal. Less than fifty men deserted that day, which the adjutant general and his assistants considered almost as welcome as a victory over the enemy.

Seventy-two hours later Harry led his men on another, similar raid, and proved that his first success had not been accidental. He took seventeen wagons, most of them loaded with fresh beef, and that night Washington's corps dined in a style to which it had long been unaccustomed. In both ventures the Fifth Troop had escaped unharmed, and word of Harry Lee's prowess spread quickly through the army. His gaudy uniform had remained unspotted, and aside from a film of dust on his knee-high boots, he was none the worse for wear.

At some time during the slow, autumn-long retreat through New Jersey into Pennsylvania, the commander of the Fifth Troop acquired the name of Light-Horse Harry. The origin of the phrase is unknown, and its original author has never been identified. But grateful foot soldiers quickly developed great affection for the Virginian who magically produced food when they were hungry, and soon the whole army knew the identity of Light-Horse Harry.

The quantities of food he captured on a half-dozen lightning raids were insufficient for the needs of so many thousands of weary soldiers, of course, but his remarkable success did more to raise the flagging spirits of the defeated army than did the relatively meager quantity of supplies he brought back to headquarters. Here, at last, was an American capable of defying the British, someone who thumbed his nose at the Redcoats and escaped unpunished and unscathed.

"Captain Lee," wrote Alexander Hamilton, one of Washington's aides, "warms the blood of the footsore more than would casks of brandywine or rum."

Some of Harry's admirers on the commander-in-chief's staff claimed that his raids were at least partly responsible for the reduced rate of desertions, but their claims were, in all probability, exaggerated. The faint-hearted had already decamped, and those who remained were determined to stand by Washington until the bitter end. That end seemed close at hand, and after crossing the Delaware River into Pennsylvania in December, the dejected commander-in-chief wrote. "Ten days more will put an end to the existence of our army."

His forecast was overly pessimistic, but not even he could have correctly judged the stamina and courage of those who had chosen to cast their lot with him and the infant United States. No one displayed greater fortitude during this grim period than the blithe and debonair Harry Lee, who would soon celebrate his twenty-first birthday.

Harry had now reduced his raids to a carefully determined science, and his success was still phenomenal, almost uncanny. In all, he conducted fifteen known raids on the British, either in the field or on supply depots, between October and the end of December 1776. His only casualties were two troopers slightly wounded and one horse shot. The boy who had been fascinated by the tactics of ancient Greek and Roman generals had won his spurs as a man.

It is difficult, perhaps impossible, to analyze and evaluate Captain Henry Lee's record. He had never received formal military training, had never commanded men and had been completely lacking in field experience when he had accepted his commission from Patrick Henry and taken charge of the Fifth Troop. Yet he was beating seasoned professionals at their own game. The British were now keeping a sharp watch for him, and had acquired so much respect for his raiders that the guard had been doubled at all quartermaster posts and installations.

Speed, stealth, and thorough reconnaissance work were the keys to Harry's triumphs. His men were capable of moving swiftly, knew each other and their horses, and had developed a blind, unquestioning faith in the captain. They knew that, when he struck, he had already acquired a thorough knowledge of the enemy's strength and dispositions, and with each success their faith in him—and in themselves—grew greater. They were truly the elite, the pride of the miserable little army that had so little reason to boast about anything, and they were quick to accept the aura of invincibility that others attributed to them.

Above all else, Harry Lee appears to have been a natural-born soldier, a trait that he passed along to his even more renowned son, Robert Edward. Both knew precisely what to do in a moment of crisis, and how to do it. Robert E. Lee attended the United States Military Academy at West Point and gained experience in the Mexican War, but neither training nor experience can explain the rare genius he demonstrated at the apex of his great career. His father, completely untrained and totally lacking in experience, performed exploits that made him the darling of all America and Washington's personal favorite. A biographer, piecing together a man's personality and accomplishments from a distance of almost two centuries, can only agree that genius is inexplicable.

Not the least of Harry Lee's talents was his ability to handle his men. Praise quickly went to the heads of his strutting young cavalrymen, and the soldiers of other units, Continentals and militia alike, resented the heroes who had never fought in an actual battle, but had won glory by stealing food from the foe. Brawls broke out in the American camp, and when Harry discovered that his men had taken part in fist fights on two successive nights, he took quick action before he himself was reprimanded by higher authority.

He mustered the troop for an inspection and, making no mention of the fights, ordered his sergeant major to pass out thistles to every man—except the brawlers. Those who had not engaged in fisticuffs proudly wore their thistles in their hats. The others, envying them, thereafter kept the peace. This simple solution enabled Harry to restore order without resorting to harsh discipline that might have injured the morale of his troop.

In its way, it was the greatest of the minor miracles he had as yet performed. He—and the hard-bitten youngsters of the Fifth Troop—were now ready for the rugged campaigning that lay ahead.

III

THE GALLANT BAND

Whether circumstances and times produce the great heroes and villains of history, or whether genius creates an era, is a little like trying to decide which came first, the chicken or the egg. Could Napoleon Bonaparte have risen to supreme power had the French Revolution never taken place? Could Light-Horse Harry Lee's son, Robert E., have won enduring fame as a field marshal had there been no war between the American North and South? Such questions can be debated endlessly—and inconclusively.

There is little doubt, however, that the eighteenth century and the early years of the nineteenth saw horse cavalry achieve their greatest glory on the world's fields of battle. The horse was no stranger to war, to be sure, from earliest antiquity. It was apparent to the ancients as well as their descendants that a mounted man had a natural advantage over one who fought on his own two feet.

Persians used cavalry to great advantage, and so did the man who destroyed their mighty empire, Alexander the Great. The horse went out of military fashion during the centuries when the infantry phalanxes of Rome conquered the known world, but Genghis Khan and Attila the Hun subsequently demonstrated anew what a trained corps of riders could accomplish.

Knighthood restored the horse to his preeminent position in the Age of Chivalry, but not until England's Revolution in the seventeenth century did the dashing Royalist leader, Prince Rupert, reveal the true capabilities of power, thrust and mobility that a cavalry corps employed.

Horsemen tipped the scales in a majority of the battles fought in the War of the Spanish Succession, and the Duke of Marlborough's great ally and good friend, Prince Eugene of Savoy, a Frenchman who became Austria's field commander, helped bring Louis XIV to his knees and later saved Vienna from the Turks, developed the use of cavalry into a science.

Napoleon's brother-in-law, Joachim Murat, who enjoyed a very brief reign as King of Naples, was the striking arm of the French legions that conquered all Europe. And on this side of the Atlantic, a genial Tennessee giant, John Coffee, a superb and unsung cavalry hero, provided the margin of victory in most battles fought by his friend, neighbor, and relative by marriage, Andrew Jackson.

Perhaps it is not accidental, then, that the two most glamorous figures of the American Revolution, Light-Horse Harry Lee and his ever-implacable foe, Banastre Tarleton, were cavalrymen. They lived and fought in the heyday of the horse soldier, and made major contributions to the portrait of the cavalryman that has survived for almost two hundred years after they rode at full tilt leading charges that were wild, romantic, and required the utmost in personal courage and stamina.

The cavalryman continued to play a major role in war after his time, however, but the accurate, high-powered infantry and artillery weapons mass-produced during the Industrial Revolution doomed him to extinction. The military student took to heart the slaughter of Lord Cardigan's Light Brigade at Balaklava in the Crimean War in 1854, and Robert E. Lee, who preferred cavalry to every other branch of service, recognized the futility of the accomplishments of his great leader of horse, Jubal Early.

A relatively little-known function of cavalry, infinitely less glamorous than the battle charge but at least equal to it in importance, was that of engaging in reconnaissance missions. The science—or art—of scouting has always been delicate, hazardous and difficult. A reconnaissance leader is required to spy on the enemy, himself remaining unseen, if possible. He must learn the foe's size and troop dispositions, destination, and intentions.

Therefore he must be more than a scout who merely reports back to his own headquarters that he has located the whereabouts of the enemy. He needs to be a student of warfare, capable of studying and analyzing opposing forces. He is the eyes and ears of his commanding general, but he is also something of a prophet, with the touch of a soothsayer and soul of an oracle.

Light-Horse Harry Lee, from the outset of his astonishing career, was a brilliant scout, and his lack of military training makes his success all the more remarkable. His superior, George Washington, was one of the most complicated of human beings, a man who never showed favoritism, tried to be calm and objective in all his judgments and in his official life held himself aloof from his fellow men.

So Harry Lee, whom the general had known from birth, had a harder row to hoe than any other officer in the American Army. The fact that his parents were close friends of the Washingtons made him suspect in the general's eyes, and he had to work harder and accomplish more than anyone else to win a place for himself in his own right.

The young captain, not yet twenty-one years of age, quickly and confidently demonstrated his worth. By late December 1776 the tattered American forces, numbering approximately forty-five hundred men, were ready to give up the struggle for independence. Their cause appeared hopeless, and the commander-in-chief knew the only tonic that would rejuvenate them would be a victory. So he and his staff, quartered in Newtown, Pennsylvania, planned a daring project.

A large enemy force, made up in the main of German mercenaries, had made itself comfortable in winter quarters across the Delaware River in Trenton, New Jersey. Washington decided to attack them on Christmas night, when they would not be expecting an assault. First, however, he wanted to know more about their strength and dispositions.

Harry Lee had shown enough talent in his raids to be chosen for the scouting operation that was a necessary prelude to an attack. It was essential that he learn all he could, and imperative that he and his men avoid detection. If Americans should be seen snooping in the vicinity of the Hessian barracks, it would be obvious to the enemy that something was stirring.

Staff members made less than helpful suggestions. One thought the Fifth Troop should wear civilian clothes on its surveillance, but Washington himself vetoed the idea. Soldiers who were not wearing uniforms when on espionage missions were candidates for a firing squad or hangman's rope.

Another urged that the cavalrymen swim their horses across the Delaware, but Harry himself refused. The river was too broad, and the weather was so cold that men and horses would become ill.

He decided to use only a small part of his Troop for the assignment, and believed it wise that he, a junior officer, and fourteen of his best men be ferried across the Delaware five miles upstream, by barge. Everyone taking part in the expedition was sworn to secrecy, and the crossing was made on Christmas Eve.

The mission was so successful that, like all good reconnaissance operations, it was totally lacking in drama. The crossing was accomplished shortly before midnight in viciously cold weather. Civilians, farmers, and townsmen alike were at home behind locked doors, and the scouts neither saw nor spoke to anyone. They made a wide circle around the mercenaries' camp, staying far enough away not to arouse the sleepy, numbed sentries, and then returned to their waiting barges. They reached the American headquarters in Newtown around five o'clock on Christmas morning, and Harry made his report to Washington a few hours later, while the general ate his breakfast.

Washington thanked him courteously for the information, but offered him no praise. He had been given an assignment, which he had performed efficiently, as expected, and the commander-in-chief was not one to lavish words on subordinates who did their jobs. Harry must have indicated his disappointment to someone at headquarters, as Henry Knox commented, "I think Captain Lee's nose was nipped by the frost of his reception."

Another year would pass before the eager, glory-seeking young officer would understand the personality of his father's friend, who had always treated him with so much kindness and charm when the Lee family had visited Mount Vernon. Washington, in the field, was as icy as the frost on the windowpanes of his farmhouse headquarters.

An even greater disappointment shocked Light-Horse Harry that Christmas Day. There was no place for cavalry in the attack on the Hessians. The barges he had used the preceding night were too few and too cumbersome for the swift recrossing of the Delaware that Washington planned. So the Fifth Troop was left behind as part of the guard assigned to stand duty at the American camp, and the young horsemen fumed in impotent dismay while their infantry comrades conducted one of the most daring raids in American history, completely surprising the Hessians and taking one thousand prisoners.

Harry's sense of frustration was intensified by the fact that his own part in the operation was swallowed up by the greater glory of the triumph. Scouts, he discovered, remained virtually anonymous, and he had no passion for anonymity. However, he was given little time to brood.

Washington decided to follow up his victory with another strike, a new action having been made necessary because Billy Howe's able, tough subordinate, Lord Charles Cornwallis, had been sent into the field. The American commander knew of Cornwallis by reputation, and decided to clip the noble eagle's wings. A direct confrontation was out of the question, as the Americans, still short on supplies, lead, and powder, were badly outnumbered.

An unexpected thaw that melted ice on roads enabled the wily Washington to repeat the tactics he had employed at Trenton. The better part of Cornwallis' force was stationed at Princeton, his lordship having requisitioned the College of New Jersey as a barracks. Washington, experienced in Indian fighting, determined to hit where least expected.

On January 2, 1777, his corps of less than five thousand began the march toward Princeton. The cavalry vanguard was commanded by Colonel Thomas Rodney of the Delaware militia, and the bulk of horse troops were supplied by the Philadelphia Red Feathers, an elite regiment of light-horse. Harry Lee's Virginians were assigned to ride with the rest.

The American column was anything but awe-inspiring, and when a heavy, cold fog set in, Henry Knox, who was bringing up the rear, was heard to remark that he was afraid the damp might melt the glue that held his artillery ammunition carts together. Relatively few of the men were fully uniformed, it was dubious that the cannon could be fired, and everyone, the commander-in-chief included, was hungry—as usual. But at least the Army was on the move, and was going forward rather than in retreat, so the men were relatively cheerful, although the wet ground soaked the boots of those fortunate enough to own footgear.

In the main body, no one except the generals knew the corps' destination. All vanguard commanders were told the secret, necessarily, and Harry Lee was pleased. Having spent three years at Princeton, he was thoroughly familiar with the surrounding countryside.

The Americans avoided the much-traveled Post Road, and marched on a connecting series of old, back roads that ran parallel to it. As they drew nearer to Princeton, Harry, who had volunteered his services as an advance scout, expected Rodney to call on him. But there were others in the column who knew the territory even better, having been born and reared in the area. So the Virginians kept their modest places in the cavalry ranks.

Washington again caught the enemy by surprise, but the Americans almost lost the battle, thanks to the inexperience of their militia, who panicked when the disciplined Redcoats quickly rallied. But Henry Knox found a way to make his guns work, and gave the infantry support at a time when it was most needed. Washington abandoned his usual role, that of the cool and detached commander who observed an operation and relayed orders to subordinate leaders through his staff assistants. Aware that he himself had to participate if he hoped to prevent his entire corps from disintegrating, he rode up and down in full view of the enemy, exhorting his troops to hold firm.

They did, and the Americans resumed their offensive, sending the enemy scurrying out of Nassau Hall. The commander-in-chief, in a rare display of emotional exuberance, led the chase in person as the British fled down the Post Road toward Trenton. Perhaps he was inspired by the sight of Redcoats in retreat, a pleasure he had seldom enjoyed since accepting the invitation of the Continental Congress to lead his fellow countrymen in the field.

According to several accounts, he was so carried away by the unique joys of the day that he half-stood in his stirrups, waved his hat in the air and shouted, "It's a fine fox-chase, lads!"

Washington's exuberant leadership gave subordinates little opportunity to share his limelight, and a junior officer commanding a small body of Virginia militia went unnoticed. If Harry Lee performed feats of valor in the Battle of Princeton, they are unrecorded. Apparently neither he nor his Fifth Troop accomplished anything of note, for he makes no mention of the battle in his *Memoirs*, an account of his career that pays attention to minute details, even though written in an impersonal, sometimes frigid style.

Nevertheless, his feelings ran deep. "*As you may have learned,*" he wrote to his parents a few days after the battle, "*we handed the Lobsters a richly deserved trouncing at Princeton. I was sick at heart when I caught a glimpse of scarlet uniforms in the window of the very room Charles and I once occupied, but we drove out the rascals, and found Nassau Hall in tolerable good shape. Our own gunners creased the masonry of that venerable structure, more's the pity, but are not to be blamed. They, like the rest of us, had to seek out the enemy wherever he was hiding.*

"*The general,*" Harry added in a diplomatic afterthought, "*fought superbly, and inspired in us all a desire to emulate his gallant conduct.*"

The ambitious young captain must have known that his mother would show his letter to Mrs. Washington, whom she saw daily, and he would have been dull indeed had he not hoped that Aunt Martha, as he called her, might mention his comments when she next wrote to her husband.

Harry Lee did nothing in the Battle of Princeton to enhance his reputation, but the engagement was a significant milestone in his career as a soldier. Only a few days from his twenty-first birthday, the captain had taken part in his first real battle, had heard the whine of American artillery overhead and had faced enemy cavalry, enemy infantry and enemy guns. The experience was not wasted.

Artillerist-bookseller Knox, himself deeply interested in a comparison of past and present, wrote to his wife, in an undated letter probably dispatched in late January 1777; "*I have had several discussions of our campaign with Capt. H. Lee, of Virginia, a learned fellow who displays as much knowledge of the maneuvers of the ancients as he does of Cornwallis' cavalry screen. I find him fluent also in Latin, and believe that unless our tribulations sap his buoyancy, he will become a valued colleague.*"

Few men, if any, shared the foresight of Knox in the first dreary months of 1777. There was little opportunity for any American to shine in that drab period. On the surface, the situation looked bright: Howe, frightened by Washington's twin victories at Trenton and Princeton, withdrew all but a few outposts to New York

Town and, technically at least, left the American Army in possession of the whole state of New Jersey.

But Washington knew, if the enemy did not, that the few regiments of Continentals and shaky militia were too weak to occupy the ground. The corps had not yet been reinforced, and neither munitions were being provided by a harried Continental Congress that, lacking authority over the states, could not fulfill its promises or meet its financial obligations.

Washington's problems were complicated by the unpleasant fact that many militia enlistments were expiring, and cold, hungry men, out of contact with their families and worried about the prospects of spring planting, were leaving for their homes. A few units replaced them, but militia recruits, as the Continental commander and his generals had learned, were almost useless. One simply could not rely on a soldier until he had smelled gunpowder and, without panicking, faced a long, cold steel line of advancing British bayonets.

While the rest of America rejoiced over the victories at Trenton and Princeton, General Washington privately wallowed in gloom. "*If the enemy do not move,*" he wrote in March, "*it will be a miracle. Nothing but ignorance of our numbers and situation can protect us.*"

Harry Lee believed that the Almighty helped those who helped themselves. Unwilling to idle away uncomfortable hours at the American winter quarters in rural Pennsylvania, he obtained permission for his troop to engage in reconnaissance operations during most of January, February, and March. What he sought was not information regarding enemy numbers, but food and arms; the foe was in New York, so he ventured north, and became an expert at raiding small garrison outposts that Howe had established to protect the approaches to New York Town.

Harry's Virginians were so active that, in mid-February, they stole stores from three different posts in three days, one in Newark, one in Perth Amboy, and one a lonely beach station at Highlands, facing the Atlantic. The alarmed Howe concluded that the Americans were sending out patrols in strength, and increased his garrisons. Not until years later did he discover the truth, that he had been pestered by a single, persistent gadfly.

The supplies Harry brought back to the American camp weren't spectacular, but he rarely returned emptyhanded, and the senior commanders became increasingly appreciative of his talents. Not surprisingly, a significant change took place in his status and that of his command when, their enlistments expiring, his troops voluntarily re-enlisted—to a man. No other militia unit could boast such a record, and the Fifth Troop deserved a reward, which was immediately forthcoming.

Colonel Theodorick Bland had arrived at headquarters with the bulk of his Virginia Light Dragoon regiment, and everywhere he heard praise for Captain Lee. He reacted accordingly, and in a brief ceremony redesignated the small unit as the First Troop. Harry was given a small blue pennant, decorated with white stars, as his insignia, and his standard-bearer carried it for the rest of the war, long after the captain had attained a much higher rank and greatly expanded command.

Colonel Bland wanted his new First Troop to rejoin the regiment. But several senior officers, among them fellow-Virginian Colonel Daniel Morgan and General Benjamin Lincoln persuaded the commander-in-chief that he was too valuable to be wasted on ordinary cavalry duty. At the personal order of General Washington, the new First Troop remained on detached service.

Washington, who never allowed himself to be moved by personal considerations, was undoubtedly thinking in broader terms. The war was entering a new and critical phase, and it was urgently necessary that he learn the enemy's intentions as soon as possible. Word had reached Washington that Lieutenant General John Burgoyne, reputedly one of the most able of British field commanders, had begun a march south from Canada with a strong corps. Apparently he intended to make his way into the United States by way of the New York state chain of lakes that Benedict Arnold and Ethan Allen had won for the Americans early in the war.

This left Sir William Howe with an option, and either choice spelled bad news for the defenders. He might march north from New York Town to link forces with Burgoyne, cut off the fertile Mohawk Valley, the American "breadbasket," and isolate all of New England. Or, knowing that the manpower-shy Washington could not let Burgoyne advance unopposed, Howe might elect to make a thrust against the weakened main body of defenders and try to take Philadelphia, the seat of the Continental Congress and the most important city in the United States.

The British held a forward position at New Brunswick, and a makeshift American division faced them at nearby Bound Brook. The intervening ground was perhaps the most sensitive area in North America at the moment, and Harry was sent on patrol there, under General Lincoln's command, early in April. Each day he and his men rode into no-man's-land, searching for any movements that might hint whether the British were intending to pull out or advance toward Philadelphia. Tempers were frayed at the command post of Lincoln, a plodding bulldog of a man, but Harry was always cheerful. Then, as later, he thrived on tensions that left other men limp.

It was a personality trait he recognized, but refused to take credit for it. Many years later, his eldest son, who was called Henry, Jr., but was actually the fourth in a direct line of descent to bear the name, wrote that his father was painfully modest on the subject, refusing to take credit for what he considered inherited characteristics.

Two weeks later he displayed another and less admirable trait, inordinate vanity. He received orders from Colonel Bland, instructing him to take up a new position on the eastern flank of the main body, at Chatham, and to proceed there by way of Morristown. Harry was dismayed. Morristown was General Washington's headquarters, and his troop, after many months in the field, no longer made a smart showing. Many were wearing ordinary footgear instead of their polished boots, which had worn out. Others had lost or damaged their plumed hats.

Harry promptly wrote a letter to Colonel Bland. "*Could the articles mentioned* (boots and helmets) *be allowed my Troop, their appearance into Morristown would secure me from the imputation of carelessness as their captain; and I have vanity enough to hope would assist me in procuring some little credit to the colonel and the Regiment.*"

General Lincoln, holding a line with untrained militia, was unhappy for different reasons when he heard of the transfer. He desperately needed experienced cavalrymen who could serve him in battle as well as on scouting missions. He directed Harry to remain, and promised to write Colonel Bland.

Events conspired to keep him so busy he had no time for letter-writing. That night Lord Cornwallis forded the Raritan River near the village of Millstone Creek on a raiding expedition. Lincoln hastily withdrew to safer ground, but his raw troops failed to act quickly enough, and sixty militiamen lost their lives. Lincoln suffered the personal humiliation of having his own personal headquarters looted, and lost his official papers and personal luggage. His aide-de-camp, who tried singlehanded to stave off the bayonet-wielding Redcoats, was killed.

Captain Harry Lee and his First Troop were sent against an enemy of unknown size. The little body of cavalry made a gallant charge, and drove forward so vigorously that it scattered a whole battalion of Redcoat infantry. As it happened, Cornwallis was merely probing, not conducting a major operation, and withdrew. Harry knew better than to take credit for the British retreat, but his unit, nevertheless, was the only organization in General Lincoln's command that behaved creditably that night.

Cornwallis' push having been successful, he determined to remain active, and the Virginia Dragoons were assigned a permanent place in the defense line. Redcoat units from platoon to battalion strength moved out against the Americans every day, and every day Harry's First Troop was dispatched to the trouble spot. For all practical purposes he fought fourteen miniature battles in fourteen days, and his men suffered their first casualties, two troopers sustaining serious wounds, while three others survived lesser injuries.

Harry was so busy during this hectic period that he had no time to make out his monthly payroll requisition to Colonel Bland. Meanwhile the flustered General Lincoln, trying to protect himself from the blows that were directed at him first from one quarter, then another, completely forgot that the junior officer on whom he was leaning so heavily had been ordered elsewhere— and that he himself had taken no action in the matter.

At the end of April, Colonel Bland sent Harry another order, repeating the instructions he had given in his first. The colonel's patience was wearing thin, and he couched his command in blunt language stripped of diplomatic and military finesse. Again General Lincoln demurred, and Harry was caught in the middle.

Well aware that he was laying himself open to court-martial charges on grounds of insubordination if he disobeyed Bland, and of the even more serious charges of desertion if he abandoned Lincoln, Harry sat down at the end of a hard day's skirmishing and scribbled a letter to Bland, explaining the situation in full.

Lincoln, he said, was intending to attack Cornwallis' Hessians the following Saturday. Therefore, assuming that all went as planned, he would be able to leave on Sunday. The assault did not take place, Cornwallis having learned of the Americans' intentions. He kept the initiative, the weary Virginians were sent in to plug holes in the line each day, and it was mid-May before Harry finally left for Morristown.

By then he and his men were too tired to care how they looked. They were unshaven, their uniforms muddy and patched, their cloaks battle-stained. But when they arrived at the commander-in-chief's headquarters they exhibited a quality that Washington appreciated far more than a smart appearance. They were professional soldiers now, men who had met and repulsed the enemy repeatedly.

They rode with a swagger, they stared the infantrymen who hooted insults at them into sudden, panicky silence and they thought so highly of themselves that they voluntarily staged an impromptu review for General Washington, cantering past him in pairs, as though daring him to criticize their ragged appearance.

Washington responded by granting the First Troop its first official commendation, which he issued to Colonel Bland in his Orders of the Day dated May 17. And that same day the instructions directing Harry to take up his position at the little town of Chatham were countermanded. General Lincoln had finally found an opportunity to send a detailed report to the commander-in-chief, and Washington decided that the First Troop of Virginia Dragoons should remain on detached service.

There was enough to keep Harry and his men fully occupied. With the coming of warmer weather, the British began to gather supplies in larger quantities, and their wagon trains once more bounced over the rutted New Jersey roads. Harry resumed his practice of raiding them, expanding and refining his techniques so successfully that one day he and his First Troop appeared in the role of cowboys as they drove a large herd of British-purchased cattle into Morristown.

It had been simple for him to capture the animals, he explained. He had divided the Troop into two squads, and while the larger had attacked the Redcoat quartermaster escort, the smaller had stolen the cattle. He had brought back enough beef-on-the-hoof to provide virtually everyone in the Army with meat for supper, and those soldiers who hadn't before heard of Light-Horse Harry Lee knew him now.

On another occasion the First Troop returned with equally interesting booty, forty carts laden with bolts of scarlet cloth obviously intended for use in the making of new uniforms. The quality and weave of the wool were good, and several New England officers familiar with the manufacture of fabrics began to experiment, hoping to find ways to dye the cloth blue. Unfortunately, their efforts failed, so General Nathanael Greene, who was as adept at performing non-combat functions as he was at fighting, decided to make blankets for the corps that was growing larger again, to the pleased surprise of every senior officer.

Howe was annoyed by the Virginians' raids—and by those of other companies of horsemen emulating them—so he sent out cavalry of his own to protect his convoys and harass the enemy. Frequent skirmishes erupted on the New Jersey flatlands, perfect terrain for the maneuvering of horse. Casualties were few in these encounters, and neither side deterred the other. But the flurries provided Harry with still more training, under actual combat conditions. He learned more, he said in his *Memoirs*, from the British officers he fought than he had picked up in all of his previous experience.

The most important of the new traits he acquired was caution. Heretofore he had charged headlong at the enemy, hoping to scatter the opposition, but he was impressed by the techniques of the British commanders, who applied pressure by flanking movements rather than direct horse-to-horse and sword-to-sword confrontations. It was obvious that a leader who rode his men straight into an enemy line was courting death so he experimented with the British tactics, and found ways to improve on them.

One was to begin an operation as a head-on charge, then sweep to a flank after gaining momentum—and before coming within the foe's pistol range. In that way he was able to utilize the best features of both methods. It is significant that he never again employed the reckless charge in his career, and relied instead on skill, utilizing his instinctive ability to think and act more quickly than his foes.

There was more than work to keep Harry busy now, and he developed something of a social life for the first time since going on active service. Mrs. Washington arrived at Morristown, and not only entertained for other wives who had come there, too, but invited various officers to dine at the general's table. The majority were generals and colonels, and virtually no juniors were honored other than members of the commander-in-chief's personal staff. But Martha Washington would not hear of excluding the son of her dearest friend.

So Harry reluctantly found himself dining rather frequently in exalted company. Mrs. Washington, who remembered his vivacity and his tendency to dominate table talk by discussing his favorite authors, was struck by his long, meditative silences. "*Henry*," she wrote to his mother, "*is much changed. He has acquired a modest grace that is most becoming in one of his years.*"

Harry had not changed in the least. But, as a professional soldier, he had learned that a captain holds his tongue when surrounded by the gold and silver epaulets of major generals and brigadiers, colonels and lieutenant colonels. When he dined with his peers, he still bored them to distraction by quoting Pope at length, from memory.

Mrs. Bland also joined her husband, and Cousin Harry received frequent invitations to sit at the table of the colonel and his lady. Another newcomer was Mrs. John Fitzgerald, the wife of a dashing lieutenant colonel from Virginia who was serving as one of the commander-in-chief's personal aides. A pretty and charming young woman, she was only a few years older than Harry; one of her younger sisters had been his companion at several pre-war dances, and was still interested in him, so she made it a point to entertain the captain, too.

"*I dine so handsomely,*" Harry wrote to his parents, "*that I no longer have an appetite for plain Army fare.*" Always painfully thin, he gained a little weight.

Meanwhile the skirmishes continued, and no one knew what Howe would do. Gentleman Johnny Burgoyne captured Fort Ticonderoga, the gateway to the Mohawk Valley, and there was gloom at the Morristown headquarters. Washington wrote letter after letter to the Congress and the governors of the states, begging for more men, supplies, and ordnance. Enlistments in the Continentals had increased, but not enough, and the new militia units were undependable, as always.

A political storm enlivened life at headquarters, too. Silas Deane, who had been sent to Paris to negotiate an alliance with the government of King Louis XVI, inadvertently touched it off. His talks were progressing, and there was hope that a pact would be concluded. In an attempt to further them, he sent communications to Washington and the Congress, recommending the appointment of a thoroughly qualified French gentlemen, Philip-Charles du Coudray, as chief of artillery. Du Coudray had excellent connections at court, and the awarding of the post to him might make it easier to obtain the much-desired treaty.

Du Coudray himself arrived simultaneously with the letters, bearing a recommendation in the busy Deane's own hand. Unfortunately, he regarded the letter as an actual appointment.

A large, genial obstacle stood in his path: Henry Knox, perhaps the most popular of American generals. His colleagues immediately rallied to his defense. Nathanael Greene sent a furious letter to the Congress, threatening to resign his own commission if Knox was superseded. Major General John Sullivan went a step further, and actually submitted his resignation, to take effect immediately on the appointment of du Coudray.

Junior officers were expected to be seen but not heard when matters of such importance were being decided. But Harry Lee was loyal to his friends, and Knox had been kind to him. He sent a letter of his own to Governor Henry of Virginia, promising to resign if Knox was ousted, and to make certain his decision was known in the right places, he delivered a copy by hand to Washington's headquarters.

The worried commander-in-chief was not pleased by the young officer's impudence, but had no time for such trifles. His concern over the fall of Ticonderoga, his worries about Howe and the new political storm, not to mention his unceasing fight for recruits and supplies, left him with no opportunity to chastise a brash youth.

Harry's impetuous gesture did him no harm in other high quarters. Knox was grateful to him, but nevertheless deemed it necessary to lecture him on military proprieties. John Sullivan sought out the Virginian and publicly shook his hand, praising him loudly. And Nathanael Greene invited him to dinner.

This occasion is the first known contact of Greene and Lee, an association that was to ripen into a professional and personal friendship of the greatest military significance. The one-time blacksmith's apprentice from Rhode Island, whose martial attitudes had led to his expulsion from the Society of Friends, and the dashing Virginia aristocrat were men of vastly different temperaments and personalities, yet they enjoyed each other's company from the start.

"Captain Lee and I spent an evening discussing the waging of the war, and I envy his sure grasp of essentials. I must study plans of campaigns and of battles before I know how to act, but he need only glance at a map of a situation to be guided, surely and accurately, by a marvelous instinct," Greene declared.

"*General Greene,*" Harry wrote, "*is perhaps the best theoretician in our Army. His judgments are based on the experiences of others, from antiquity to the present, and if he does not recommend new strategies, neither does he forget the errors of those who went down in defeat. He well remembers all the great victories of history.*"

In less than four years the team of Nathanael Greene and Harry Lee would make history of their own.

For the present, however, each went his separate way, with Harry spending his days on patrol duty.

One problem was settled by the ever-diplomatic Washington, who recommended that Congress grant du Coudray an appointment as "Inspector General" of artillery, a meaningless title. Knox remained as chief of the department, his colleagues were satisfied and Silas Deane was able to report to the French government that du Coudray had been given a post of honor.

Intelligence reached Morristown that the enemy was landing vast numbers of fresh troops at New York Town, and that each day transports arrived carrying Redcoats and mercenaries. Some said that there were as many as fifty thousand men disembarking, but these stories were exaggerated. The actual number was eighteen thousand, itself an imposing figure, but of these, approximately one-third were seriously ill of "shipboard fever."

Then, finally, Sir William Howe made his intentions clear. He started preparations for an active campaign, and it soon became apparent that his goal was Philadelphia.

IV

THE CAPTAIN WINS HIS SPURS

General Washington expected the enemy to march through New Jersey from New York Town, but Billy Howe had tasted more of the Americans' hit-and-run tactics than he enjoyed, and wanted to march as short a distance to his objective as possible. Hoping to fool the enemy, he bundled his entire corps onto troop transports and, protected by the mighty fleet of his brother, Admiral Lord Howe, sailed south.

The Americans were not fooled. Washington had too many spies in New York, and General Howe made preparations for his campaign that were too elaborate and protracted. Some of his regiments went on board the transports in July, and sweltered there for the better part of two months.

Not until August 28 did the British and their mercenaries finally land on the shores of Maryland. Cavalry and light infantry, heavy infantry and artillery, supply columns and ordnance troops came ashore in waves, and Howe, accompanied by Cornwallis, established his temporary headquarters in the little town of Elkton.

The Americans were as ready as circumstances permitted. Knowing they were outnumbered, they nevertheless prepared to defend the capital of their country. Washington moved up to a forward position, making his headquarters at Wilmington, Delaware, and ordered all available cavalry units to harass the foe.

Virginia's First Troop of Dragoons went into the field only a few hours after the initial British landing was reported, and Harry ventured so close to the landing area that he actually saw some of the British units coming ashore. He sent a courier to Wilmington with a report to General Washington of what he had observed, and remained in the vicinity, spoiling for a fight.

The next day he got one. Howe threw out a cavalry screen to protect his corps while he consolidated his position before advancing, and Redcoat patrols spread out through the gently rolling Maryland countryside. They, too, were eager for combat after being cooped up on the evil-smelling transports for weeks. More than two thousand strong, all of them veterans, they had no reason to fear the three to four hundred American horsemen Washington had sent on scouting and harassment assignments.

Neither then nor at any later time in his career was Harry Lee concerned about the inferior size of his own forces. His First Troop currently mustered one lieutenant, one ensign, and fifty-nine enlisted men, the others being absent on sick leave. All shared their commander's yearning for glory and, a scant forty-eight hours after the British vanguard had come ashore, they enthusiastically followed him when he sighted a full battalion of British cavalry in the distance.

The enemy force was comprised of three full troops, more than two hundred men in all, and few commanders would have deemed it prudent to attack against such odds. But there were factors working in Harry's favor. The Redcoats had just ridden into the open from a patch of woods, and were riding parallel to it, four abreast. The Americans immediately cut into the woods, and had no difficulty concealing themselves, as the enemy, with a disdain of the New World born of ignorance, were shouting to each other as they rode.

They were observing no security precautions, either, as Harry was quick to note. All carried carbines, lightweight muskets with short barrels that had been expressly designed for cavalry, that were infinitely superior to the Americans' weapons. But they were harmlessly slung in holsters, and appeared to be unloaded. The Virginians, on the other hand, kept loaded, primed pistols in their belts, as they had done from the days of their initial recruit training.

Harry was relying on the element of surprise to help him, and incredible as it seemed, he and his men had not been seen by the British before disappearing into the woods. Either the Redcoats were not expecting opposition, or were indifferent to it. They soon learned to respect their foes.

The Americans took up positions behind trees, and Harry waited until approximately one-half of the enemy force had ridden past before raising his own pistol. A silent signal was passed up and down the line, each of the Virginians selected his own target and then fired at will. Thirty Britons fell to the ground or drooped in their saddles, all but three of them dead.

Harry shouted an order, and the First Troop advanced into the open immediately, the men drawing their spare pistols. They concentrated their fire on the British rear, and again took a heavy toll before increasing their pace from a canter to a gallop. Sabers flashing, they cut and slashed, and before the bewildered, disorganized Redcoats realized what was happening, the troop at the rear was cut off from the rest of the battalion.

Long months of working together in raiding parties enabled the Virginians to time their thrust perfectly, and, following the instructions Harry had given them, aimed their deadliest blows at the officers. All but one were either killed or wounded, and the Redcoats lost more than fifty troopers as well.

The bewildered survivors, virtually leaderless, milled around in helpless disorder, while the shocked members of the other troops watched from a distance, unable to fire for fear of hitting their comrades. Harry behaved as though he had been conducting such operations all his life, and displaying a skill that won him a grudging commendation in the British battalion commander's report to Sir William, he shepherded the uninjured members of the rear troop into the woods.

Speed and coordination were essential, and the Virginians demonstrated both. By the time the stunned Redcoats still on the field recovered sufficiently to form their lines anew and charge, the Americans had vanished into the woods, taking one embarrassed officer, a sheepish captain, and twenty-three enlisted men with them as prisoners.

Harry remained under cover until long after night fell, aided by a knowledge of the district that was the result of thorough advance scouting. Then, certain at last that he wasn't being followed, he took his prisoners to Wilmington, appearing at General Washington's headquarters at ten o'clock that night.

The commander-in-chief had just sat down to a late dinner,

and sent Lieutenant Colonel Alexander Hamilton to determine the cause of the commotion outside. On learning what had happened, Washington interrupted his meal long enough to see the prisoners for himself, shake Harry's hand and express his approval to the entire First Troop.

The following morning the Virginians enjoyed the privilege of hearing themselves praised in the General Orders of the Day. And Harry Lee became the hero of the army—for the moment. There was little cause for cheer in the camp, and everyone spoke of his exploit. With the loss of only one man slightly injured, he had killed or wounded more than fifty Redcoats and captured twenty-four others.

The triumph was a minor incident, as every officer in the Army knew, and in no way affected the basic problem that the Americans faced. Its only significance, other than winning recognition for the First Troop of Virginia Dragoons and their commander, was the promise it held out to others, particularly the untried recruits who had yet to face the enemy in combat, that the British were not invincible.

Some took the lesson to heart, but others had to relearn it in the days that followed, when Howe began his drive toward Philadelphia and Washington grouped and regrouped his forces before taking a stand. Gradually the engagement known as the Battle of Brandywine developed, and was fought on September 11. Nathanael Greene held center of the American line, commanding a division of Continentals, most of them Virginians, augmented by several smaller units of Virginia militia. The First Troop of Dragoons was assigned to his command, and received no instructions other than those given to everyone.

"The enemy," Greene said in an Order of the Day, "must be halted."

General Anthony Wayne held the left flank with Continentals and militia, and the right was placed under the command of John Sullivan, who had suffered in the past because of the ineptness of green militia, and was to suffer again.

Howe's plan of battle was simple—and effective. He sent Cornwallis with a strong force around Sullivan's right, and the Redcoats then doubled back to hit the unsuspecting militia recruits from the rear. The inexperienced men panicked, and the entire American line was in danger of collapse. Washington was forced to retreat, but the situation wasn't hopeless, and the frightful rout of the Battle of Long Island was not repeated. First the commander-in-chief sent an extraordinary young French volunteer, the Marquis de Lafayette, to rally Sullivan's men, and finally dispatched Greene's whole division to the sector while several tough, independent brigades continued to give as good as they received in the center.

The withdrawal of Sullivan forced the rest of the army to retreat, but the maneuver was accomplished in good order, the center pulling back slowly and Wayne giving up ground with great reluctance. The battle was lost, to be sure. Howe was certain to take Philadelphia, and the Continental Congress prepared to travel far to the west, to the frontier town of York, Pennsylvania, a move that began on September 19. But the army had not disintegrated under an attack by a vastly superior corps, and so many brigades gave good accounts of themselves that there was hope they would do better another day.

Harry Lee's First Troop fought doggedly at Brandywine, but did nothing to distinguish itself. The maneuvering ability of cavalry was strictly limited under circumstances which forced horsemen to help cover a slow retreat.

Washington hoped to rally his battered troops and make another stand on the Schuylkill River approaches to Philadelphia, and his senior commanders worked so diligently that less than a week after the Battle of Brandywine the army was ready. Harry Lee's troop was stationed with the vanguard, in advance of the main body, but the expected battle did not take place. A wild gale roared up the Atlantic coast, and in six hours dumped as many inches of rain on the Americans and British alike. Gunpowder was soaked and rendered useless, and Washington, who could ill afford the catastrophe, lost most of his supplies.

On September 27, Howe, virtually unopposed, took Philadelphia.

Sir William immediately set up two supply lines, one between the city and his brother's fleet, which was still hovering off the Maryland coast, and the other between the fallen American capital and New York Town. Harry Lee was immediately granted the right to resume the raids which had been so successful in the past, and brought in a steady trickle of supplies and munitions.

He and his men may have felt a sense of urgency in their mission that had been lacking in the past, and they no longer confined their efforts to taking enemy carts, but began to visit the storehouses of farmers suspected of loyalty to the Crown. Harry's zeal was greater than his judgment, and after he had burned several barns and destroyed some fences, the commander-in-chief found it necessary to issue an order forbidding the destruction of civilian property.

Washington soon made it clear that his young Virginia neighbor was not out of favor, however. Enough powder and lead came in from various sources for the commander-in-chief to challenge Howe once again, and on October 5 the Battle of Germantown was fought. The First Troop of Dragoons saw no active combat that day, having been granted the honor of serving as General Washington's personal bodyguard. Harry appreciated the privilege, but would have preferred action.

Late in the day the Americans were forced to withdraw once more, pulling back about ten miles to the north. But the First Troop remained behind on a surveillance mission that was far more to Harry's liking. For forty-eight hours he and his men hovered close under the noses of the enemy, keeping a close watch on the Redcoats and sending frequent intelligence reports to the commander-in-chief.

By now Harry knew the enemy well, and often allowed his men to be seen in the open. He knew that, provided he kept his distance, the Redcoats would not pursue him, and made good use of their careless indifference. They had no idea that the reports he sent to headquarters were detailed, thorough, and so precise they became a major source of information treasured by the American high command.

By now Harry had acquired a reputation as a man capable of performing dangerous and difficult missions. Therefore, when Joseph Reed, head of the Pennsylvania Committee of Public Safety, wanted information on the situation at a small American outpost on the New Jersey side of the Delaware River, Fort Mercer, which was under heavy enemy attack, Virginia's First Troop of Dragoons won the hazardous assignment.

Harry obliged by leading his men safely past the enemy in an operation that required a combination of superb horsemanship and courage. He found Fort Mercer more than holding its own, and on his return to headquarters noted the main British supply route, which he mapped with care and presented in person to the commander-in-chief. Thereafter he resumed his careless gadfly raids.

Early in December he was given a similar assignment on a larger scale. The First Troop and Dan Morgan's Virginia Rifles, perhaps the finest body of infantry marksmen in the entire American Army, were sent into New Jersey to harass the enemy and capture supply trains. The expedition was under the command of Nathanael Greene, who was again doubling as the American Quartermaster General, and Greene himself went into the field with the Virginians.

Here the general had an opportunity to watch Harry Lee in action, and was increasingly impressed by his cool, unflustered efficiency. *"The captain's instinct,"* Greene wrote to Washington, now making his temporary headquarters at the dreary village of Whitemarsh, *"is as sure and swift as that of the eagle that drops out of the skies to snatch its prey. No convoy within range of his horses is safe from his depredations."*

Greene was soon recalled by Washington to help prepare the battered army's winter camp, a "natural fortress" in the Pennsylvania hills called Valley Forge, and Harry and Morgan were on their own. One of their assignments was that of preventing British requisitioning parties from stealing the produce of American farmers, and they accomplished the mission so successfully that most of the platoons Howe sent from Philadelphia to gather supplies in the neighborhood were decimated.

"An American named Lee," Sir William declared in annoyance, "is a damned nuisance! I expect the rebels to nip at our heels, but this fellow always draws blood."

The American corps withdrew to Valley Forge in a grim march that left the survivors exhausted and ill. American spirits had reached their lowest ebb, food was so scarce that soldiers lucky enough to own boots boiled them and ate the leather. Few men expected the weary Patriot forces to remain banded together until the end of that terrible winter of 1777–78.

But Washington himself did not abandon hope. The fainthearted had already deserted, and the men who stayed at the camp burrowed into half-underground huts of logs and frozen mud. If they could get enough food to stay alive, they would continue the fight when warmer weather came.

Harry Lee was recalled to Pennsylvania, and was assigned the task of finding grain and meat for the starving army. He made a survey of the area in the vicinity of Valley Forge, studied the enemy supply routes and set up his own tiny headquarters at the once-prosperous farm of a Patriot named Scott, six miles from the army's winter bivouac.

Here he established an unvarying routine. Every morning, no matter how vile the weather, the men of the First Troop left the blazing fires in the comfortable old farmhouse long before dawn, saddled their horses and went "fishing." Every night, long after sundown, Harry led them into the camp at Valley Forge, bearing their "catch."

The British at Philadelphia were vulnerable, and no one knew it better than Harry Lee. Howe, far from his bases of supply, needed food for his corps. He also had to provide for the civilian population of the largest city in North America. Therefore convoys came from New York and the Maryland coast in a never-ending stream. Some were protected by large escorts, others were given smaller companies of armed troops and still others, of necessity, had to take their chances alone.

Harry attacked them indiscriminately, and his success was phenomenal. It was during this period that he truly came into his own, and the Americans at Valley Forge could not have survived until spring without his unfailing help. He was brilliant, audacious, and untiring, and he won the devoted admiration of everyone in the Patriot camp from the commander-in-chief to the ragged, fever-stricken private soldiers whose lives he saved with medicines and elixirs stolen from the enemy.

It is difficult to measure the true worth of his achievements that winter. Not only did the army depend on his raids, but their unflagging success was a repeated demonstration to dispirited, sick men that the enemy could be beaten. If the young Virginians could outsmart, outride, and outfight the Redcoats, others would be capable of following their example when spring came.

Illness had reduced the ranks of the First Troop to forty-seven effectives, sometimes aided by the most unexpected of allies, eleven warriors of the Iroquois Federation, braves who rode their own horses and took part in the raids for sheer sport. Harry, glad to have their help, rewarded them liberally and returned the compliment by learning to speak the language of the Oneida. When he had time for such studies is something of a mystery, as he was fortunate when he could sleep as long as four to five hours in a night.

Sir William Howe lost patience, and his reaction is an indication of the importance he attached to Harry's foraging. The British commander sent out reconnaissance parties of his own, learned the location of Harry's headquarters and then dispatched a full regiment of cavalry, more than three hundred strong, to take the American gadfly, dead or alive.

The Redcoats set out from Philadelphia on the night of January 19, 1778, and traveled by a circuitous route in order to avoid various American outposts that might warn Harry of what was in store. They reached Scott's farm just before dawn, just as Harry and his men were finishing a hasty breakfast and preparing to leave for their day's "fishing."

One of the troopers happened to glance out of a window and saw the scarlet tunics and plumed brass helmets of the enemy vanguard. He shouted a warning, and Harry immediately put his house in order. The doors were barred with furniture, and men were stationed at every window. But the prospects were dim. The Iroquois were at their own camp, about two miles away, and forty-seven defenders faced a force six times their own strength.

Harry knew that extraordinary measures were required, and took them. First, he ordered his men to crouch low behind the windows and remain hidden, no matter what the provocation. Even more important, he instructed them not to fire on the foe until he gave the word.

He watched row after row of Redcoats emerge from the woods, and as he wrote many years later in his *Memoirs*, "*Captain Lee deemed it unlikely that his strategem of defense could succeed, so great were the numbers of the enemy. The vicissitudes of war offering a commander of troops no choice and compelling him to deal with a situation as he found it, the captain was given no alternative, and perforce carried out the scheme he had envisioned.*"

That scheme was based on many factors: his knowledge of the stamina and courage of his own men and their response to pressure, his awareness of the enemy's attitudes and, equally significant, a careful weighing of the physical factors that favored each side. In a real crisis, Harry Lee was less impetuous than he seemed. Others believed him rash, not understanding that his mind worked at great speed, enabling him to analyze a situation far more rapidly than could military plodders.

The British opened fire, but the bullets lodged in the soft pine logs of the farmhouse wall, and the volley was wasted. The commander of the attacking party urged his men forward, and a second round buried itself harmlessly in the wood. Now the Redcoats were within close range, and Harry called, "Fire at will."

The Virginians didn't need to be told to take careful aim at individual targets, as they had been doing little else on scores of raids. They took such a heavy toll that the British, with only two small apple trees in the farmhouse yard to serve as cover, retreated to the protective shield of the woods.

After a brief pause for regrouping, the enemy advanced a second time, and Harry employed the same technique he had used to repulse the first assault. A major, the deputy commander of the British regiment, led the charge, the regimental sergeant major beside him. Both were severely wounded when the Americans replied to the fire, and had to be carried to the woods. Of the six troopers in the front line of attackers, three were killed and the other three badly wounded. Understandably, the Redcoats lost their zest for close combat, and again withdrew.

The First Troop suffered only one casualty. Lieutenant Lindsay, Harry's second-in-command, sustained a wound in his left hand, but obtained help in reloading his pistol and insisted he could still fire with his right.

He proved it when the British advanced a third time, and for the third time were repulsed. Approximately thirty minutes had passed since the "Battle of Scott's Farm" had begun, and the Redcoats decided they'd had enough of the Virginians' marksmanship. Before leaving, however, they rode around to the barn at the rear of the house, intending to steal or drive off the Americans' horses.

Harry and his men raced to the windows on that side of the house, and after firing a deadly round at the foe, the captain called out in a tone that carried conviction, "Fire away, lads, here comes our infantry! We'll have them all."

With that, he and his men fired again and again, as rapidly as they could reload their weapons.

The ruse proved effective, and the British withdrew permanently, not bothering to ascertain for themselves whether American reinforcements had actually arrived at the scene. And they departed in such panicky haste that they left most of their dead and wounded behind, a cardinal sin rarely committed by experienced soldiers.

The Americans stripped the dead, and buried them in a common grave, then tended the wounded as best they could, and relieved them of their weapons. The prisoners were sent off to Valley Forge under escort, along with the badly needed clothing, boots, carbines, and ammunition. And Harry then went off for his day's "fishing" with the bulk of his Troop, annoyed because the interruption had delayed him by more than three hours.

News of the battle created a sensation that alleviated the gloom at Valley Forge. Generals toasted the victors with rum and brandywine they had been hoarding for a special occasion, and men strong enough to leave their huts danced and sang. Many wept without shame, and in spite of the bitter cold, a warm reception was planned for Harry.

When he and his foragers finally arrived at Valley Forge that evening, however, the captain, having accomplished the truly spectacular, revealed his innermost character by reporting quietly to Colonel Hamilton at the commander-in-chief's headquarters, then leaving again for Scott's farm before anyone else knew he was there.

Before he could set out at dawn again on the morning of January 21, a messenger arrived with a letter written in General Washington's own hand:

My Dear Lee:

Although I have given you my thanks in the General Orders of this day, for the late instance of your gallant behaviour, I Cannot resist the inclination I feel to repeat them again in this manner. I need no fresh proof of your merit, to bear you in remembrance. I waited only for the proper time and season to show it; those, I hope, are not far off. I shall also think of and will reward the merit of Lindsay, when an opening presents, as far as I can consistently; and I shall not forget the corporal (who gave the alarm),

*whom you have recommended to my notice. Offer my sincere
thanks to the whole of your gallant party, and assure them, that
no one felt pleasure more sensibly, or rejoiced more sincerely
for your and their escape, than*

Your affectionate, etc.
G. WASHINGTON.

The letter was official notification, in a sense, that Captain
Harry Lee had become a person of consequence in the American
Army. Two weeks later, as he was about to leave the farm for
Delaware, having learned that British quartermasters were collecting large herds of cattle there, he also received letters of congratulations from Governor Patrick Henry of Virginia and his
own distinguished cousin, Richard Henry Lee. Sir William Howe's
dispatch of a regiment to make him captive, and his escape from
a force of that size, thanks to his own efforts, had at last made
him famous outside the Army. The story of the adventure, told
and retold in increasingly exaggerated form, appeared in newspapers throughout the United States, and men everywhere delighted
in the tale of the brave and resourceful captain who had out-
witted and outfought Billy Howe's finest.

In February, Harry and the First Troop rode off to Delaware,
where they enjoyed their usual success, collecting several hundred
head of cattle for the ravenous troops at Valley Forge. During his
absence, General Anthony Wayne, the tough, resourceful, and
somewhat eccentric Pennsylvanian, submitted a formal request to
General Washington, asking that the now renowned First Troop
of Virginians be attached to his command for as long as they
could be spared from other duty.

The most unusual aspect of the request was that it was made
without Harry's knowledge. According to eighteenth-century military etiquette, an officer received an invitation from a superior
before such a request was submitted. But "Mad Anthony" Wayne
was too anxious to avail himself of Harry's talents to bother with
courtesies.

Washington called Wayne to headquarters, and conversed with
him privately. No record of the talk was kept, but the gist of it
is known. Wayne was informed, politely, that the commander-in-
chief had plans of his own for his fellow Virginian, so Wayne

withdrew the application. If he was told anything more detailed, he kept the information to himself.

At the beginning of March the First Troop returned to Valley Forge, shepherding more than two hundred head of cattle. The men were grimy, tattered, and tired, but the hungry army gave them a riotous welcome. Harry borrowed a razor, someone supplied him with a bucket of hot water and a cup of soft, rank-smelling soap, and he made himself relatively presentable before going off to report at headquarters.

There he was informed that the senior aide-de-camp wanted to see him, and Alexander Hamilton closed the door of his private office before opening the conversation. They chatted for a few minutes, Harry submitted an informal report, and then Hamilton exploded his bombshell.

The commander-in-chief was extending to Captain Henry Lee, Jr., the high honor of an invitation to join his official family as a member of his staff. He would serve as a personal aide-de-camp, and would act as liaison officer between General Washington and all American cavalry units.

Washington had indeed remembered his old friend's son, who had won his spurs in his own right, and had offered him the most glittering of prizes.

The post carried with it a variety of awards. The most obvious was a double promotion in rank to a lieutenant colonel. The prestige, of course, would be great. Living would be comfortable; aides slept in beds every night, and ate hot meals daily. Aides also knew virtually all of the commander-in-chief's closely guarded secrets.

Most officers dreamed in vain of such an assignment. But Harry Lee refused to be rushed, and asked for the privilege of a little time to consider the matter. The surprised Hamilton went off to learn the general's pleasure, and returned with word that the commander-in-chief was in no hurry. He would be delighted to receive Captain Lee's decision at Captain Lee's convenience.

V

THE PARTIZANS

Harry Lee knew from the moment he received George Washington's invitation that he had no desire to become the general's aide-de-camp. After eighteen months of active service, he thought of himself as a fighting man, not an administrator. He enjoyed the work at which he had become so adept, and longed for an opportunity to assume greater responsibility. He felt a fierce loyalty to the men he had recruited and who had served under him so faithfully. To abandon them now, he felt, would be a betrayal of their trust.

However, it was risky to reject an honor offered by a man as sensitively thin-skinned as George Washington. An officer could ruin his military career if his reply lacked the precise blend of delicacy, tact, and respect that the commander-in-chief expected from his juniors.

All through the month of March 1778 Harry procrastinated. He spent his days raiding British supply columns, and at least a portion of his short nights composing, editing, and rewriting his carefully balanced letter of refusal. Twice Alexander Hamilton hinted that it would be wise to communicate with the general as soon as possible, and twice Harry indicated that his letter would be forthcoming very soon.

At last, on March 31, he carried it to headquarters himself. It read:

Sir, I should do violence to my own feelings, was I to depart from Camp, without testifying the high sense of gratitude I feel for your Excellency's approbation of my conduct. I assure you, sir, to deserve a continuance of your Excellency's patronage, will be a stimulus to glory, second to none in power, of the many that operate on my soul. "It is not in mortals to command success," to deserve it shall be the object of my unwearied attention.

I must here take the liberty of laying before your Excellency, the reasons which have influence on my judgment, respecting the proposal you was pleased to make me through Colonel Hamilton.

Permit me to premise that I am wedded to my sword, and that my secondary object in the present war, is military reputation. To have possessed a post about your Excellency's person is certainly the first recommendation I can bear to posterity, affords a field for military instruction, would lead me into an intimate acquaintance with the politics of the states, and might present more immediate opportunities of manifesting my high respect and warm attachment for your Excellency's character and person. I know, it would also afford true and unexpected joy to my parents and friends.

On the contrary I possess a most affectionate friendship for my soldiers, a fraternal love for the two officers who have served with me, a zeal for the honor of the Cavalry, and an opinion that I should render no real service to your Excellency's arms.

Having thus shortly stated the reasons which operate on my mind, I will only say, that I most cheerfully will act in any character your Excellency may call me to, and that the second satisfaction I can possibly enjoy is my knowledge that my behaviour has met with your Excellency's approbation.

I have the honor to be, with the most profound respect and perfect esteem,

> *Your very obdt. servant,*
> H. LEE, JR.

General Washington was duly flattered by the tone of the young man he had known since infancy, and was equally adept at reading between the lines. He wasted no time, and early the following morning his reply was delivered to the anxious Harry:

Dear Sir:

By your favor of yesterday I am made acquainted with the feelings of your mind on the subject of my proposal communicated

*to you by Colonel Hamilton; the undisguised manner in which
you express yourself cannot but strengthen my good opinion of
you.—As the offer on my part was purely the result of a high sense
of your merit, and as I would by no means divert you from a
Career in which you promise yourself greater happiness from its
affording more happy opportunities of acquiring military fame, I
entreat you to pursue your own Inclinations as if nothing had
passed on this subject, and to be assured of the good wishes of,
Dear Sir,*

Yours, etc.
G. Washington

The exchange of correspondence was closed, but Washington
was not content to let the matter drop, "as if nothing had
passed on this subject." Instead he sent a messenger with an urgent
communication to the Continental Congress, sitting at York, and
for once those gentlemen responded promptly.

Harry was promoted to the rank of major—in the Continental
line. He was now a field-grade officer in the Regular Army.

His officers and men were also transferred to the Continentals,
and Lieutenant Lindsay was promoted to captain.

In addition, by authorization of the Congress, Major Lee was
given command of a special "Partizan Force of Cavalry," responsible only to the commander-in-chief.

Washington was quick to create the Partizan Force, which was
comprised, initially, of two troops. The First was the Virginia
unit, now commanded by Lindsay. The Second was a band of
raiders that had been almost as successful as Harry's own men.
Its captain was Allan McLane of Delaware, a wealthy, dashing
aristocrat who, like his new superior, had grown up in the saddle.
Not all of his troops were horsemen, however. Some were rifle-
bearing frontier scouts who preferred buckskins to uniforms and
resented any attempts to subject them to military discipline.

Also closely associated with the dashing McLane were forty
Oneida Indian warriors, who were impressed by the fact that
Harry, like McLane, had taken the trouble to learn their tongue.
After a slight hesitation, followed by a conference with McLane
and Lindsay, Harry consolidated the Oneida with his own braves,
and granted them the distinction of organizing into their own
troop, the Third.

The bizarre quality of the Partizan Force attracted a number of adventurous and daring young men serving elsewhere, and Harry screened their applications, interviewing each man himself. He accepted only those whom he wanted—and whose commanding officers willingly released them. In all, the Partizans numbered approximately one hundred and seventy hard-riding, exceptionally courageous men, and Harry put them to work immediately.

The intensity of the raids on British supply columns increased, close watch was kept on all enemy troop movements in and out of Philadelphia, and accurate intelligence as well as additional supplies poured into the American camp. Meanwhile, at Valley Forge itself, a series of miracles had taken place, and a shabby corps of amateur soldiers, the survivors of the most cruel winter imaginable, had been transformed into an elite fighting force.

Not the least of the miracles was that the hardships the men from thirteen states had endured, together, had imbued them with a new spirit that caused them to put aside their parochial differences and think of themselves first as Americans.

Another miracle, less appreciated by the men at the time, manifested itself in the person of Baron Friedrich von Steuben, a one-time junior officer in the Prussian army of Frederick the Great during the Seven Years' War, whom Washington had made his Inspector General. A drillmaster without an equal in the New World, von Steuben had taught the Americans manuals of arms, drills, disciplines, and, above all, had inspired in them the pride of professional soldiers.

Harry Lee and Allan McLane had made their own miracles, bringing to Valley Forge the food and supplies, blankets and medicines they had taken from the enemy. Nature assisted them, and men were stunned by the "miracle of the shad." Fish by the thousands appeared in the rivers that marked the boundaries of the bivouac, and everyone, even staid generals, waded into the cold waters to net mountains of shad, some to be eaten fresh, others to be smoked and salted for future use.

Early in May, General Washington announced the greatest of all the miracles. Thanks to the victory achieved by Benedict Arnold over Gentleman Johnny Burgoyne at Saratoga, New York, the previous October—a victory for which General Horatio Gates claimed the credit—Silas Deane, aided by that wisest of Americans, Benjamin Franklin, had finally secured a treaty of alliance with

France. Soon a great French fleet would cross the Atlantic, bringing troops, money and precious weapons, lead and gunpowder. The United States no longer faced England alone, but had made common cause with a powerful ally.

Harry Lee's Partizans showed their own appreciation of the new state of affairs by first doubling, then trebling, the quantity of the booty they stored in Nathanael Greene's newly-built log warehouses. They made life so miserable for the British that General Sir Henry Clinton, who had just replaced Howe, decided he was overextended. In June he evacuated Philadelphia, and the Partizans celebrated by capturing two major wagon trains, each of more than four hundred carts.

Washington had no intention of letting Clinton return to New York unopposed, and the two armies met on the New Jersey plains in what came to be known as the Battle of Monmouth, a clash in which the Americans proved their worth as soldiers but were unable to win a clear-cut victory. The Partizans, to Harry's dismay, were so busy foraging they missed the fight.

Thereafter Washington imposed what was tantamount to a blockade of Clinton, who was bottled up in New York, and Harry Lee became a principal instrument in that prolonged siege. The Partizans roamed at will, capturing and cutting off supply columns that ventured into the countryside from New York Town in search of food. Clinton was forced to dispatch large bodies of troops to protect his foragers, and late in September Harry met and defeated a regiment of Redcoat dragoons at Tarrytown, on the Hudson, sending the British fleeing for their lives.

Clinton increased the size of his escorts, and Washington countered by assigning a regiment of tough Pennsylvania infantry from General Anthony Wayne's brigade to work with the Partizans. The regimental commander, Colonel Richard Butler, was a mercurial but cautious hothead whose temperament matched Harry's, and between them they drove Clinton to distraction.

"Lee," the British general said in October, "immobilizes a division, and Butler another. I'd give my soul to see them killed or captured."

Later that autumn Harry transferred his base of operations to Long Island. Although frequently harassed by Redcoat dragoon units sent to search for him and clip his wings, he managed, between November and January, to cut off nearly all of Clinton's sources of food supplies on the island.

Early in 1779, with the Americans in winter quarters at various bases, Harry was transferred with his men to New Jersey, where his chief role was that of keeping watch on all enemy movements in and out of New York Town. The intelligence reports he sent direct to the commander-in-chief were so crisp, authoritative and complete that Washington used them as models when he exhorted other officers on reconnaissance duty to send in similar data.

Spring found the Partizan Force ranging up and down the Hudson River, as Washington had reason to fear that the British, who still clung to the hope of taking the Mohawk Valley and cutting off all of New England, might soon launch a new offensive. A quick reconnaissance indicated that something was indeed stirring, but was only in its initial stages. Clinton, comfortably ensconced in New York, was in no hurry to fight new battles.

Washington read the thorough reports, and suggested that, as the situation wasn't yet urgent, Harry might enjoy a brief leave of absence. Someone had called to the commander-in-chief's attention the fact that Major Lee hadn't taken a single day's leave since first joining the Army three years earlier.

The thought of a holiday hadn't crossed Harry's mind, and he wrote to Washington that he was in no need of either a rest or a change of scene. The general felt otherwise, and ordered him to take a furlough, leaving McLane in charge of the Partizans during his absence. Immediately concerned, Harry was afraid he was being replaced, and needed assurances from Colonel Hamilton that he still enjoyed the commander-in-chief's confidence and esteem.

The orders granting the furlough were issued, but Harry refused to leave until he wrung a promise from McLane that a messenger would be sent to Virginia for him if anything untoward developed. McLane gave his word, and Harry started out for home. En route, a new thought struck him. Perhaps his parents had taken advantage of their friendship with General Washington to obtain the furlough for him, behind his back. He was horrified.

He flung the accusation at them immediately after exchanging greetings with them. His father, no play-actor, obviously didn't know what he was talking about. But Mrs. Lee admitted, wistfully, that she had told Martha Washington she was anxious for a brief visit with her eldest son, whom she hadn't seen in almost three years. Harry, afforded a glimpse of women at work, knew this was one battle he couldn't win, and forgave her.

Like so many families in so many wars, the Lees scarcely knew their son. An exuberant youth had ridden off to war, and a grim, taciturn young man who seemed far older than his twenty-three years had come home. He spoke and thought of nothing but the war, and couldn't be distracted. He dutifully went out to inspect the plantation with his father, but wasn't interested, and when shown the books for the past year, confessed he had no head for agricultural figures.

He had changed in other ways, too. He never quoted the poets, and he retired early every night, sleeping until late the following morning. And he disturbed the routines of Leesylvania by sending servants to Alexandria for the latest war news. But in some respects he was still the same. He ate anything, at any hour. He paid "duty calls" on relatives in the neighborhood, but made no attempt to conceal his boredom. He spent an entire morning cleaning, polishing, and adjusting the hair-spring triggers on a brace of pistols he had bought in Baltimore.

He tried out several colts, advising his father that several were valuable and that others should be sold. And when he learned that farm animals were difficult to procure, he promised to send home the first pair of work horses awarded to him as booty. It was his prerogative, as a field-grade officer, to keep five percent of the loot he captured, but as worldly goods had always meant so little to him and the army's needs had been so great, he had never bothered to exercise his rights.

Mrs. Lee had entertained fond hopes that her son might become interested in an eligible young lady. It was no accident that a half-dozen or more of the most eligible happened to drop in for coffee and a chat at the homes of relatives he was visiting. But Harry scarcely bothered to look at any of them. He was civil to them, of course, his gallantry making it impossible for him to treat any woman rudely, but one of the girls later complained that he was unaware of her existence, even when looking straight at her.

Had Mrs. Lee been a trifle more perspicacious, she would have wondered why Harry paid three calls at Stratford, a large estate on the Potomac owned by distant, wealthy cousins, and why he made no protest when, on each of these visits, he was taken on long tours of the property by the eldest daughter of the house, Matilda Lee. Perhaps Harry's mother did know of these rides, but dismissed them from her mind as insignificant. After all, Matilda was a girl of only sixteen, just approaching womanhood, and Harry was an experienced soldier who had endured the privations and horrors of war for three years.

It is unlikely that an active romance was sparked during these calls of Harry's at Stratford in 1779. Harry would have been able to keep quiet if he and Matilda had realized they were drawn to each other, but Matilda enjoyed babbling everything she knew to a large circle of confidantes, most of them relatives. And the secret undoubtedly would have made the family rounds, particularly in an age when everyone wrote long letters and when women had nothing better to occupy them while the menfolk were off at war.

Nevertheless, Matilda made an impression on Harry, and he didn't forget her. Occasionally, in his infrequent letters to his parents following his 1779 furlough, he asked them to tender his affectionate regards to Cousin Matilda at Stratford.

Apparently a soldier's life had not altered Harry's basic attitude toward women. Ladies still found him fascinating, but he thought flirtation cheap, and refused to indulge in it. Several more years would pass before he would show that he was a one-woman man— or, at least, that he was interested in only one at a time.

His father was mildly puzzled because Harry paid no visits to the brothels of the area during his visit, and finally asked him why he was abstinent. According to a letter the elder Lee wrote to his brother, Harry replied, "*I am ever sensible of the good name this family enjoys in the county, sir.*" Being a Lee was a full-time job.

No messenger came from New York to disturb Harry's furlough, but he found himself incapable of waiting and wondering on the sidelines. So, instead of spending nineteen days at Leesylvania, he left after fifteen, and returned to duty by the shortest routes. His leave of absence had been useful, of course. He had satisfied his mother, gained a few pounds and spent several interesting hours with Cousin Matilda, who had been a mere child in 1776.

Also, the family tailor had made him a set of handsome new uniforms, which he had badly needed. So, all in all, the furlough had been a success.

Sir Henry Clinton had obligingly done nothing significant during Harry's absence from his post. But it became evident, during the late spring of 1779, that the British hoped to extend their hold up the Hudson. Their pivotal headquarters on the river was a virtually impregnable fort, Stony Point, which sat astride the crown of a rugged, high hill. It was surrounded by a stone wall, it was protected by artillery as well as infantry lookouts and was defended by a large but unknown number of men.

Of late there had been more activity than usual at Stony Point, and Harry reported this fact to Washington. The commander-in-chief pondered for a time, and reached some conclusions of his own. He had grown strong, and was becoming more powerful with each passing day. It was no longer necessary for him to wait fearfully for each new enemy attack, and he saw no reason he couldn't launch an offensive or two of his own.

He took two simultaneous steps. First, he formed a new infantry unit, an elite corps of the sort the Americans had always lacked. Every soldier enlisted in it was a veteran of at least two years' combat service, and every officer selected for command and staff positions was known personally to Washington and his staff.

Anthony Wayne, restlessly killing time on furlough, was summoned by Washington to take command of this new brigade of light infantry, which was given the best and most modern of equipment. Picket lines were established to keep out all outsiders, both military and civilian, and the brigade went into intensive training.

Meanwhile Harry Lee received secret instructions in Washington's own hand, ordering him to find out everything he could about Stony Point, its garrison and the approaches to it. The Partizans went to work, and Harry scouted every inch of the ground himself, one night approaching so close to the stone wall that he could count each heel click of the Redcoat sentry's heels on the stone ramparts.

The Partizans' Third Troop, composed exclusively of Oneida, set up a round-the-clock watch on the fort, and Allan McLane established a lookout post in the woods across the Hudson. An hour-by-hour log was kept on every visitor, every departure, every arrival of bargeloads of supplies carried up the Hudson by boat.

But there were some facts Harry could not obtain. He could only guess at the garrison's size, and he knew nothing of its interior bastions. There was only one way to get the information he sought, and he wrote Washington, asking for permission to hire a spy. He warned that the expense might be great.

The commander-in-chief sent a reply by return courier, granting Harry the right to do whatever he deemed necessary and authorizing him to spend any sum he deemed appropriate. But a word of caution was added: under no circumstances should the spy allow himself to be caught.

Harry found his spy, and the man went into the fort. It is one of history's more vexing frustrations to discover that no details of this phase of the operation are available. Neither then nor later did Harry—or McLane, the only other man who knew what was happening—write a single word on the espionage operation.

It was sufficient for military purposes to send a dispatch five days later to General Washington. Major Lee had the honor to report that the garrison consisted of seven hundred seventy-two officers and men, that there were eleven artillery pieces mounted and ready for use, and that he acquired accurate maps of the post's interior.

Washington was satisfied, and Wayne's elite light infantry began a march so secret that only the commander and his colonels knew the brigade's destination, although the men realized they were on more than a training march and were in for a fight. Washington had warned Wayne that, based on the information Harry had supplied, the fort would be impregnable if the enemy learned of the assault even ten minutes before it was made. Therefore the Partizans, acting in close coordination with Wayne, took the most careful and elaborate security precautions of the war.

Allan McLane's Troop cleared all traffic, both military and civilian, from the road leading to Stony Point and an area one mile inland from the Hudson. Grizzled Partizans tapped politely at farmhouse doors and told the residents that, for the sake of their health, it would be wise to remain indoors for the night.

No detail was overlooked, and the Third Troop was given a highly unusual assignment, that of clearing all dogs from the vicinity of Stony Point. It had occurred to Harry that the barking of just one animal might arouse the entire garrison.

The First Troop, meanwhile, accepted a difficult land-and-water mission. Some Virginians ranged up and down the shore on both sides of the Hudson, while those familiar with small boats were given the task of hiding in canoes and preventing all craft, large and small alike, from approaching the fort. The men were under strict instructions, however, not to use firearms under any circumstances. Precisely how unhorsed cavalrymen in canoes were expected to halt a British gunboat, for example, had one appeared, was not made clear in Harry's orders.

Shortly after Wayne's march had begun, Harry, who was concealed in thickets near the base of Stony Point, learned from Captain Lindsay that a member of the First Troop had deserted. No one knew the man's destination, but if he chose to alert the enemy, hundreds of Americans would be killed.

Harry handled the crisis at once, and gave instructions that later subjected him to a great deal of criticism. A small squad under the command of a trusted sergeant from Virginia was sent in pursuit of the deserter, and the unfortunate man was caught a short time later, less than two miles from the Partizans' bivouac deep in the woods west of the Hudson.

He was hanged immediately, without benefit of trial by court-martial or any other legal procedure. Later, when the incident became known, Harry shrugged off the protests of humanitarians. "The lives of more than thirteen hundred Americans were at stake," he declared, "and if faced with the same situation again, my conduct would not be altered one whit from the decisions I made that night."

The time agreed for a rendezvous with Wayne approached slowly, and at ten o'clock Harry was waiting for the general at the edge of a marsh about a mile and one-half from the fort. The two men, each an admirer of the other, met on schedule and shook hands. Harry requested a favor. The Partizans had spent many days in the most grueling, unrewarding labor, and were anxious to join in the attack. He requested permission to place his troops under Wayne's command for the operation.

The general regretfully refused. Horses could not climb the Stony Point slope, as Harry had pointed out in his reconnaissance reports, so cavalry would be an encumbrance rather than a help. However, as a personal mark of esteem, Wayne agreed to let the horsemen act as a reserve on whom he could call in case of dire need.

Harry, McLane, and two Oneida acted guides, leading the twelve hundred men of the brigade around the edge of the swamp toward the Hudson, then up a tortuous path on the west slope of Stony Point. There, while Anthony Wayne waited with his vanguard for the rest of the brigade, Harry and McLane retraced their steps down the slope and went off to assemble the Partizans in the woods.

The attack was a brilliant success. Wayne launched simultaneous assaults from two directions, the element of surprise was complete and the British garrison was forced to surrender after a brief flurry of fighting in which General Wayne himself suffered one of the night's few casualties, a minor scalp injury. The services of the Partizans were neither needed nor utilized.

The capture of Stony Point was of little strategic importance, as events transpired, and had virtually no direct influence on the outcome of the war. But its psychological significance was enormous. For the first time since the outbreak of hostilities in 1775, Americans had taken the offensive in a major operation and won a clear-cut victory. Newspapers hailed the feat as equal to the defeat of Burgoyne at Saratoga which was nonsense, and also pointed out that, at Saratoga, Gates and Arnold had been on the defensive, while at Stony Point Wayne had been the attacker. In this respect the contemporary accounts were accurate.

The country went wild with joy. "Mad Anthony" Wayne became America's darling, and Harry Lee received his due share of glory, which was considerable. The Continental Congress ordered a gold medal struck in honor of the victory, and for some decades thereafter, September 15 was celebrated as a holiday in New York, Pennsylvania, Virginia, and Delaware. About one-third to one-half of Wayne's brigade came from Connecticut, but the legislature in Hartford delayed in taking action to proclaim the day a holiday until the end of the war, by which time the victory was seen in its proper perspective.

Harry shared in the additional fame achieved at Stony Point, but received no direct rewards. The Congress, in its wisdom, treated him in the same indifferent, unjust manner that had so infuriated many other officers of merit, leading some to resign their commissions and, in the case of Benedict Arnold, contributing to the dissatisfaction that caused one of America's finest officers to become a traitor and transfer his allegiance to the Crown.

Anthony Wayne, his colonels and their staffs, received official commendations from the Congress, which neglected to mention either Harry or his Partizan officers in the praise-filled document. Vast quantities of supplies and a huge sum of gold and silver was captured at Stony Point, and the Military Affairs committee of the Congress voted a share of $170,000 to the officers of the brigade, to be divided according to rank. The Congress subsequently ratified the committee's bill, and again the Partizans were excluded.

As a final blow, all officers of the brigade lower than the grade of lieutenant colonel were promoted one rank. The names of Partizan officers, from Harry down, were not on the list.

General Washington delivered a stinging oral rebuke to members of the Military Affairs committee who visited his headquarters, and Wayne went a step further, writing a long letter protesting that the Partizans who had made his victory possible had been cruelly ignored. But Harry Lee, McLane, and Lindsay reacted with dignity, tact and, above all, remarkable restraint. All of these hot-blooded young men had the good sense to keep their mouths shut.

Washington, always vexed by his relations with the Congress, did his best to compensate for the oversight. His first move was to add still another Troop to the Partizan Force. Its captain was Henry Peyton and its second-in-command was Lieutenant George Handy. Both were Virginians, friends whom Harry had known most of his life, and he realized they and their veterans were trustworthy, dependable in any situation.

The Partizan Force was now the single largest body of cavalry in the Continental Army. In some state militia units it was as big as a regiment, and in all it was the equal of a battalion. By definition its commander deserved the rank of lieutenant colonel, even though the Congress had not yet seen fit to promote Harry.

In the reorganization of the Partizans, Harry offered the permanent post of second-in-command to McLane, but the Delaware horseman had few personal ambitions, and preferred to remain in command of his own troop. So, as Lindsay was outranked in length of service by Peyton, the latter was given the position, and hence would be the first to be granted the grade of major, if and when the Congress saw fit to recognize the enlarged status of the Force.

A sympathetic Washington made it still easier for his favorite cavalryman to achieve greater glory. No major operations requiring the services of horse troops were pending, so Major Lee was given orders as extraordinary as they were surprising. By command of the General himself, the Partizans were granted the privilege of originating and executing any project of their own that struck their fancy and would be "useful to the nation's cause." Washington stipulated only one condition: he required Harry to obtain his permission before planning and executing any operation.

After three years of serving others, Harry Lee was on his own at last, and was determined to make the most of his opportunity. *"I lose no sleep over the Congress's snub,"* he wrote to his parents late in July, 1779. *"My officers and I spend all our waking hours studying maps of the enemy's positions, and tomorrow we ride to inspect a site that offers the promise of as great a victory as any achieved by our cohorts in the war. We have in mind a scheme so daring that if it but bears fruit, we shall rattle the teeth of Sir Henry Clinton so loudly that even the fine gentlemen dozing in the halls of the Congress shall hear the sound.*

"Pray for me, I beg you, that all goes well with my Grand Enterprise."

VI

THE GRAND ENTERPRISE

Major Harry Lee and Captains McLane, Peyton, and Lindsay set
out from the Partizans' headquarters on the Hudson, each accompanied by a personal servant whose saddlebags were filled with the
silver, plate, and spare linen of the elegant young gentlemen. Also
included in the party were two Oneida officers of the Third
Troop, who may have marveled at the airs assumed by their
colleagues. But Harry and his subordinates did not think it unusual to be traveling in such style, nor did the members of infantry units they encountered on their journey south.

The cavalry had been a special corps of the gentry from the start
of the war, and now that the army was in more comfortable circumstances and still expanding, it was only fitting that the elite
should behave according to their station. When the group halted
for the night, the servants cooked supper over a wood fire, and the
officers were served on chinaware, drinking their small beer and ale
from cups of sterling and eating with knives that bore their mono-
grams. Presumably the Oneida, who dined with them, used their
fingers.

The following morning the party put aside its grand manners
as it circled south of Manhattan Island, and concentrated on the
business at hand. Ahead of them, on a small isthmus known as
Paulus Hook, bounded on one side by the Hudson River and on
the other by the little Hackensack, stood a sturdy log fort manned
by a full regiment of British Regulars. The Redcoats had been
firmly entrenched there ever since Billy Howe had captured New

York Town, and no one had ever dreamed of dislodging them—
for obvious reasons.

On one side was the Hudson, where great ships-of-the-line
and sleek frigates of Admiral Lord Howe's fleet rode at anchor, the
fort within striking distance of their great guns. The ships could
sail closer to Paulus Hook, easily and quickly, in case of attack,
and would be able to pour a murderous fire at Americans stupid
enough to brave their wrath. Also, the regiment at the garrison
could call for help in case of need, and approximately ten thousand veteran Redcoats stationed on Manhattan Island were close
at hand.

The rear of the fort enjoyed unusual advantages, too. The
muddy Hackensack formed a natural moat, difficult to ford, and
the nearest bridge connecting the isthmus with the mainland was
more than twelve miles away. On one flank was the hook of
land from which the place took its name, and the deep waters
there were patrolled by Royal Navy sloops designed for operations in just such waters. Each of these ships carried fifty marines,
members of a fighting force that had won its well-deserved reputation in scores of battles fought over the period of more than a
century.

The remaining flank enjoyed even better protection. A muddy
creek formed a natural barricade, and had been widened by the
British, who had made passage across it doubly difficult by stud-
ding it with irregularly placed rows of sharpened stakes driven
into the ground. Royal Engineers had built an old-fashioned drawbridge across the creek, and protected it with a large sentry detachment, two sets of gates as thick as those used to prevent
access to great European castles and, it appeared, three batteries
of six-inch cannon, each consisting of four guns.

The fort looked impregnable, and Captain Peyton, after making
a close study of the position, expressed the opinion that it could
not be taken. "*Major Lee disagreed,*" Allan McLane wrote. "*In his
opinion the obstacles created by Nature offer an irresistible challenge to the resourceful, and those conspired by man can be overcome by man. His confidence inspired in us the determination to
wrest the fort from the foe.*"

Paulus Hook had a strategic importance out of proportion to
its size. By maintaining a strong garrison in New Jersey, Clinton was in a position to threaten any American units that tried

to operate in the area. And, at the same time, he enjoyed the comfort of preventing a surprise assault on his main body in New York Town itself.

The very odds against the possibility of carrying out a successful operation at Paulus Hook made the venture attractive to Harry. He had been robbed of his fair share of the rewards granted by the Congress with such a lavish hand after the capture of Stony Point, and he sought a victory that even the most obtuse civilian could neither ignore nor denigrate.

He and his officers rode north again, up the Hudson, and spent several days discussing the project. Every conceivable angle was considered and weighed, every prospect of success analyzed, every chance of failure examined. Then Harry called in his junior officers for a council of war, and broke precedent by inviting an enlisted man, Sergeant Major John Champe, to sit in on the meeting. Champe, in Harry's opinion, was worth "any three Ensigns or two Lieutenants" in the Partizan Force.

All who attended the council were sworn to secrecy. The project was laid before them, and the risks frankly discussed. Then Harry called for a vote, and his subordinates unanimously declared themselves in favor of going ahead.

Next they needed Washington's approval, and Harry sent a formal note to Lieutenant Colonel Richard K. Meade, the general's appointments aide, asking for the privilege of an interview. Washington was busy, as always, but one day in early August, Harry was summoned to headquarters at West Point. The complacency of the usually serene commander-in-chief was shaken when he heard the idea, but he had gained enough respect for Harry's military talents to listen attentively.

Finally he agreed to give the project every consideration, provided that the chances of attaining success were fairly good and the risks relatively light. However, he said, he wanted a detailed plan spelled out for him before making a final decision.

Harry returned to his own headquarters farther down the Hudson and sent McLane back to Paulus Hook to gather as much intelligence as he could. The scout from Delaware did his usual, thorough job, and several days later the senior officers of the Partizan Corps gathered again to make and refine a plan of attack.

In order to obtain as many points of view as possible, Harry asked each officer to draw up his own individual plan. He did the same, and then the group assembled again to argue, accept, reject, and coordinate the various thoughts. Accustomed to working at high speed, under pressure, the Partizan chiefs completed their entire task within a very few days, and Harry sent a long, minutely detailed plan to General Washington.

Of primary importance was Harry's conviction that victory could not be obtained by the Partizans alone. The nature of warfare, he wrote, had become so complicated that cavalry required strong infantry support in any major operation. Therefore he requested that at least three hundred and fifty light infantry troops be placed under his command for the operation.

His basic plan of assault was relatively simple. He proposed that a bridge, pre-built in sections, be thrown across the Hackensack at one of its narrowest points. Then, he wrote, the cavalry, closely followed by infantry, should take the drawbridge by surprise and follow this move immediately by fanning out inside the post and making the soldiers of the garrison captive before they could fire their cannon and alert either the British fleet or the troops in New York Town across the Hudson.

An effective withdrawal would be as essential as a rapid attack, so cavalry would keep open the line of retreat. Everything would depend on secrecy, speed, and timing.

General Washington thought the plan ingenious, but found much at fault with it. "*Upon the whole, in the present position of the enemy's army*," he wrote to Harry, "*I should deem the attempt too hazardous, and not warranted by the magnitude of the object. We should lose more in case of failure than we could gain in case of success; and a single deserter, or disaffected inhabitant, may disclose the design and involve the party in ruin.*"

The commander-in-chief believed that a water-borne operation might enjoy a better chance of success, but was afraid the attention of the British fleet would be drawn to a string of transport ships. Lastly, he declared, the Continentals, although stronger than in previous years, had too few troops to spare three hundred and fifty infantrymen for a hit-and-run mission.

In spite of his objections, however, he indicated that he had no desire to call off the project, and urged Harry to give the matter more thought.

Harry Lee needed no urging. Already convinced that the plan

he and his officers had prepared was sound, he sought ways to improve it. The risk of discovery would be minimized, he believed, if the assault began at midnight or later. Post-midnight raids were unusual in eighteenth-century warfare, but the Americans had become expert in the use of unorthodox techniques to compensate for the inferiority of their numbers and armaments. He also suggested that a fleet of small boats be made available to stand by, in case of need, thus giving the attackers an alternate mode of retreat.

He wrote a long, persuasive letter to the commander-in-chief, and followed it with another personal visit. His salesmanship was persistent, and Washington finally capitulated, approving the scheme. He wrote Harry a brief note, which contained a final warning: "*No time should be lost in attempting to bring off cannon, stores, or any other articles, as a few minutes' delay might expose the party to imminent risk.*"

The infantrymen Harry wanted were sent to him on detached service from the division of the American nobleman, Lord Stirling of New Jersey, all of them combat veterans. Many were alumni of the winter at Valley Forge, and were enthusiastic at the prospect of serving directly under Harry Lee. But their ardor cooled somewhat when, on the afternoon of August 18, 1779, they gathered at his camp on the Hudson and learned they were going to participate in an operation as dangerous as any conceived in the four years the country had been at war.

A council of war was summoned, and Harry read his battle orders to the officers. The corps would be divided into three sections, two of which would perform security and holding missions. The third, a combined cavalry and infantry force, would operate under the personal command of Major Lee, and would dash into the fort, take prisoners and supplies, and then leave hurriedly while protected by the other two columns. These units would form a rear guard and, if necessary, fight a delaying action while retreating to the boats that Henry Peyton would have in readiness.

Stirling's officers, to whom the whole scheme was new, made it clear they were less than wildly optimistic. They were as willing to fight as any other group in the Army, but had no desire to commit suicide. Harry tried to win them over with a patriotic speech, which he repeated in somewhat broadened form shortly thereafter to the troops. His words were greeted with mild applause, but no one cheered. Experienced troops were far too aware of the risks to think in terms of loot and glory.

One officer, however, thought of little else. A major named Clarke was in charge of the infantry, and realized that if the project succeeded, its commander would emerge as a man of considerable stature. Clarke had served under Lord Stirling since the catastrophic Battle of Long Island in '75, and although faithful, loyal, and hard-working, had never won a single citation.

Aside from Harry, he was the only field-grade officer taking part in the expedition, and the thought occurred to him that if he should prove to be the senior, the command of the party rightfully belonged to him. He felt certain he had already been a major while Lee had been a captain, and just before the march began he asked the date of Harry's promotion.

Harry Lee was in no mood for trifles. He had been granted command of the expedition by General Washington himself, and after all his planning, hard work, and sales efforts had no intention of taking second place, at the last minute, to a nonentity. He muttered a reply intended to silence the infantry officer.

The march began shortly before sundown on the evening of August 18, each of the three columns traveling separately. The night was sultry and dark, with thick clouds overhead and a threat of rain in the air. Harry and his cavalry-infantry assault troops were supposed to arrive at a point directly opposite Paulus Hook at midnight, but lost their way in the gloom, and even the junior officers became panicky. The commander, aware that his reputation and future were at stake, pushed on doggedly, and finally led the column to its appointed place at three o'clock in the morning.

There a detachment of Virginians quickly erected the bridge, and a small, mounted scouting force under Lieutenant Michael Rudolph was sent ahead to determine whether the enemy had been alerted. Time was now the most precious of all factors; if the British discovered the presence of the raiders after daybreak, the whole attacking force could be cut off and either killed or captured. Tension was running high, and dawn was only two hours away.

Rudolph had returned with word that the Redcoats were sleeping, and the assault party started off at once, one platoon ordered to take the drawbridge while the others waded across the waist-high, muddy waters of the ditch. Contrary to custom and common sense, Harry rode with the vanguard.

More than fifty men had already scaled the stone wall of the fort when the attackers drew fire from blockhouses and the drawbridge. By then it was too late, Harry's reserves were moved up and the raiders fanned out, their bayonets ready. So far the Americans had not fired a single shot.

Redcoats and Hessian mercenaries began to surrender by the score, giving themselves up so quickly that something of a traffic jam developed as they were sent across the bridges. There was another, unexpected complication, too. The wives and children of many British officers and sergeants were living at the fort, and had to be evacuated with care. An officer could ruin his good name forever if he failed to treat noncombatants with elaborate courtesy. They were evacuated, too, all of them shown every consideration.

Harry was frantically busy. More than two hundred and fifty prisoners had been taken in the first charge, but the Redcoat colonel in command of the fort was not among them. Someone discovered that he was absent at a meeting in New York Town, where he had remained overnight, and Harry had to be satisfied with taking the person of his deputy, a major.

No one could find the key to the powder and ammunition magazine, so Harry ordered two detachments to batter down the strong wooden doors of the chamber, warning the officers to whom he gave the assignment, however, not to use firearms. Daylight would soon break, and several junior officers reported that although the cannon could be moved, they would slow the American retreat. Harry ordered them moved immediately, but insisted that first priority be given the prisoners, women, and children.

It proved impossible to break into the munitions stores in the time available before daybreak, so that attempt had to be abandoned. Harry, the last man to leave the fort, rode across the drawbridge a scant twenty minutes before dawn.

Now a new and unexpected hitch developed that put the entire operation in jeopardy. Captain Peyton's boats were nowhere to be seen near the rendezvous point. Harry's raiders were badly outnumbered by their prisoners, and were exhausted after their long march. No one had eaten a bite of food since the previous afternoon. And, to make matters still worse, most of those who had forded the ditch had taken insufficient precautions to protect their own powder, which had been rendered useless.

British reinforcements were only a short distance away, and the sky was growing lighter. Harry ignored the grumbling and carping of Major Clarke, and sent a courier galloping off to the headquarters of Lord Stirling, at the village of New Bridge, for reinforcements. Soon thereafter the raiders faced their first test when a company of Redcoat infantry appeared on the road directly ahead of the vanguard.

Harry knew of only one way to deal with the situation. A half-troop of horse rode down the foot soldiers, sabers flashing in the early morning light, and the attack was so rapid, so ferocious, that the British infantry surrendered. Only a few American officers, including Harry, who had led the charge himself, knew that his entire party was suffering from a critical lack of powder.

Stirling responded at once to Harry's plea for help, and a full battalion of American infantry appeared to give support and protect the raiders' rear. It was almost noon, and Harry expected the enemy to retaliate in force at any time. He ordered that the march continue, even though some of his men were now so weary they were staggering.

Early in the afternoon a strong detachment of Redcoat cavalry appeared, but Harry dispersed the foe by dividing his own small force of horsemen into two columns and attacking the British flanks. These tactics were so unorthodox they bewildered the enemy, who withdrew.

Peyton's men, who had gone through a difficult time of their own, finally joined the column, increasing its strength. And late in the afternoon Harry finally marched into Lord Stirling's camp with nearly four hundred prisoners. He had lost one man killed and two wounded in the entire operation.

He, his Partizans, and the infantry who had accompanied them were fed a hearty meal and threw themselves on the ground to sleep. In spite of near-disaster, mishaps and the confusion that seemed inevitable in military operations, they had won a clear-cut victory against great odds.

General Washington responded at once with, for him, lavish praise. In a letter to the Continental Congress, he declared, *"Major Lee fulfilled his trust with great address, intelligence and industry."*

He was even warmer in a personal letter he sent to Harry, saying, "*You will find my sense of your conduct, and that of the officers and men under your command, expressed in the General Orders of yesterday, and in my letter to the Congress. I congratulate you on your success.*"

Stirling quickly congratulated Harry, too, and so did Anthony Wayne, Nathanael Greene, and Henry Knox, generals whose opinions he valued highly. Another who wrote him was the young Marquis de Lafayette, the French volunteer who was a kindred spirit, and who declared, "*The more I have considered the situation of Paulus Hook, the more I have admired your enterprising spirit and all your conduct in that business.*"

Newspapers in Philadelphia, Boston, Baltimore, and the other major cities of the nation hailed the triumph, and Harry Lee was now assured of the esteem he sought from his fellow countrymen. He was no longer an officer who showed mere promise, no longer one who helped others attain victories, but had won laurels of his own in a manner that could be denigrated by no one.

Even Sir Henry Clinton, embarrassed and unhappy, issued an order to his own outpost commanders telling them to be more alert in the future. And at a dinner given in his honor by New York Tories, he said, "I wish I had a few more officers of my own who display Major Lee's spirit. He is no Marlborough, but his gallantry and our slovenliness make him appear great."

Harry had every reason to anticipate that he would receive his due rewards from the Congress. He would be made a lieutenant colonel, and his officers would be promoted one rank. Even though he had captured no booty, his victory had been as great as that won by "Mad Anthony" Wayne at Stony Point.

Instead he received notice that he was under arrest, and would be tried by a court-martial board on eight serious charges, any of which, if proved, would subject him to immediate, dishonorable discharge from the Army.

VII

THE TRIAL

Harry Lee had been too successful for his own good at Paulus Hook, and the security precautions taken prior to the launching of the enterprise had been so thorough and complete that not even high-ranking American officers had known of the venture. Two of them were furious, each believing that he should have been given the opportunity to win such glory. Brigadier General Peter Muhlenberg, sometimes known as "the pastor," and Brigadier General William Woodford were competent, loyal officers. Both commanded infantry brigades, and both were doubly upset because an officer who had never held a major command and was much junior to them had been granted the privilege of making the raid.

They complained in formal letters to Lord Stirling, their superior, who was required under Army procedures to forward the communications to Washington. Their statements were based in part on hearsay evidence, and they were fed all the ammunition they wanted by the disgruntled Major Clarke, who declared that he would have assumed command of the expedition himself had Harry not lied to him about the date of his promotion from captain to major.

The actual charges were varied. One specified Clarke's complaint. Another stated that Harry had ordered a retreat before capturing a redoubt still in enemy hands at the fort, a failure that had placed the entire mission in jeopardy. He was also charged with having taken no steps to destroy the British storehouse, arsenal, and blockhouses.

Another charge stated that he had given various commands to junior officers rather than to men senior to them, and that in so doing he had defied rules of military procedure. Even those he had favored, the indictment said, had been given their appointments in an "irregular manner."

One long charge was devoted to the retreat from Paulus Hook, and declared that he had carried it off in "such a confused, irregular, unmilitary manner" that the Americans would have suffered great losses had they been intercepted by a large body of the enemy. Finally, Harry was accused of conduct unbecoming an officer and gentleman.

The arrest had been ordered by General Washington, as Harry reported direct to the commander-in-chief, and Washington also directed that a court-martial board hear the charges and pass on them.

Harry Lee's first reaction was a stunned disbelief, which quickly gave way to wild anger. No matter what the board might rule, he wrote his parents, he intended to resign from the Army and return home. His letter stating this resolve was dated September 3, the day he received the unhappy news.

Within twenty-four hours, however, he had simmered down enough to experience doubts about the wisdom of such a course. The Army had been his only love, and he didn't know what to do. Deeply disturbed, he wrote a personal letter to General Washington, asking for advice and stating that, if it would help restore unity in the ranks of the highly placed, he would send his resignation to the Congress at once.

Washington sat down and penned a reply the instant Harry's letter reached him a few hours later. "*As you request my concurrence to the step you propose,*" he said, "*I do not find myself at liberty to give it, because it appears to me to be premature and unnecessary. From the time your report was dispatched to the Congress, there is no reason to suppose delay. I am firmly persuaded the event will show you they cannot possibly intend you injustice. I should be sorry you would suffer your sensibility to betray you into an error—which on reflection you would condemn.*"

Washington, that most impartial of men, had leaned far to

assure a worried subordinate of his support. Rarely had the commander-in-chief been so firm in his profession of friendship.

But Harry, having decided to face a court-martial board, couldn't help stewing. Most of the charges against him were false, and he felt confident he could prove his innocence. But several were serious. One concerned his failure to burn the enemy's stores and fortifications, another was that his retreat had been disorganized and unmilitary—which at least hinted at cowardice, and still another was Clarke's allegation that the young Virginian had lied in order to gain command of the expedition.

Harry had acted in accordance with the verbal instructions given him by General Washington, but as September wore on while he awaited trial, he couldn't help wondering whether he had understood those orders correctly. Again he wrote to the commander-in-chief, and again received an immediate reply.

Washington recalled their conversation in complete detail, he wrote, and said he had directed that *"no time should be lost in attempting to bring off cannon, stores, or any other articles, as a few minutes' delay might expose the party at least to imminent risk. I further recollect, that I likewise said, that no time should be spent, in such case, in collecting stragglers of the garrison, who might skulk and hide themselves, lest it should prove fatal; also that, if the post could not be carried in an instant by surprise, the attempt must be relinquished. My objects were to surprise it, to bring off the garrison immediately, and to effect a secure retreat."*

Harry's Partizan colleagues were overjoyed when he showed them Washington's letter. The commander-in-chief, writing in his own hand, had dispelled several of the charges. He took still another step, too, as Harry and his friends soon discovered.

Although unwilling to censure two generals who had proved themselves dependable, Washington wrote a letter to Lord Stirling that stopped just short of a rebuke to Muhlenberg and Woodford, while simultaneously disposing of other charges. *"The transactions in the Virginia Line,"* he said, *"in consequence of the enterprise against Paulus Hook, are to me as painful as they were unexpected.*

"The only point I shall take notice of is the giving the command to Major Lee. This could be exceptionable, but on three principles, his being a horse-officer—his being unconnected with the

division from which the greatest part of the detachment was drawn, or the number of men employed being too large for his rank." All three objections, the commander-in-chief admitted, were reasonable, as they had no foundation in military custom or common sense.

Then he went on to destroy the arguments. *"Major Lee's situation,"* he said, *"made it most convenient to employ him to make the necessary previous inquiries: It was the best calculated to answer the purpose without giving suspicion. He executed the trust with great address, intelligence and industry—and made himself perfectly master of the post with all its approaches and appendages.*

"After having taken so much pains personally to ascertain facts, and having from a series of observations and inquiries arranged in his own mind every circumstance on which the undertaking must turn, no officer could be more proper for conducting it; and as the command was not to exceed what any officer of his rank might decently be intrusted with, it would have been a piece of hardship if not injustice to have given the honor of the expedition to another."

The communication was a private one, theoretically, but copies mysteriously found their way into every command of consequence in the Army. Greene and Knox soon added their views, both expressing firm opinions that the commander-in-chief had been right. It was time, they said, that the talents of Harry Lee were recognized. Lafayette became furiously partisan, and argued with anyone who dared to say a word in favor of the position taken by Muhlenberg and Woodford.

Another who raced to Harry's defense was Alexander Hamilton, and the mere fact that he spoke up on the subject was an indication that the gods were smiling on Harry Lee. It was Hamilton's place, as Washington's senior aide-de-camp, to maintain a discreet silence in all controversies within the military establishment. The staff of the commander-in-chief, like the commander himself, was expected to remain neutral, and no one knew the rules of the game better than Hamilton, who had developed a talent for keeping his mouth shut, a difficult feat for a fiery, ambitious, and brilliant young man to perform.

Hamilton appears to have spent the better part of several days in mid-September 1779 writing letters to brother officers on the justice of Harry Lee's cause. The Army thought it unlikely that he would have spoken so freely without the consent, or even the encouragement, of General Washington. There were many, consequently, who believed that Harry would be vindicated.

But Muhlenberg and Woodford continued to grumble, and in spite of the heavy artillery the other side had unlimbered, a large number of brigadier generals and colonels sided with them. These officers, all eager to win renown in their own right, disliked the prospect of watching glory snatched from them by their energetic juniors.

Major Clarke still complained, too, forcing Lord Stirling to silence him with the reminder that the matter would be settled by the court-martial board. Stirling's intervention seemed to place him in Harry's camp, and created fresh complications.

Major General William Alexander, still known to all of his colleagues as Lord Stirling, was a courageous, hard-driving officer of Scottish descent who would have won even greater renown than he achieved had he not been a shade too fond of brandy-wine. He never drank on duty, nor did he allow liquor to interfere with his calling in any other way, but, on those occasions when he had nothing better to occupy him after eating a supper of the beefsteak and oyster pie that was his favorite dish, he liked to settle down for an evening with a jug of French or Spanish brandy.

On these nights he was inclined to speak his mind freely to any subordinates who had been invited to share a cup with him. He was particularly free in his conversation one evening in mid-September. Until then, no one had known of his rebuke to Clarke, nor had he indicated his own stand in the controversy. Now, however, he made it plain that he thought Muhlenberg and Woodford were behaving like disgruntled old maids.

The news that Stirling, too, had taken sides reached the commander-in-chief's headquarters. And Washington was forced to revise his plans. He had intended to ask Lord Stirling to become president of the court-martial board, but his lordship had disqualified himself, so someone else had to be found. It wasn't easy, as virtually every senior officer seemed to be unburdening himself on the subject.

Meanwhile the Continental Congress was in an embarrassing predicament. Major Lee had won a brilliant victory, and his admirers in that august body were demanding that his feat be recognized and rewarded. One of the most persistent of his advocates was the powerful and universally respected Richard Henry Lee, his kinsman, and when Richie Lee spoke, the Congress listened. The distinguished legislator had the good sense not to make a public issue of the matter, however, but confined himself to private conferences with small groups of his fellow Congressmen.

The Congress, never noted for the speed of its deliberations, artfully walked a fence, marked time and busied itself with other matters. No one ever knew the outcome of a military trial in advance, even though Major Lee apparently had strong support in the Army. And the Congress, which had made more than its fair share of blunders through the years, saw no reason to put itself on a spot. If the major was exonerated, something could be done to commemorate the capture of the Redcoat garrison at Paulus Hook. On the other hand, if the major should be found guilty, the Congress would happily forget his victory.

Congressmen were politicians, by nature a cautious breed, so their reluctance to join in the fray was both sensible and natural. But Harry didn't see their position in that light. The facts of his victory spoke for themselves, he wrote to his parents in a candid letter, and he was bitterly disappointed over the refusal of the Congress to take cognizance of his triumph.

"If they are so cowardly they dare not embrace me," he wrote, "let them at least reward the heroism of those fine officers and men who served with me and made possible our victory. Whether I was right or wrong, a scheming usurper of command and a pusillanimous poltroon in my conduct, it cannot be controverted that the joint force of cavalry and infantry did take possession of the fort, march the garrison into captivity and behave in such a manner so as to escape with fewer casualties than those marked in any other engagement since the war's commencement.

"I know not whether I am more disgusted with jealous officers who lust after my scalp, or weakling politicians who are afraid to admit the facts of a victory already known to all the world."

The elder Lees wisely showed his letter to no one, and for once Martha Washington was not called in as a confidante. Harry's parents seemed to understand that someone—probably their son —would be stung if the hornet's nest was jarred too hard.

The end of September came, and the board had not yet been summoned. Harry's patience was at the breaking point, but Washington had not yet found the officers he wanted to sit on the tribunal. Perhaps, too, he was deliberately allowing passions to cool. When he acted at last, on September 29, he once again revealed his genius.

The president of the board was Brigadier General Anthony Wayne, the whole nation's hero since his triumph at Stony Point. While it was true that he was Harry Lee's friend, close associate and long-time admirer, it was generally conceded—even by the supporters of Muhlenberg and Woodford—that he was a patriot who would put justice ahead of personal considerations.

The deputy president was Colonel Dan Morgan of Virginia, soon to be made a brigadier general, and his choice was hailed as a master stroke. Morgan was an infantryman, the leader of a band of expert riflemen whose exploits were legendary, and no one could accuse him of being overly partial to the cavalry. As he was a Virginian, he was a native of the same state as the major participants in the quarrel. A rawboned giant with a violent temper, no one would dare accuse him of taking sides in advance. And best of all, he had not expressed an opinion in the case, probably because he had been suffering from a painful and incapacitating attack of arthritis.

Four lieutenant colonels and three majors made up the rest of the panel. All were infantrymen, and Captains McLane and Peyton complained bitterly that no horse-soldiers had been selected. In justice to General Washington, there were no horse-soldiers of Harry's own rank or higher in the vicinity and, therefore, available for court-martial duty. Army protocol required that a man be tried only by his peers and superiors. It was possible, too, that the commander-in-chief deliberately tipped the scales in favor of the infantry to prevent still more outcries from Muhlenberg and Woodford at a later date.

Harry received a message late in the evening of September 29, summoning him to Smith's Cove, a village on the Hudson, and he appeared there early the following morning. General Wayne informed him of his right to employ counsel, either military or civilian, but he surprised the court by stating that he preferred to conduct his own defense. It was the first time in his life that the young man who had once hoped to become an attorney had practiced law.

The court spent the morning hearing the testimony of the defendant and that of a number of witnesses, all of them officers who had taken part in the Paulus Hook attack. The court then cleared the hall to deliberate in private, and after less than two hours Harry was called in to hear the verdict.

Most of the charges against him were dismissed, the tribunal commenting repeatedly that they were totally without foundation. They neatly disposed of the charge that he had assumed command of the expedition through trickery by expressing the opinion that "Major Lee did through inattention give Major Clarke a wrong date of his commission, but by no means intending of emposing on Major Clarke by assuming the command of him, having Express orders from his Excellency, the Commander-in-chief, for that special command." The court therefore deemed him honorably acquitted of the charge.

In dealing with this subject, the board was treading on delicate ground. It was extremely unlikely that Harry, even though otherwise occupied, could have forgotten the date of his promotion to major. In all probability he let a false date "slip out," in order to prevent an argument that might have disrupted his carefully made plans. The crux of the matter was that Washington had indeed given him supreme command of the party. He knew it, his own officers knew it and he had no intention of allowing a busybody from Stirling's division to usurp his rightful place.

On the eighth charge, that Harry's conduct had been unbecoming an officer and gentleman, the tribunal expressed itself firmly. "Major Lee's conduct," the findings read, "was Uniform and Regular, supporting his Military Character, magnanimity & judgment, and that he by no means acted Dorogatory to the Gentleman & Soldier, which character he fills with honor to his country and credit to the Army."

For all practical purposes, Harry had won, but was not free until the findings of the board were verified. The report was taken straight to General Washington, who again acted immediately, writing in his own hand on the last page, *"The Commander-in-Chief confirms the opinion of the Court. Major Lee is released from his arrest."*

Harry's exoneration was complete, and he returned to duty with his Partizan Force that same evening.

General Muhlenberg had the grace to bury the hatchet with a flourish, and wrote Harry a letter of congratulations. General Woodford maintained a stiff-necked silence, but when his path and Harry's accidentally crossed about five months later, he, too, made amends. In the presence of several officers, General Woodford offered his apologies for any inconvenience and embarrassment he might have caused. Harry accepted with the courtesy of one who was a gentleman and a Lee, just as he had replied in the same manner to General Muhlenberg's letter. Perhaps it was coincidental that he did not serve again with either officer at any time before the end of the war.

Now it was the turn of the Continental Congress to react, and that body responded at once, spurred by the prodding of Cousin Richard Henry Lee. Several lieutenants whom Harry had commended were promoted to the rank of captain, and the sum of fifteen thousand dollars was voted for distribution among the sergeants, corporals, and privates, "in such manner as the Commander-in-Chief should direct." This meant, for all practical purposes, that General Washington would accept Harry's advice in the matter.

Major Harry Lee himself received the warm congratulations of the Congress, "for the remarkable prudence, address and bravery displayed." Even more important, a special Congressional medal of gold was struck, and was subsequently presented to him in a ceremony held in General Washington's presence.

Inexplicably, however, he did not receive a promotion to the rank of lieutenant colonel. Still raw after his court-martial, Harry was at first inclined to believe that the slight had been deliberate, but General Washington made inquiries into the matter on his behalf, and Alexander Hamilton specifically assured the major that the Congress' failure to promote him had been nothing more than a technical oversight.

Such mishaps were common, and Harry accepted the disappointment with admirable philosophical detachment. He wore his gold medal on his tunic, a distinction that only a tiny handful of heroes enjoyed. He had acquired an international as well as a national reputation, and was known as a brilliant and courageous officer in England, France, and the German states. Eager mothers sought ways to interest him in their daughters, and he was regarded as the most eligible bachelor in the Continental line.

Most important of all, he had won the unqualified confidence of George Washington, who assured him that his talents would be utilized to the full. His promotion would be granted in due time—and, until then, there was work to be done for his country—and for greater glory.

VIII

"LEE'S LEGION"

Major Harry Lee's duties in the months following his vindication were dull, anticlimactic, and could have been performed by any competent junior officer. He threw a ring of Partizans around Manhattan Island, and kept watch on all British land and sea movements, reporting anything of significance to General Washington. He maintained a special lookout for a powerful French fleet sent to aid the Americans, and was the first to greet its eccentric commander, Admiral Count D'Estaing.

Only one phase of his activity interested him in the autumn of 1779. As the officer in charge of reconnaissance, he was given responsibility for maintaining the American espionage network in New York. He hired spies and gave them their missions, helped them slip undetected into the British-occupied city and then received their reports when they escaped.

Very little is known of this operation other than that it was extensive. The names of spies, the records of their accomplishments and of the sums paid them were—then, as in later wars—deemed so confidential that Harry's reports, both verbal and written, were submitted direct to General Washington, and were seen only by the commander-in-chief and a few of his personal aides. Within the confines of a small, select circle, Harry became known as a highly efficient spy master, and no doubt this experience prepared him, in part, for the great challenge that lay ahead.

Few Americans knew that Harry was directing an espionage

network. But Sir Henry Clinton was well aware of the young Virginian's activities, and in December wrote to the War Office, "*I have just hanged a spy, aged forty years or thereabouts, but was unable to find means of obtaining information from him before he was executed. For each of Major Lee's spies I capture and execute, a half-score must slip through my fingers. Would that Lee had been sent home in disgrace by his judges three months ago. The wretched fellow gives me no peace of mind.*"

In January 1780, Clinton may have breathed a trifle more easily, as Harry went home to Virginia on his second leave of absence since the start of the war. The conqueror of Paulus Hook was given the reception due a hero, and in spite of wartime shortages a ball was held in his honor soon after his arrival.

He happened to arrive during a relative lull in military operations, so other officers were visiting their homes, too, and Leesylvania echoed to the music of fiddles, the rumble of baritone laughter—and the excited whispers of the ladies who watched the handsome major single out his cousin, Matilda, as his partner for every quadrille.

The "divine Matilda," as her friends called her, was maturing rapidly, and was reputedly the most skilled flirt in a band of young women who made an art of toying with the affections of the opposite sex. Almost as tall as Harry, slender and vivacious, with dark brown hair that she piled high on her head, Matilda was perhaps the loveliest heiress in Virginia.

Rumors that abounded that January have become romantic legends. According to one, Matilda made a wager with a friend that she could fascinate Harry to such an extent that he would look at no other girl. If she set a net, she was caught in it herself. No one, not even a young lady whose intimates considered her a goddess, dared to deal lightly with the dashing Harry. He took himself too seriously, and if there was one quality of character in which he was conspicuously lacking, it was a robust sense of humor.

Harry spent much of his leave at Stratford, and his mother quietly breathed a sigh of relief. "*There is as yet no formal betrothal,*" she wrote Mrs. Washington, "*as Matilda is still too young for Marriage. But I believe there is a private Understanding between them, and that a Union will follow when next he returns to Virginia.*"

A long time would elapse before Harry again saw Matilda—or his own family's estate. The nature of the war was changing in 1780, and as one theatre of operations atrophied, another became active. Sir Henry Clinton's enclave at New York Town became an isolated bastion, and virtually all of the northern portion of the United States was now safely in American hands.

The War Office in London was directing a new strategy: the southern states were to be captured and the area made secure; thereafter a concerted drive would be made on the more heavily industrialized north. The British plan unfolded gradually, and the most able of Clinton's generals, Lord Cornwallis, was made the director of field operations.

Washington countered by sending his steadiest, most dependable comrade, General Nathanael Greene, to head a new corps in the south. He was given three thousand men, with a promise of more to follow, and Brigadier General Dan Morgan became his deputy in command of infantry.

But it soon became evident that foot soldiers alone could not stem the new Redcoat tide. The British made repeated landings everywhere in the southern states, and the harassed Americans didn't know where the enemy would strike next. Above all, they loathed and feared the man they considered the Devil incarnate, whom they called "Butcher" Tarleton.

Lieutenant Colonel Banastre Tarleton, the son of a Liverpool merchant, had been closely associated with Cornwallis ever since accompanying the general to America in 1776. He was a superb horseman, and displayed organizational talents that had won him a post as Cornwallis' brigade-major of cavalry. Now, with his lordship holding a higher post, Tarleton had been promoted, and headed a force which the newspapers in England fondly called the British Legion. It was made up in part of cavalry, in part of light infantry and, occasionally, called on the services of American Loyalists.

Tarleton specialized in the lightning raid, attacking communications and supply centers in surprise assaults, then withdrawing again very quickly. He spread havoc and terror wherever he went, and had a hand, in May of 1780, in the conquest of Charleston, South Carolina.

Nathanael Greene quietly and firmly took up the reins laid down by his incompetent predecessor, Horatio Gates, but he soon realized he needed fire to fight fire. South Carolina was occupied by the enemy, Cornwallis was planning a sweep to take North Carolina and Greene needed help.

Specifically, he needed a fast-moving legion of his own, made up of cavalry and light infantry that could operate as a vanguard, meet Tarleton's force with counterforce and harass Cornwallis as he himself was being badgered. He and General Washington considered only one man for the post of commander, and reached a joint decision more or less simultaneously.

Harry Lee, who had been one of the first to recognize the merits of combined cavalry-infantry operations and had utilized just such a force at Paulus Hook, was summoned to headquarters. There General Washington asked him if he would like to become Commandant of such a Legion and Chief of Cavalry in the Southern Department. The question, of course, was a rhetorical formality.

Washington renewed his application to the Continental Congress for Major Lee's promotion, asking that it be granted with dispatch, and meanwhile Harry went to work. He was given his choice of cavalry units, and naturally took most of the troops who had served with him in the Partizan Force. He was also granted the privilege of selecting his own infantry.

In all, he was promised five hundred men, but the usual delays and military mishaps made it possible for him to go into the field with no more than three hundred and fifty officers and men. The Legion was an elite body, made up in entirety of Continentals who had enlisted for the duration of the war. All were issued new equipment, the best of the arms and supplies now arriving from France. And Harry, ever-conscious of appearance, ordered a new uniform for the Legion: plumed helmets, dark green tunics, white breeches, and black boots.

"Lee's Legion," as the unit was immediately dubbed by the newspapers, was organized in a single month's time. Harry was so busy hurrying from place to place in New Jersey, gathering provisions, blankets, saddles, and arms that a courier needed two and a half days to catch up with him and hand him his commission as lieutenant colonel, granted by the Congress and countersigned by Washington. Ironically, Colonel Lee was too busy to reply to the many messages of congratulations he received on his belated promotion.

Generals Washington and von Steuben reviewed the Legion in a hastily arranged ceremony, and late in November 1780, Harry began his long march south to join General Greene—and win himself a permanent niche in American history as a field commander of great distinction.

From the outset the Legion was forced to prove its mettle. Greene and Morgan were in trouble, and there was no time to waste. Harry set a furious pace, riding at the head of the column himself, and his cavalry and infantry learned how to work together by marching together. Quartermasters were sent ahead each day to buy food and arrange for overnight bivouacs, and those who were serving with Harry for the first time learned that he gave an order just once, expected it to be obeyed instantly and without question, and would dismiss any man who failed to do what he was told, when he was told to do it.

Early in December the Legion, tired and dusty, reached General Greene's headquarters on the banks of the Pee Dee River in North Carolina. The men were given a night to themselves, and Harry immediately joined Greene and Dan Morgan at a dinner conference that lasted most of the evening.

The situation was discouraging. The British held a number of small outpost fortresses in the Carolinas, and used them as headquarters for raids on the countryside intended to disrupt the American defenses and allow Cornwallis to move north unimpeded. At the moment the British were opposed only by a band of irregulars and militia under the command of a forty-eight-year-old brigadier general of South Carolina militia, Francis Marion.

Greene and Morgan praised Marion lavishly, although they called his guerrilla fighters undisciplined and sometimes undependable. Certainly the "Swamp Fox" was proving himself an elusive nuisance to the British, and Tarleton had made several unsuccessful attempts to capture him and disband his irregulars. Harry was instructed to find Marion in the swamp country and join him in his assaults on the Redcoat outposts.

The situation was a delicate one, and required great tact. A lieutenant colonel of the Regular Army who was also Chief of Cavalry in the South had more authority than a brigadier general of state militia, and the Continentals had learned to regard all militia with contempt. But a young man in his mid-twenties had to be careful in his handling a middle-aged eccentric who happened to be performing a vitally needed service for his country. General Greene authorized Harry to take precedence over Marion, in case of need, but urged him not to exercise his prerogative of command.

The Legion set out at dawn the following morning, after a night's rest as short as any spent on the march south. All baggage wagons and other encumbrances were left behind at Greene's headquarters. *"In accordance with Colonel Lee's orders,"* Harry much later wrote in his *Memoirs, "each man carried his fair share of ball and powder, emergency supplies of hardtack and jerked beef, and provisions for the horses. Colonel Lee found it repugnant to common sense and common militarism for a light corps to expect to operate advantageously with even a single wagon."*

The Legion moved cautiously but swiftly into the territory between the Pee Dee and Santee rivers, and Harry sent an officer ahead with a letter to Marion suggesting modes of conducting joint operations. The courier found Marion without too much difficulty, but the dour South Carolinian who daily drank several drams of vinegar and led a Spartan life was astonished by the appearance of a lieutenant who looked like a toy soldier on parade—or worse, like a British officer.

Marion's reply to the suggestion of conducting joint operations was vague. Although he didn't decline the invitation in so many words, he didn't accept, either, and after sending the Legion courier off with a hazy verbal message rather than a written communication, he vanished deeper into his swamp country.

Harry's first report to General Greene was guarded, but he made no attempt to hide his discouragement. He would approach Marion again at the first opportune moment, he said. Meanwhile he would continue to survey the area, and he urged Greene to march farther south. "Here," he said, "are plenty of provisions and a direct centre to the crossroads. It is country well suited to the type of operations you contemplate."

His route "happened" to take him farther into the swamp country, and again he sent out couriers, requesting the privilege of a meeting with General Marion. The need for a show of courtesy to a fellow American prompted the unenthusiastic Marion to agree. The Legion and irregulars met in a valley at sundown one cold evening in mid-January, and each immediately bristled. The Continentals were disgusted by the shabby creatures with long, unkempt hair, ragged clothes and beards, and the guerrillas in linsey-woolsey looked coolly down their thin noses at the "toy soldiers."

Harry Lee and the brigadier general who was twice his age found an immediate rapport, however, to their mutual surprise. Harry's son, Henry, Jr., writing years later in his definitive book, *The Campaign of 1781 in the Carolinas*, repeatedly stressed that his father and General Marion were always in accord and became fast friends. There is no positive evidence to the contrary and much to substantiate this view, in spite of rumors subsequently spread by men who had not served with either commander.

The record of their joint achievements indicates that Harry Lee and Francis Marion understood each other and worked well together. There was much, to be sure, that drew them together. The first consideration was the desperate state of affairs that American men at arms faced in the Carolinas. Cornwallis, commanding a corps of ten thousand to fifteen thousand men—no one could be sure of the exact strength of his army—faced a force that at best could muster five thousand men, including irregulars. The British were supported by artillery and buoyed by cavalry; their quartermaster and ordnance officers supplied all their wants, both personal and military.

It was essential that Americans work together. Francis Marion was a shrewd judge of men, and so was Harry Lee, who, in spite of his youth, had spent almost five years in command of troops. The Continental lieutenant colonel and the militia brigadier recognized kindred spirits in each other. Each was cautious, yet daring. Each held sound military views. Each was firmly in command of his own men, and each was blunt and honest.

The longer Harry and Marion talked, the more they warmed to each other. They shared a beefsteak, eaten on a trencher of bread, and soon found themselves planning a joint operation. Marion even offered the Virginian a nip of his vinegar, and Harry manfully drank it without shuddering, which won him a high place in Marion's esteem.

They decided their first joint venture should be an attack on the British garrison at Georgetown, South Carolina, a fort located in the delta below the mouth of the Pee Dee River. The seeming impregnability of the post attracted both men. The fort was protected on the east by boulders and the tides of the Atlantic, and on the west by patrols sent out in strength by the garrison commander, a Redcoat colonel named Campbell.

Marion knew of several chinks in the fort's armor. On the northeast, where the post faced a bay, the terrain on the opposite shore was too swampy to permit patrols to operate too near the shore. Even more important, there were several small, heavily wooded islands that studded the bay and provided natural steppingstones to the Georgetown garrison. With a lack of foresight typical of British operations in the still-primitive New World, the Redcoats had neither established small sentry detachments on these islands nor erected defense works of any kind there.

Harry and Marion were in complete agreement: Georgetown was ripe for a surprise attack. A simple plan was worked out. The Legion's infantry would travel down the Pee Dee by boat, at night, and conceal themselves on the island nearest to the fort. The following night they would cross the water to the post in two separate units, and would launch a frontal attack on the "open" side of Georgetown, where the wharves were located. Meanwhile Harry's cavalry and Marion's irregulars, also mounted, would be waiting just past the line of sentry patrols at the rear of the fort, and would charge the instant they heard the Legion infantry open fire.

The plan was submitted to General Greene, who approved it—with misgivings. The hardest task was that of obtaining boats for the enterprise, but Marion's guerrillas were able to get their hands on virtually anything they wanted, and they borrowed a fleet of small craft, taking some without the owners' knowledge or permission.

The Legion infantry was placed under the command of Captain Pat Carnes, a cool-headed, dependable officer, and Captain Rudolph, who had served with such distinction at Paulus Hook, was made his deputy. The infantry sailed down the Pee Dee on schedule, and the horsemen followed at a slower pace, guided by volunteer civilians who lived in the area and were familiar with every tree, every patch of marsh in the deep woods.

The attack was scheduled for midnight on the second night, but not until an hour later did the waiting cavalry hear the crack of musket fire. They charged, Marion's men and Harry's riding shoulder to shoulder, but the sound of fire died away before they reached Georgetown. When they raced through the streets to the log fort, they found Captain Carnes at the parade ground, with Captain Rudolph's men stationed at the approaches to the fort. One prisoner had been taken—Colonel Campbell himself.

The Redcoats had retired in haste to the fort at the first sounds of fire, and had barricaded themselves there. Now Harry and Marion were faced with the problem of what to do next. It hadn't occurred to either to bring battering rams or other equipment to smash the walls of the fort, and they had no supplies for a protracted siege.

What had begun as a glorious bid for victory ended on a sheepish note. The Americans withdrew up the Pee Dee, taking their one prisoner with them. The "Battle of Georgetown" had been a mockery, but in their embarrassment Harry and Marion tightened the bonds of their friendship. Both remembered the lessons they learned that chilly January night, and thereafter their joint enterprises were far better planned. The failure at Georgetown was the prelude to later successes.

General Greene had far more than Georgetown on his mind. Cornwallis was intending to invade North Carolina in force, and was using Tarleton to goad the Americans into making a stand. Greene, who was being reinforced slowly by Washington, wasn't yet ready for a major battle, and was playing for time. He decided to retire slowly into Virginia behind a vanguard made up of Morgan's riflemen, light infantry from Maryland and Delaware under the command of Colonel John E. Howard, a battalion of cavalry led by the able Lieutenant Colonel William Washington, and Harry's Legion.

Dan Morgan was given over-all command of the screening force, but the American cause suffered a severe blow when he came down with an attack of arthritis that forced him to leave the field. The "light corps" was placed under the officer next in rank, Colonel Otho H. Williams of Maryland, who had been on active service since 1775, and was a dependable but uninspired leader.

Lee's Legion was given the difficult task of bringing up the rear of the light corps, which meant that he was expected to deflect or blunt every blow delivered by the enemy cavalry. On February 13, 1781, Lee's Legion and Tarleton's Legion had their first encounter near the town of Guilford Courthouse. The Americans, warned by a farmer that the enemy was making a wide sweep around a flank in an attempt to bring off a surprise, hid themselves in a patch of woods.

An unarmed Yankee bugler boy, a lad of fourteen, had the misfortune to appear in the open and was instantly cut down by the Redcoats. Harry was so angered by the murder that he led his men in a ferocious charge, giving no quarter, and dispersed a force twice his strength, taking forty prisoners as well.

A running engagement continued all day and far into the night. General Greene was taking the bulk of his army down a main road, hoping to pull back across the Dan River, and the light corps was under orders to slow the enemy advance at all costs. Lee's Legion performed superbly. Harry's infantry twice captured bridges over rain-swollen streams and, after the cavalry had crossed to the north, destroyed them. Harry and Tarleton constantly maneuvered for position, like two swordsmen feinting, and the two Legions were in plain sight of each other for hours at a time.

Although within mutual musket range, neither wasted the ammunition. The stakes were too high, and both commanders were intent on their main tasks, Harry's that of delaying the foe, Tarleton's that of harassing his enemy.

Late on the evening of February 13, Harry and Colonel Williams, who had dropped back and was riding with him, had a severe fright. Directly ahead they could see scores of campfires blazing. They had done everything in their power to delay the Redcoats, but if Greene had tarried too long, he would be compelled to fight a major engagement before the night ended.

To their great relief, the two officers found the camp deserted. As they discovered soon afterward, Greene had abandoned it that morning. But Lord Cornwallis continued to advance, not knowing that Greene had now crossed the Dan to the relative safety of the far bank. The light corps moved to the rear more rapidly when Williams received word that the bulk of the army was safe, but Lee's Legion remained behind to pick away at the British as long as possible.

Not until dawn the following morning, after almost twenty-four consecutive hours in the saddle and on their feet, did the cavalry and infantrymen of Lee's Legion finally cross the Dan and rejoin the rest of Greene's army. During that long retreat they had eaten no food, drunk no water and had made no more than a handful of five-minute halts. Thanks to their protective cover, the Army of the South was safe, and Harry Lee had performed in a manner that would go down in military annals as a classic in the difficult maneuver of retreat. Every potential thrust had been parried, and hence prevented, and not one member of Greene's main body had been injured or killed. Harry's men had suffered two casualties, the bugler boy and a lieutenant who had been cut down in the day's one hot action.

Cornwallis now knew that the enemy screen was protected by a professional soldier of exceptional talents, and the self-confident Tarleton, who had heard rumors of Harry's prowess but had refused to believe them, realized he had a foe worthy of his best efforts.

For four days the Army of the South rested in Virginia, and Nathanael Greene pondered his future. He literally couldn't afford to abandon North Carolina, and knew it. There were too many Loyalists in the state for comfort, and many would be certain to join Cornwallis or, at the very least, accept the new, liberal amnesty terms that the Crown was offering. There were fewer Loyalists in South Carolina and Georgia, but in those states, too, thousands of citizens would give up the fight and pledge their fealty to George III if the only American force in the entire region continued to huddle in Virginia.

No matter how small his army, Greene concluded, he had to go back into North Carolina. But his dilemma was that with which so many American commanders before him had wrestled: How could he contain Cornwallis, yet refuse to fight in a decisive engagement until he obtained reinforcements?

General Greene conceived a new plan, and dined at Harry's Legion bivouac to discuss it with the lieutenant colonel on whom so much would depend. Greene had decided, he said, to recross the Dan into North Carolina, but would keep his army in the rugged western highlands, where the British would find marching too difficult and the settlers were fiercely partisan to the Patriot cause.

But Cornwallis could not be allowed clear passage to the north across the eastern lowlands. His progress had to be slowed and, if possible, he had to be "teased" in a series of delaying actions that might even tempt him into marching to the hill country where the Army of the South could meet him on terms more favorable to the Americans.

The delaying, or containing, action would be performed by a new corps, Greene had decided. Its head and striking arm would be Lee's Legion, its body a tough brigade of South Carolina militia, a unit as well-disciplined as Continentals and commanded by an exceptionally able militia officer, Brigadier General Andrew Pickens.

Harry unhesitatingly accepted the new assignment, even though the odds against him would be tremendous. He then accompanied Greene on a visit to the bivouac of General Pickens, who was frank to admit that the mission was a desperate one. But he, too, agreed; there was no real choice.

While the two generals and Harry conferred over maps in Pickens' tent, a Legion scout who had been a member of a small party that had remained in North Carolina to keep watch on the enemy, arrived with bad news. "Butcher" Tarleton was roaming through North Carolina enlisting Loyalist recruits to serve with Cornwallis, and his methods were effective, although sometimes crude. Farmers who refused to enlist were sometimes shot, and at the least their stores were looted and their homes, barns, and other outbuildings burned to the ground.

Almost needless to say, Tarleton was enjoying great success, and the men he recruited were being subjected to British discipline, which meant that those who had enlisted to save their skins and property were executed if they tried to desert, and sent to hard-labor penal battalions in chains if they failed to respond to their new mode of living with enough enthusiasm.

Obviously time had become a vital factor again, and the new corps recrossed the Dan at daybreak the next morning, in search of trouble and Tarleton.

IX

DUEL OF THE LEGIONS

Harry Lee and Andrew Pickens marched rapidly through the pine-covered hill country of North Carolina in search of Banastre Tarleton, and after several days learned from Patriot sympathizers that he was in the neighborhood. Scouts were sent ahead, and discovered that the Redcoat was leading a force of considerable size and strength. He had about two hundred cavalrymen, more than four hundred foot soldiers and an artillery battery of several brass cannon. As nearly as could be determined, he was operating alone, and was not merely leading a vanguard of Cornwallis' main body.

The Americans decided to attack, with Pickens on one flank, the Legion infantry under Harry in the center, and the cavalry on the other flank under the command of Rudolph, who was constantly rising higher in Harry's esteem and had been given a brevet, or temporary, commission as a major.

To the intense disappointment of the Americans, Tarleton had just evacuated the farmhouse at which he had been making his headquarters. Two of his staff officers were still there, however, putting their papers in order, and were taken prisoner. These officers revealed, under questioning, that Tarleton intended to establish a new camp six miles to the east.

The region was one in which Loyalist sentiments were strong, so Harry decided the corps should pose as part of Tarleton's command, and Pickens agreed. In this remote backwoods area, many settlers literally were unable to distinguish the uniforms of one

army from those of its foes. But, to be on the safe side and for the
sake of window dressing, the two captured British officers were
given conspicuous places in the line of march. Harry warned
them that if they failed to play the roles assigned to them, they
would be killed on the spot.

After moving a mile or two toward Tarleton's new bivouac,
the vanguard, which Harry himself was leading, came across two
young farmers who assumed they were Tarleton's men and informed them they were leading four hundred recruits under a
"Colonel" Pyle to join the British.

Harry instantly declared that he was Tarleton, and asked that
the Loyalists, who were about a mile away down a side road,
present themselves for his congratulations and inspection. Then,
hurriedly, he sent back word to General Pickens, requesting that
the South Carolina militia conceal themselves in the woods to the
left of the Loyalists. He proceeded to lead his Legion toward the
spot, taking up a position on the right of the Loyalists.

"Colonel" Pyle and his would-be British recruits were lined up
at the side of the road, and Harry reviewed them, taking his time
in order to enable Pickens to move into place. The deception
was successful—until some of the Loyalists, themselves woods-
men, heard the South Carolinians in the brush behind them.
They opened fire on a troop of the Legion commanded by one
of Harry's recently promoted officers, Captain Joseph Eggleston,
whose grandson, Major General Joseph Eggleston Johnston, was
to become one of General Robert E. Lee's most valued and trusted
subordinates.

Captain Eggleston did not hesitate. He gave a sharp order,
sabers were drawn and the troop went into action. At Harry's
command, the rest of the Legion did the same. The slaughter of
the Loyalists was, in Harry's own words, even after the lapse of
many years between the incident and the writing of his *Memoirs*,
"sickening." The Legion killed about ninety of the Loyalists, and
the South Carolina militia shot down those who fled in sudden
panic. "Colonel" Pyle was gravely wounded, and so were the vast
majority of his followers who survived the initial assault. Only a
handful managed to escape.

Eighteenth-century light corps traveled without surgeons, and
there was no way of tending the Loyalist wounded. The Continentals had no liking for men they regarded as traitors, but were

sufficiently professional to feel a sense of responsibility for the injured. Pickens' men did not agree, however, too many of them having seen their own families butchered by Loyalists. So the Loyalist wounded were left where they had fallen, and the most Harry could do for them was to send several men to farmhouses in the vicinity for aid.

The corps had suffered virtually no casualties worthy of the name in the brief, bitter encounter. A few men were scarred by powder burns, but otherwise the corps was intact. But several hours had elapsed since the two farmers had first appeared on the road with word of a Loyalist column in the vicinity, and it was late in the day by the time the Legion and militia finally arrived at its goal, the British bivouac.

Tarleton had gone, and his camp looked as though it had been abandoned in great haste. Perhaps his pickets had heard the sounds of rifle fire, or it may have been that some of the Loyalist survivors had found their way to his headquarters and given the alarm. Either way, he now knew that an American force was in the vicinity, searching for him.

Harry and Pickens had lost their greatest advantage, the element of surprise. Henceforth he would be more difficult to contain, infinitely harder to beat.

The Americans camped beside the main road leading to the town of Hillsboro, and less than an hour later were joined by three hundred Virginia militiamen, volunteer rifle sharpshooters who had heard that Cornwallis was in the vicinity and were searching for General Greene. When they learned the mission on which Harry and Pickens were engaged, they enthusiastically voted to join the party.

They were made welcome, and Harry sent out scouts to find Tarleton and pinpoint his position in the hills. The corps had greater numerical strength than the enemy now, a situation that Americans rarely enjoyed, and both Harry and Pickens were sure they would win a decisive victory the following day.

Tarleton's own scouts had informed him that the enemy had received reinforcements, and he had no intention of being over-whelmed. In the early hours of the morning he quietly evacuated his bivouac, and by the time Harry learned of his flight, roused the corps and started a pre-dawn march, the Redcoats had vanished.

For the next few days the two Legions played cat-and-mouse, the Americans seeking, the British eluding, a reversal of a situation that had been virtually universal since the beginning of the war. A clash between the two cavalry leaders seemed inevitable, but their generals had other ideas. Greene had recrossed the Dan with his main body, which was being reinforced each day with new militia units from Virginia and the Carolinas, so the basic situation was altered.

Cornwallis needed Tarleton's Legion to act as his vanguard, and Greene reactivated his light corps under Colonel Otho Williams to act as a screen between him and the Redcoats. And Lee's Legion was better equipped than any other unit to give life to the light corps. The two cavalry leaders reluctantly accepted their new assignments and rode off in opposite directions, their showdown battle postponed until another day.

The basic situation was fluid as each side jockeyed for an advantageous position. For the immediate moment, Cornwallis held a slight edge. His corps was at full strength, and he held a number of forts in South Carolina and Georgia that kept those states more or less under his control. In North Carolina genuine Loyalists and opportunists willing to swing either way with the tide of victory were encouraged by his proximity, and he was anxious to win them permanently into his camp before a military accident or an American victory caused them to change their minds.

Greene, on the other hand, was forced to behave cautiously. He was still receiving reinforcements, most of them militia, and their records were spotty. Some were veterans who had given an excellent account of themselves in the frontier Battle of Kings Mountain the previous October 1780, and had virtually destroyed a strong British force that had made the mistake of fighting a formal, European-style battle in the American wilderness better suited to guerrilla operations. Others were eager but raw recruits, and Greene had watched such troops buckle too often in the past. So, although preparing for definitive action, he continued to delay as long as possible in order to give green men the benefit of field experience before sending them into combat.

Under these conditions Cornwallis decided to take the initiative again, and on March 6 sent a strong vanguard against the American screening force. Colonel Williams' men were almost totally unprepared for the assault, so Lee's Legion was thrown into the

battle against a Redcoat battalion of light infantry aided by several
auxiliary units. Harry's men performed with quiet efficiency, and
held the enemy at bay while Williams retired across a small river
to regroup his forces. After a fight of about an hour, Williams
sent word that all of his units had made the crossing, and Harry
retired, too.

He and Williams made a quick review of their situation, and
decided they were in an untenable position. They knew they were
outnumbered, and the Redcoats could cross the little river at
too many places where the water was shallow. Williams decided
to continue his retreat, and the Legion once again was given the
unenviable task of delaying the enemy. It was assisted by a battalion of mountain men, many of them Kings Mountain veterans,
and together they managed to hold off the Redcoats.

After two more hours of brisk fighting, however, the British
light infantry managed to gain a foothold on the American bank
of the river. Almost immediately Tarleton's dragoons appeared,
riding in formation down to the water's edge, ready to lead a
decisive sweep.

Here was the opportunity for direct combat that Harry and
the British cavalry leader had sought. Harry sent his infantry to
the rear, and put his horsemen in battle formation to repel
Tarleton's charge. But, before the British could move, a courier
arrived with orders from General Greene, who directed that a
major clash be avoided. Lee's Legion, humiliated and deeply frustrated, was compelled to withdraw.

According to several accounts that may be no more than romantic legends, Harry and Tarleton stood in their stirrups and saluted
each other with their sabers before the Americans drew off. At any
rate, it appeared that the fates were conspiring to prevent the confrontation both men sought.

On March 14 the light corps reported to General Greene at
his new headquarters, a spot in the North Carolina hills known
as Guilford Courthouse because a red brick building used by the
judges of the circuit courts in more peaceful times was located
there. The general called a meeting of his senior subordinates and
told them he was as ready to fight as he would be later. He had
received a letter from Dan Morgan telling him that the only way
he could beat Cornwallis would be in battle, and he agreed.

His greatest problem, he told the colonels, was his green mi-

litia. Once again taking Morgan's advice, he planned to put the recruits well forward, in the center of his lines, with tough veterans
behind them, ready to shoot down any who fled from the field
in panic. The solution was far from ideal, but Americans had
suffered too many unpleasant experiences in battle to place much
reliance on untried militia.

On the morning of March 15 Lee's Legion was given its usual
difficult assignment of riding south to act as a screen and, this time,
to draw Cornwallis into a major engagement. Harry was supported
by the dragoons of Lieutenant Colonel William Washington, an
exceptionally energetic, able officer whose men were seasoned
horsemen. Although senior to Harry in the date of his commission, Washington was placed under the command of the Chief
of Cavalry.

Recruits held the van of the infantry positions, with experienced
Virginians giving them backing, and tough Continentals, Marylanders, and Virginians held the right. Greene stationed them at
the crest of the hill that dominated the area, and indicated that
this sector would be his anchor. Motley militia units were placed
on the left, the weakest portion of the line, and Harry Lee was
ordered to fall back and give them support after accomplishing
his initial mission.

Harry pushed forward cautiously, and about an hour before
dawn heard the approach of enemy cavalry. His scouts told him
that Cornwallis' entire column of more than three thousand men
was on the move, and in a sense the Legion's mission was ended.
General Greene was destined to have his battle.

Couriers were dispatched to the rear with the news, a ride of
about five miles, and Harry turned to wait for the foe. Now it was
his task to slow the Redcoat advance in order to give Nathanael
Greene enough time to finish building breastworks and make
ready for the battle.

The Legion was divided into three separate units, the bulk of
the cavalry under Major Rudolph, with separate troops commanded by Captain Eggleston and Captain Joseph Armstrong
strung out in a thin line before them. There were about two hundred and fifty men under Harry's over-all command.

The advance unit of the British vanguard was a battalion of
light infantry, supported by Tarleton's Legion. Word was passed
back through the Redcoat lines that Americans in green tunics

and plumed helmets had been sighted in battle formation, and Tarleton refused to be denied the pleasure of fighting the duel he had so long awaited. He pushed forward, his three hundred and eighty horsemen in a double battle line.

Harry was outnumbered, and chose to resort to trickery. The main body under Rudolph pretended to hesitate, then turned and galloped off in simulated panic. Eggleston's troop then did the same. Armstrong was the bait being used to tempt the enemy, and he played his role with courage, retiring slowly, his men walking their horses sedately.

Tarleton was unable to resist the opportunity that seemed to present itself. His dragoons gathered speed, and thundered toward Armstrong's troopers, who coolly continued to pull back at a crawl. An instant or two before the British came within pistol range of the troop, Harry called an order, and his main body wheeled, with Eggleston make a sweeping turn on the flank. Armstrong waited until his comrades were almost even with him, then he also made a sweep toward the other flank, and the entire Legion galloped toward the enemy at breakneck speed.

Tarleton was caught completely by surprise, and the two troops leading his charge were decimated, riders and horses falling as the Americans cut and slashed viciously. It was impossible to estimate the number of Redcoat casualties, and the American drive was so strong that it carried deeper into the British lines before slowing.

Even the best disciplined of horsemen were unable to resist the force of their foe's momentum, and one troop of Tarleton's Legion scattered. Their commander demonstrated his versatility and courage by rallying his other troops and leading them in an orderly retreat.

Harry immediately swung his men in a semicircular, scythe-like movement in an attempt to cut off Tarleton from the British units behind him. The two Legions raced madly, one seeking protection, the other trying to destroy it, and Tarleton was able to reach the sanctuary of the light infantry lines with the loss of only a few more men.

The British foot soldiers opened a brisk fire with their muskets, and Harry's horse was either shot from beneath him or bolted. In the excitement of the moment, he never learned which had happened. In any event, he had sufficient presence of mind to leap to the ground, throwing himself clear, and although he was the target of a number of enemy marksmen, managed to leap into the empty saddle of a slain British officer's mount.

Urging his cavalry forward again, he called up the Legion infantry and a battalion of North Carolina infantry that had been following close behind. The foot soldiers moved into the center of his line, and he split his cavalry into two divisions, each covering a flank. Tarleton, maneuvering frantically, arranged his men in roughly the same formation, and the two forces engaged in a furious slugging match.

After a few minutes of intensive fire, American marksmanship proved superior, and the British withdrew slowly from the field. Thanks to Tarleton's presence everywhere in their ranks, they maintained good order.

Harry had to make a rapid decision. He was tempted to follow the enemy in close pursuit, but knew that the farther he went, the closer he was drawing to Cornwallis' main body and the more distance he was putting between himself and Greene. Eventually he would come within range of the Redcoat heavy infantry and artillery, and would be subjecting his men to risks greater than the situation warranted. In an admirable display of level-headed judgment, he broke off the engagement and returned to Greene's lines far to his rear, his infantry marching first, his cavalry providing cover behind them.

At last he and Tarleton had met—under conditions ideal for both forces—and Lee's Legion had won an emphatic victory. It was the first time Tarleton had suffered a clear-cut defeat in all the years he had been fighting in North America, and Harry's men sang *Yankee Doodle* in triumph as they marched.

But the Battle of Guilford Courthouse was still in its opening phase. It was only eight o'clock in the morning, and an hour later the two main bodies collided, Cornwallis sending his heavy British and Hessian infantry forward in solid waves after trying to soften the Americans with a fifteen-minute artillery barrage, an attempt that failed because of his gunners' poor marksmanship. To the surprise of the Redcoats, the entire American line held firm. Tarleton, who had been sent to the rear to act as a reserve, asked for the privilege of redeeming himself, but the situation did not call for the utilization of cavalry, and he was to brood in sheepish despair.

The entire American line remained in place behind its breastworks, and the two armies pounded at each other, each taking a heavy toll. Occasionally Cornwallis paused briefly to regroup his attackers, but continued to maintain a heavy pressure. Greene remained unwavering in his defense, and no Americans had better demonstrated their professional skill and stamina than the men who served under him that day.

Then, finally, the inevitable happened, and several companies of militia on the American left wavered, buckled, and fled. Harry Lee made a desperate attempt to rally them, even using his cavalry in an effort to force them back into the line, but his efforts were unavailing. A battalion of Welsh Fusiliers and another of Hessians poured through the gap.

It was up to the cavalry now to stem the enemy tide before the entire flank was turned, and with the infantry of Lee's Legion still in position, Harry's horsemen and those of William Washington's battalion charged straight into the ranks of the foot soldiers. Again and again they cut through to the rear, turned and fought their way back to their own lines, and after almost three hours of a struggle without a respite, managed to close the hole.

By that time, however, the basic situation had changed. The other action had moved farther to the right, and the Legion, together with several seasoned companies of Virginia militia, was holding the left alone. Elsewhere American men-at-arms were accomplishing wonders. The Continentals on the right flank of Greene's line pushed back several severe attacks and then themselves assumed the offensive. Colonel Washington's dragoons were sent to help them, and the combined force made a forward thrust that resulted in hand-to-hand combat with the cream of Cornwallis' corps.

His lordship was in danger of losing the field, and in a gesture that later subjected him to severe criticism in England, took the only course open to him and ordered his artillery to fire into the mass of struggling men. The two forces separated, but Cornwallis achieved no advantage, for Greene's men continued to drive forward. The American center was more than holding its own, too, and the prospects of victory were improving.

On the left, however, Lee's Legion and the Virginia companies, who were ultimately joined by a battalion of North Carolina militia, were fighting for their lives against almost incredible odds. This was still the weakest American sector, and Cornwallis sent two of his best regiments, one of elite Grenadier Guards, the other of experienced Hessians, against that portion of the line.

Between mid-afternoon and sundown that day, Harry Lee fought what many military students have believed to be his finest battle. Outnumbered by approximately four to one and completely cut off from the rest of General Greene's army, he waged what was tantamount to a separate action. First, forced to retire, he retreated into pine woods and there fought Indian-style, with his men concealing themselves behind trees and brush, then firing at close range when the enemy rushed into the forest.

After inflicting severe losses on the enemy while himself suffering only five casualties, a record almost too good to be true, Harry launched a vicious counterassault and sent the enemy into retreat. He was achieving something of a miracle, but he and his men were too busy to realize it at the time.

It cannot be emphasized too strongly that Harry Lee and Nathanael Greene were unable to communicate with each other during this last part of the Guilford Courthouse battle. Their respective forces had moved far apart, and each was still locked in combat with strong British forces that separated them.

In the years following the battle, Harry's personal foes charged that had he notified Greene of his success, the American army could have won a victory so smashing that Cornwallis would have been forced to surrender, ending the war in the southern states. This stand is groundless.

Greene might have been able to follow up on his advantage had he been able to call on several regiments of reserves, but he had already committed every man in his army to battle. There were literally no fresh troops available. Also, even had he driven the enemy from the field, Cornwallis was far from beaten. He still held a number of strong forts in occupied South Carolina and Georgia, and in the months that followed was able to summon his strategic reserves from Charleston and other towns where he maintained large personnel pools.

Nevertheless, neither Harry on the left nor Greene on the right knew what was happening to the other. General Greene realized only that he had inflicted a severe trouncing on the Redcoats, and had rendered Cornwallis incapable of continuing the fight. Uncertain whether Lee's Legion was still active or had been

destroyed, he withdrew, leaving Cornwallis in technical possession of a portion of the field.

Meanwhile Harry cut the proud Guards regiment and the
haughty mercenaries to shreds. His men accomplished more than
any Americans had done since the start of the war, with the exception of the troops that had destroyed Burgoyne's corps at
Saratoga. The remnants of the two enemy units pulled back to
rejoin Cornwallis, and Harry rode to the courthouse, his weary
men in formation behind him, only to discover that Greene had
retired about four miles.

Both armies had fought until exhausted, and it was impossible
for either to renew the battle. Both sides claimed victory, but
Greene's arguments were by far the more impressive. The better
part of his army was intact, save for the militia companies that
decided they'd seen enough fighting and went home. But Cornwallis' corps had been shattered, and he was forced to retire to the
town of Wilmington, on the Cape Fear River, North Carolina's
chief seaport, which was located about thirty miles from the Atlantic. There he licked his considerable wounds—and sent urgent requests to Sir Henry Clinton for fresh troops so that he could continue to fight the war.

At the time, few Americans were aware of the magnitude of
Nathanael Greene's triumph at Guilford Courthouse, and the
newspapers in England congratulated Cornwallis on his victory. If
it be true that he won, his "triumph" was the turning point that
cost him the campaign and, eventually, the war.

No one knew it better than the tired officers and men who
gathered at Greene's headquarters to rest and, after catching their
breath, plot their future course. Every unit that had distinguished
itself won a commendation from Greene, and none won more
praise than Lee's Legion, without whom, the general informed the
commander-in-chief, "our achievements would have been negligible."

Lieutenant Colonel Harry Lee was awarded the highest laurels.
*"Of all officers who served their country and the cause of liberty
on this day,"* Greene wrote Washington, *"Colonel Lee towers
above the rest. He well deserves every mark of gratitude &
affection that a grateful nation can give him."*

For once in his short life, Harry cared nothing for glory or
praise. He was so tired that, after reporting to the general and

making the rounds of his Legion's bivouac to see for himself that his men were comfortable, he ate a few shreds of jerked beef, dampened some hard biscuits with small beer, and rolled himself in his blanket to sleep until late in the morning on the damp, cold ground.

X

THE GRAND DESIGN

In the days that followed the Battle of Guilford Courthouse, Nathanael Greene and his principal subordinates held a running council of war. They were agreed that their strategy might be the decisive factor in determining the outcome of the war in the southern states, and the scent of ultimate victory was in the air. But there were unceasing arguments, with no two colonels advocating the same course.

One wanted the Army of the South to march into Virginia, where Benedict Arnold, now a brigadier general in the British Army, was burning towns and scattering civilians. It was obvious, however, that such action would leave Cornwallis in complete possession of the South.

Another of the colonels believed that Greene should remain in his present position, ask Washington for still more reinforcements and force Cornwallis to come to him. But General Greene exploded this potential. Washington, he said, had literally no more troops to spare. The bottom of the manpower barrel had been scraped, and was empty.

Still another suggestion was somewhat more daring. The Army of the South should pursue Cornwallis and compel him to fight again. Greene vetoed the idea. He simply wasn't strong enough to meet Cornwallis in another major engagement.

Harry Lee remained silent through most of the discussions, which his colleagues considered unusual. An extraordinary scheme was forming in his mind, but he wanted to be sure of his ground before submitting it for the consideration of Greene, who alone was charged with the responsibility of making the final decision. Finally, on March 31, he presented Greene with a formal, written memorandum.

His plan was extraordinary. He suggested that Greene march into South Carolina, and head toward the town of Camden, in the central part of the state, where a large British garrison was stationed. Meanwhile Lee's Legion, accompanied by any light, fast-moving troops that the Army could spare, would rejoin Brigadier General Francis Marion and, with his active cooperation, take a string of sturdy British outposts, among them Forts Watson, Motte, Granby, and Galphin.

Three separate American units were operating in South Carolina, and Harry advocated that their irregulars and militia—among the best in the nation—be utilized to the full. Marion in the east, Colonel Thomas Sumter in the central portion, and General Pickens in the west were shrewd, resilient men, and were currently being wasted.

There were risks, Harry admitted. Nothing would prevent Cornwallis from moving into Virginia if he wished, and he both hoped and believed that his lordship would march north. South Carolina and Georgia—assuming that the Legion and its allies could eliminate the British outposts—would be restored to the Union. The Loyalists of North Carolina, already disheartened by the battering Cornwallis had taken at Guilford Courthouse, would take to heart the return of the other southern states to the Union and would be still less inclined to join the British.

Cornwallis' possible march into Virginia became the crux of the decision. Harry said, in effect, "Let him go there. He'll be cut off from the South, and will get no reinforcements from the garrisons there. General Washington stands between him and the British in New York. There are virtually no Loyalists in Virginia; the entire population enthusiastically supports the Patriot cause. Washington can move into Virginia with his Army of the North and live off the land—while Cornwallis starves there."

In brief, the scheme was predicated on the thesis that Greene would recapture the South and leave Cornwallis to Washington.

Several of the colonels were won over to the strategy, but Nathanael Greene needed time to ponder. He refused to give an opinion, and retired to his own tent for twenty-four hours of solitary agony. Then, on the night of April 1, he summoned his colonels to dinner, and told them he was making the strategy his own. His decision was an act of great personal courage. If the plan failed, he alone would be blamed; if it succeeded, he would have to share the credit with his brilliant subordinate. It was a sign of Greene's greatness that his only concern was victory that would bring the long war to an end. He cared little or nothing for applause.

The entire plan was kept secret from everyone except the top commanders. Special couriers were sent to Marion, Sumter, and Pickens—with verbal messages. Greene refused to take the chance that a written communication might fall into British hands.

On the morning of April 2, Lee's Legion marched out of camp, accompanied by an augmented company of Continental infantry from Maryland commanded by Captain Edward Oldham. Only Major Rudolph, now Harry's deputy, and Major Eggleston, who had been given a brevet promotion after the Battle of Guilford Courthouse, had been told the Legion's destination.

Before heading south, Harry deliberately perpetrated a trick on the British, acting on his own initiative. The Legion strung out on the road as though on parade, making itself conspicuous, and headed east on the road to Wilmington. There were enough Loyalist sympathizers in the area to insure that the word would be passed along to Lord Cornwallis, who would assume that Greene was marching against him and had sent the Legion ahead as a vanguard.

Then, after making the long detour, Harry silently and swiftly turned south after sundown and headed through wooded country for South Carolina. His first task was that of finding Francis Marion, which proved more difficult than he had anticipated. No one in the delta country seemed to know the Swamp Fox's whereabouts, and only an accidental meeting with several of the general's men finally led the Legion deep into the marshes. There, after still more delays, Marion finally appeared, explaining he was taking particular care to remain in hiding because a special British task force of several hundred men had been sent out to capture him.

He promptly forgot his own safety, however, and joined forces with the Legion. Their first target was Fort Watson, a stout outpost of logs built in a forest of scrub pine. Aware of the long, difficult mission ahead, Harry and Marion were reluctant to make a frontal attack on the post and risk heavy casualties. A reconnaissance of the area surrounding the fort indicated that the Redcoat garrison depended on water from a nearby lake, so a simple scheme was devised.

Sharpshooters were stationed in the woods near the lake, with orders to shoot anyone from the garrison who came out for water. Two Redcoats were wounded, and the plan seemed assured of success, but the British countered by digging a ditch within the protecting shadow of the fort's walls. The ground was so soggy that a trickle of water sufficient for the garrison's needs dribbled under the fort's wall.

The Americans were stymied, but soon devised another trick of their own. Soldiers substituted axes for rifles, and cut down trees in the forest to build a clumsy but effective tower higher than the walls of the fort. Then, while Marion's best marksmen climbed into the tower and sent a steady rain of rifle fire down into the fort below them, Harry led the Legion's infantry to the water ditch and took possession of it.

The Redcoat commander saw that his position had been rendered hopeless, and surrendered his entire garrison. The prisoners were marched off to the headquarters of General Greene, who had followed the Legion into the state and established a camp near Camden, where he had laid siege to the fort held by General Lord Rawdon, the British commander in the area.

A crack battalion of Redcoat light infantry was marching to Rawdon's support, so Harry and Marion postponed their assault on their next objective, Fort Motte, in order to head off the British. The battalion eluded them, however, and the situation was further complicated by the reluctance of General Sumter to give up his reconnaissance patrols and put his brigade at Greene's disposal.

The commander of the Army of the South suffered momentary doubts, and was on the verge of giving up his campaign in South Carolina, but changed his mind overnight and sent Harry a battery of six-pounder artillery. The Lee-Marion march was resumed.

Fort Motte, once a private mansion, had been transformed into a New World version of a castle, complete with high walls, turrets, and a wide moat. A garrison of more than one hundred and fifty Redcoats held the place, a vitally important bastion in the British defense scheme, as it was the principal communications and supply station linking Charleston on the seacoast with Camden and with the principal forts inland and farther south.

The reduction of the fort promised to be a formidable task. A siege was undertaken, Marion's irregulars taking up a position north and east of the "castle," with the Legion on the west and south, where there was a slight elevation. Harry immediately ordered the erection of a trench and breastworks just past the crest of the rise, about four hundred yards to the south of the walls.

The two commanders enjoyed a welcome respite when Mrs. Rebecca Motte, who had been evicted from her home by the enemy and was living in a smaller house on the far side of the property, invited them to make their headquarters with her during the operation. They declined, but were pleased to accept a dinner invitation from the lady, an ardent Patriot, and on the first night of the siege ate the most sumptuous meal they had tasted in many months. Several wines were served, and for once Francis Marion drank no vinegar.

While the trench was being dug and the breastworks thrown up, Harry's six-pounder guns were moved into place on the hill, and a courier was sent under a flag of truce to the British commander, urging him to surrender and thus avoid casualties. He declined, contemptuously, and the co-leaders of the American task force suspected that Lord Rawdon was sending a relief column from Camden to help preserve the vitally important post.

Their guess was confirmed by a letter from General Greene, who informed them that Rawdon himself was in command of the troops from Camden. Greene urged them to take Fort Motte with all possible haste, and said that he was coming to support them with his entire Army. It appeared that the area might become the site of a decisive battle, so it was more important than ever that the key fort be taken immediately.

But the trench and breastworks were only partly completed, and another week of hard labor might be needed before the job was finished. The attackers couldn't afford to wait that long. Harry and Marion held a council of war with their senior commanders, and it was decided to burn down the fort and literally smoke out the defenders.

Harry took upon himself the unenviable task of informing Mrs. Motte that the necessities of war required the destruction of her home. She not only accepted the news with monumental calm, but gave him a large bow and sheaf of arrows, gifts from the East Indies that she treasured, and asked they be used to start the fire.

Again a messenger was sent to the British commandant, warning him of what was in store, but for the second time he refused to consider surrender. So, without further delay, flaming torches tied to arrows were shot onto the roof of the fort by some of Marion's men, who were expert archers.

British troops immediately appeared from the attic to extinguish the fires. Harry called on his artillery to drive them below, and on the second volley his six-pounders found the range. The British were trapped and, realizing it at last, hoisted a white flag. The garrison marched out, surrendering its arms, and a special guard detail was mounted to keep watch on the prisoners.

The imperturbable and gracious Mrs. Motte invited victors and vanquished to dine with her, and in true eighteenth-century style, Harry had a spirited, interesting conversation with the Redcoat commandant, a Captain McPherson. During their talk McPherson asked for the privilege of marching to Charleston with his men on parole, a favor Harry and Marion readily granted, as they had too few men to set up a prison camp.

That afternoon Nathanael Greene arrived with his vanguard, and was elated, establishing an American garrison at the post. With Rawdon in the field, capable of sending support anywhere he elected, it was essential that the remaining British forts be taken as quickly as possible. The assault team was dissolved, with Marion sent to capture Georgetown and the Legion to reduce Fort Granby, on the flat banks of the Congaree River, where a very strong force of three hundred and fifty Redcoats was stationed.

Harry gave marching orders immediately after the Legion finished its evening meal. Armstrong's troop was assigned screening duty to determine whether Rawdon would try to support his outpost, and the Legion made its longest and hardest forced march of war, stopping for only a few short rest periods in the next thirty-six hours. It was Harry's plan to take the fort before Rawdon could get there.

Once again, his mission appeared extremely difficult. Fort Granby had high walls of soft logs that would absorb rifle and musket fire, and a storming operation would cost the attackers many casualties. Harry thought there might be a quicker, cheaper way to achieve victory.

The commandant, a major named Maxwell, had acquired a reputation for greed, and had requisitioned horses, livestock, and even jewelry from residents of the area. Presumably he regarded this loot as his private property.

The cannon were unlimbered, and two shots were fired over the walls into the fort. Then the Legion infantry advanced to a point just beyond musket range, bayonets affixed to their rifles. There they halted, and Captain Eggleston was sent to the fort with a demand that the commandant surrender.

Maxwell replied that he was willing to give up Fort Granby and its public stores if he and his men could go off to Charleston under parole—and could keep whatever private property that had accumulated. The propriety of the request was debatable, even under the most liberal and elastic interpretation of the military codes of the era. But before the terms could be relayed to Harry, one of Armstrong's troopers arrived with word that Lord Rawdon was marching toward Fort Granby. It was far better to let the unprincipled Maxwell line his own pocket than to lose all chance for a victory without heavy bloodshed, so, when Eggleston brought Harry the conditions, he accepted them.

The Redcoats and a small detachment of Hessian mercenaries marched out, the officers guarding wagons piled high with booty, and were sent off to Charleston. Less than a day's march from Fort Granby they encountered the dismayed Rawdon, who discovered that, once again, Harry Lee had beaten him to the punch.

The stores and arsenal at Fort Granby proved to be treasure houses. General Greene arrived the day after Harry had taken possession of the place, and both were delighted by the supplies of salt, meat, and grain that had been taken, along with precious bags of powder, long bars of lead used to fashion bullets and hundreds of muskets, small arms, and knives.

There was good news from other areas, too. General Sumter had decided to cooperate, after all, and had captured a British outpost at Orangeburg. Meanwhile General Marion had laid siege to Georgetown, and its fall was expected momentarily.

The only major strongholds still in enemy hands were the city of Charleston, the town of Savannah, in Georgia, both impregnable as long as Admiral Lord Howe's fleet controlled the Atlantic; a very strong fort called Ninety-Six and several smaller posts, Forts Galphin, Cornwallis, and Grierson. Meanwhile Lord Cornwallis and his corps had not followed Greene into South Carolina, just as Harry had predicted. Almost inexplicably, his lordship continued to sit at Wilmington, North Carolina, uncertain what to do next, and with each passing day his southern flank grew weaker as Rawdon's strength was sapped.

All this had been accomplished in less than a month, and a new optimism pervaded Greene's temporary headquarters at Fort Granby. General Greene and his Chief of Cavalry sat down to plan their new tactics, and believed it possible to gain possession of all Georgia except the coastal strip. Ninety-Six and Fort Grierson, at Augusta, were the key points, and Greene had already sent General Pickens' brigade of veterans to the vicinity of Augusta.

It was possible that the enemy might decide to evacuate its post at Ninety-Six, and reinforce the troops at Grierson. So Harry was ordered to make a reconnaissance of Ninety-Six and, if he found the garrison already gone, to find the Redcoats on the road and force them to fight. Inasmuch as the detachment there was the strongest in the South, Greene promised to come to his subordinate's aid.

The Legion was on the march again within a short time after the meeting, and had become so hardened to travel across rough country that more than thirteen miles were covered between early afternoon and sundown. Harry had evolved a technique that no one else, apparently, had ever thought of using. At intervals the cavalry dismounted and the infantry rode, thus enabling every man to obtain enough rest to push ahead farther and faster than could most columns that included foot soldiers.

The following morning Major Rudolph went ahead with a reconnaissance patrol, and returned late in the day to report that Ninety-Six was still much occupied, and was bristling with defenders. Harry dispatched a courier to Greene with the information, and pushed on toward Augusta, arriving in the vicinity of the town a scant seventy-two hours after leaving Fort Granby.

A chance meeting with a reconnaissance patrol from Pickens' brigade gave him an opportunity he was quick to grasp. The garrison at Fort Galphin, twelve miles to the south, was being careless in maintaining its sentry outposts in the forests surrounding the lonely post. Harry decided to take the place before engaging in more important business.

Having discovered that trickery was infinitely preferable to costly frontal attacks, he employed still another ruse. Fort Galphin stood in a forest clearing, and the cover afforded by the trees could be used to good advantage in a scheme that various Indian tribes had often utilized.

A small party of Legion infantry was sent to the rear of the fort, on the south side, with instructions to play the role of a detachment of raw Georgia militia. The men were ordered to open fire on the defenders with a ragged volley, tempt the Redcoats into a chase and then retreat through the forest, making just enough noise to insure that the enemy would follow. Meanwhile the cavalry, under Major Rudolph's command, hid in the forest just north of the fort.

The infantry played its role perfectly, the detachment drawing close to the walls, firing and then withdrawing again before making another advance. As the British well knew, only untrained militia behaved in this erratic manner; when professional soldiers launched an assault, they sustained it.

The gates of Fort Galphin opened at last, and two companies of Redcoat infantry came out to disperse the impudent militiamen. The infantrymen led them a merry chase to an open field about a mile away, and there the rest of the Legion infantry and Captain Eggleston's troop of horsemen were waiting. Harry, directing this part of the operation himself, made the Redcoats captive without firing a single shot.

Meanwhile Major Rudolph and the rest of the cavalry rode unopposed into Fort Galphin and overwhelmed the remainder of the garrison. By the time Harry arrived, no more than a half-hour later, the place was completely under American control and the British flag had already been hauled down.

The Legion found a bonus in the form of unexpected supplies in the fort's storerooms. Fifty kegs of powder and another fifty of shot were quickly loaded onto wagons taken from the enemy's barns. There were large quantities of salt, stacks of new muskets and a surprisingly large number of swords. Only when Harry found several huge bales of unused blankets and, in one chamber, barrels of rum and brandywine piled almost to the ceiling, did it occur to him that the stores had been gathered for presentation to the local Indian tribes, whose friendship the British bought at frequent intervals.

The supplies were sent off to General Greene, along with the prisoners, Harry keeping only a little of the salt and munitions. Inasmuch as his men had grown unaccustomed to drinking spirits during the campaign, he didn't keep a single barrel of liquor.

The day was hot and the Legion was tired after its long march, which had culminated in the capture of Fort Galphin. But Harry was eager to maintain the momentum he had achieved, and after giving the men only a few hours to eat and rest, left a company of Pickens' militia to man the fort and went off to join the militia general outside Augusta.

The town stood in a flat clearing on the south bank of the Savannah River, the forest behind it, and was protected in an unusual manner. In the clearing, facing the forest, was a log-walled enclosure containing several buildings, known as Fort Cornwallis, which stood guard against a surprise attack from the woods. The main bastion, however, was Fort Grierson, named for a Loyalist officer who had erected an exceptionally well-constructed fortress a half-mile to the northwest, at the edge of a swamp that stood between the river and a smaller stream. Fort Grierson was manned by a full battalion of Loyalist militiamen who feared execution if captured by Patriots, and hence were prepared to fight ferociously. Fort Cornwallis was occupied by professional Redcoats, and the defenses as a whole were under the command of a British lieutenant colonel named Browne, who had acquired a reputation as a tough, able officer.

Harry Lee and Andrew Pickens met in the forest, and were pleased to see each other again. Former comrades-in-arms who had fought and marched together, they enjoyed the same kind of rapport that made Harry's relations with Francis Marion so pleasant. Neither was disturbed by the question of whether the over-all command should go to a lieutenant colonel of Continentals or a brigadier general of state militia. There was a difficult, joint task to be performed, and they were prepared to work together.

As a preliminary to actual operations, Harry followed the procedure he had used at the other British outposts he had taken, and sent Joe Eggleston ahead with a small detachment, under a flag of truce, to demand the surrender of Augusta. Colonel

Browne not only refused to even consider the matter, but threatened to violate the flag of truce and shoot down the couriers unless they withdrew at once.

Good manners were still an important factor in wars during the eighteenth century. General Pickens cursed aloud when he heard Eggleston's report, and Harry, speaking in icy, clear tones, promised to teach Browne a lesson. Harry's subordinates had rarely seen him lose his temper, and Eggleston, writing about the incident some years later, said he had felt distinctly uncomfortable—and sorry for Colonel Browne.

The biggest question facing the Americans was that of deciding which of the forts they would attack first. Pickens and most his officers favored Fort Cornwallis, believing the Loyalist volunteers would be easier to handle if they were denied the support of Redcoat regulars. The Legion commanders disagreed, arguing that the undisciplined Loyalist militia would buckle under siege far more rapidly than would professionals.

Harry let the others say what they pleased before expressing himself. His speech, in Eggleston's opinion, was "a model of military teaching and deportment."

The basic weakness of the enemy's position, he said, was that the British forces were split. Therefore the operation would consist of two separate operations—two attacks—in which one of the principal objects would be to prevent one Redcoat fort from giving substantial assistance to the other.

In order to isolate the two garrisons, he said, he would station the Legion—with its priceless pair of six-pounder cannon—halfway between Fort Cornwallis and Fort Grierson. He then agreed with General Pickens that the latter was more vulnerable, and suggested that the bulk of the South Carolina militia take up positions in the forest on one side of Fort Grierson, with a single battalion of militia going around to the rear to prevent the Loyalists from escaping.

The plan was put into operation at once, the South Carolina units marching off, while the Legion moved into the open, within plain view of Fort Cornwallis. Colonel Browne immediately proved he was not a man who could be intimidated, and countered by marching a large detachment out of Fort Cornwallis. The Americans put their cannon in place, and Harry was both surprised and impressed when British gun crews dragged two fieldpieces into the open plain.

A race developed to see which cannon would be operable first, but Harry disappointed his men by telling them he had no intention of engaging in a gun duel. His immediate aim was no more and no less than that of preventing the Redcoats from relieving Fort Grierson. His silence puzzled Browne, who made no attempt to fire, either, at least for the moment, and the scarlet-uniformed Britishers and green-clad Legionnaires stared at each other across less than a half-mile of open, flat field.

Suddenly Pickens began his assault on Fort Grierson, and the steady rattle of rifle fire broke the silence. Harry, using his field glass, was able to see the Loyalists responding, but at a much slower pace. And, although outnumbering Pickens' brigade, the Loyalists' fire was also more scattered.

Browne started to move across the field toward Fort Grierson, but the Legion cavalry, under Rudolph, moved into battle formation, and the Redcoats returned at once to their original positions just outside the entrance to Fort Cornwallis. Now Browne understood Harry's tactics, and reacted accordingly by opening fire on the Legion with his artillery.

His gunners lacked practice, and their aim was short, but they kept Harry's cavalry and infantry pinned down, so for all practical purposes neither the American nor British professionals were able to take an active part in the battle. As it happened, Pickens required no help.

His men kept up a steady, murderous fire, edging ever closer to the log walls of the fort, and after two hours of preparation, two companies erected scaling ladders. The Loyalists tried bitterly but in vain to repel the invaders, and soon the entire brigade had swarmed into Fort Grierson.

The hand-to-hand combat that followed was one of the most ferocious struggles of the entire American Revolution. Many of the militiamen and Loyalists knew each other; some had been neighbors, and, in a few instances, were related by blood or marriage. Feelings on both sides were violent, and neither gave quarter.

Pickens' men gradually assumed the upper hand, and the slaughter that followed was known thereafter as the "Massacre of Fort Grierson." None of the Loyalists' senior officers survived, and in many instances men who surrendered were shot down. General Pickens lost control of his troops for almost an hour, and the very few Loyalists who were either taken prisoner or managed to escape and swim down the river to Fort Cornwallis were fortunate.

When Colonel Browne realized what was happening on his flank, he withdrew his force into Fort Cornwallis, the guns moving in under the protecting cover of other cannon mounted in permanent places on parapets behind the outer walls. The handful of escaped Loyalists were taken in, and the gates were barred for a protracted siege.

The victorious South Carolina militiamen were now in possession of Fort Grierson, and Pickens, after posting a strong detail there, retired to bivouac in the forest. Meanwhile Harry established siege lines around Fort Cornwallis and, accompanied by his staff, moved into a brick mansion, the property of a Loyalist sympathizer who had fled, that stood between the fort and the river.

At dawn the following morning the Legion went to work setting up stronger siege lines. A courier went off to Fort Galphin for all shovels, picks, and spades available there, and cavalry details scoured the neighborhood for more. Meanwhile all the tools carried by the Legion itself for purposes of raising breastworks were utilized, and Harry began to dig a ditch between his headquarters and the river, shielding it from enemy fire with a breastworks that rose three feet the first day and two more the next. Gradually, in the week that followed, the ditch and breastworks were extended, and it was Harry's hope that in time he would surround the fort.

The work was hard labor in the sultry heat, and the troops were thoroughly unhappy, as all soldiers have been throughout recorded history when establishing siege lines. The task at Fort Cornwallis was complicated by the soft, sandy quality of the soil, and by swarms of mosquitoes and gnats that appeared from the forest and bedeviled the men.

General Pickens wanted to stay on and help the Continentals, but his troops refused. They had achieved the vengeance they had sought, their terms of enlistment were expiring, and they insisted on returning to their homes. Before they left, however, Pickens insisted they dismantle enough of Fort Grierson to render it inoperable.

Harry, alone now at Fort Cornwallis with his Legion, was worried because he had no natural emplacements for his artillery. Remembering the tower he had used so effectively at Fort Watson for his riflemen, he ordered a much larger and sturdier one built on the Augusta plain. The men cursed under their breaths, but went to work cutting down trees.

On the night of May 28 Colonel Browne made his first sortie. Shortly after midnight a party rode out of Fort Cornwallis in force, intending to trample down the breastworks in a surprise raid. But Harry had been expecting the enemy to try to break out of his net, the sentries were alert and the Legion infantry formed quickly behind the breastworks and opened a heavy fire on the approaching foe. The British wavered, and Harry ordered an immediate bayonet charge, an action that was extraordinary when infantry were facing cavalry, and unique when carried out at night. Browne retired at once to Fort Cornwallis.

The following day General Pickens returned with the better part of his brigade. He and his senior officers had been furious with the militia for deserting comrades in a time of great need, and the overwhelming majority had voted in favor of taking part in the siege. Some returned to Fort Grierson, and the others took places in the gradually expanding lines around the fort.

On the night of May 29 Colonel Browne again made an attempt to break out, but was driven back to the fort by combined detachments of cavalry and infantry.

The logs were now ready for the making of Harry's artillery tower, and construction began late that night, the platform rising behind an old house Harry was planning to tear down after it served its purpose, that of screening his operation from the enemy. Work crews labored night and day on the huge structure, patiently building up the walls a foot at a time, then filling the interior cavity with sand, stones, and anything else at hand.

Harry was afraid that the enemy would make a desperate attempt to demolish the tower, once they knew of its construction, and he was uncertain how much Browne could see from the towers of Fort Cornwallis, so he posted a full company of Legion infantry to stand guard over it.

Early on the morning of June 1 the Americans discovered that the enemy had learned the tower was being erected. A large party of Redcoats drove out of Fort Cornwallis in what proved to be the most vicious sortie they had yet conducted. They drove straight for the tower, cutting almost at will through two companies of Pickens' militia. But Oldham's Marylanders and a company of Legion infantry moved up quickly, and after a brief, hard fight, sent the Redcoats reeling back to their fort.

By sunrise on the morning of June 1 Colonel Browne once again demonstrated his resilience and ingenuity. He had worked all night hauling three four-pounder cannon into position on the parapet opposite the tower, and began a furious cannonade with heated iron balls.

Harry had two choices. He could order his men to crouch behind breastworks until the Redcoats exhausted their ammunition, but that alternative meant a delay in completing the tower that might last weeks. His other choice involved the risk of suffering casualties, but he elected to complete work on the tower as rapidly as possible, and put every available man on the job.

Work on the cumbersome structure was finished shortly before noon that same day, and the six-pounders were hoisted to the top of the tower in slings the artillerymen had devised for the purpose. The combined efforts of more than one hundred soldiers were required to move the American guns into position.

Powder and shot were carried up to the tower, and the American gunners went to work immediately, while every man not on sentry duty stood below to watch. In less than an hour all three of the British four-pounders were silenced. The cannon remained active throughout the afternoon, sending volleys crashing into Fort Cornwallis every fifteen to thirty minutes until sundown.

Harry was hopeful that Browne would realize he was trapped, and would surrender now, but the silence from the fort was discouraging. The British commander had already proved himself an exceptionally stubborn man, and he quickly demonstrated again that he had no intention of giving up. He also showed himself capable of matching the enemy trick for trick.

That same evening, as Harry was eating dinner at his headquarters, word was brought to him that a British sergeant had escaped from the fort and was giving himself up. The man was a grizzled Scotsman who had spent years in service. His story was that he himself had become discouraged because of Browne's intransigence. The garrison would hold out to the last man, but he was being sensible.

Harry questioned the prisoner at length, and finally persuaded him to identify the location of Fort Cornwallis' powder magazine. Accurate artillery fire could explode the powder and make it impossible for Browne to hold out any longer. The sergeant climbed the gun tower and pointed out the magazine inside the walls, but insisted on going below again at once, pointing out that his recapture could lead to his execution on the grounds of treason.

Some of the Legion's younger officers were elated by the sergeant's revelations, and predicted that Fort Cornwallis would fall by mid-morning. Harry was less certain of the outcome, and believed it possible, if not likely, that the sergeant had been sent by Colonel Browne to tell his glib story—for some as yet unexplained purpose.

At dawn the shelling was resumed, but the powder magazine remained untouched. Meanwhile three unoccupied houses that stood near Fort Cornwallis were on fire, the Redcoats sent flaming torches attached to arrows into them from the parapets. Two other deserted houses were still standing, which made Harry wonder if the resourceful Browne was up to some new tricks.

The bombardment continued for six hours, and although the Americans were unable to assess the damage inside the walls, they knew it was necessarily heavy. Harry thought the time ripe for another surrender demand, and wrote a brief letter in his own hand. He signed it, as did General Pickens. It read:

"Sir, It is not our disposition to press the unfortunate. To prevent the effusion of blood, which must follow perseverance in your fruitless resistance, we inform you that we are willing, though in the grasp of victory, to grant such terms as a comparative view of our respective situations can warrant.

"Your determination will be considered as conclusive, and will regulate our conduct."

Captain Armstrong rode alone to Fort Cornwallis, carrying a white flag on the point of his saber. In the event that the Redcoats fired on him, Harry declared, he would take no prisoners when the stronghold was captured. Armstrong was courteously received, however, and although blindfolded, was taken into the fort while Colonel Browne wrote a brief reply, which the Captain then carried back to the American commanders:

"Gentlemen, I have the honor to acknowledge the receipt of

your summons of this day, and to assure you, that as it is my duty, it is likewise my inclination, to defend the post to the last extremity."

The uncompromising rejection made it necessary to take Fort Cornwallis by storm, Harry believed, and Pickens agreed with him. They called a council of war, and planned their tactics. It was decided that the Legion infantry, supported by cavalry, would assault the barricades at nine o'clock the next morning, after an intensive artillery barrage, which would be maintained until American troops had scaled the walls. The Continentals of the Legion would not buckle under enemy fire, even though they would have to advance a considerable distance in the open, but their officers agreed that they would be able to hold their lines and keep the left side of the American line firm.

Meanwhile a carefully selected battalion of militia, made up of the best fighting men in Pickens' brigade, would assault the fort from the right, and their task would be a trifle simpler. They would hide in the two unoccupied houses near Fort Cornwallis, and hence would have less ground to cover in the open.

Harry set the time for the storming operation at nine o'clock the following morning, the late hour giving the artillery a chance to further soften the defenses, beginning at dawn. A short time after daybreak, however, there was a violent explosion that knocked men to the ground and sent a shower of burning wood and debris high into the air.

When the dust settled, Harry learned that the two unoccupied houses had been demolished, and now he understood Browne's trickery. The sergeant had been a decoy sent out to buy time. The burning of the three houses near the walls had been a deliberate move to keep the Americans preoccupied while a party sneaked out of the fort and planted mines in the other two houses. The detonating mechanism, probably a fuse, had been strung from the houses to the fort. This morning Browne had seen unusual activity in the enemy camp, had guessed that a storming assault was near and, assuming that the two houses, a natural place of concealment, were already filled with troops, had blown them up.

Pickens' infantrymen had been saved from death only because Harry had chosen an unusual hour for the beginning of the attack. Thanks to an accident, scores of American lives had been saved. Many of the militiamen were jittery, but Harry and Pickens planned to carry out the operation on schedule, even though Pickens' battalion would now have to advance on the fort across a great area of unprotected, open ground.

But Colonel Browne had played his final card, and when he saw the Americans continuing to prepare for their assault, he knew he could do no more. A Redcoat lieutenant rode out of Fort Cornwallis under a flag of truce, carrying a note jointly addressed to Harry and Pickens. It read:

"Gentlemen, In your summons of the 3rd instant, no particular conditions were specified; I postponed the consideration of it to this day.

"From a desire to lessen the distresses of war to individuals, I am inclined to propose to you my acceptance of the inclosed terms; which being similar to those granted to the commanding officers of the American troops and garrison in Charleston, I imagine will be honorable to both parties."

Under his terms, parole would be granted to the members of the garrison, who would be allowed to carry their arms with them to Charleston. Officers would be permitted to retain their horses and personal property.

The artillery remained silent while Harry and Pickens wrote their reply: *"Sir, There was a time when your proposals of this day ought to have been accepted. That period is now passed. You had every notice from us, and must have known the futility of your further opposition.*

"Although we should be justified by the military law of both armies to demand unconditional submission, our sympathy for the unfortunate and gallant of our profession has induced us to grant the honorable terms which we herewith enclose."

The Americans were willing to let the garrison go to the seacoast on parole, meaning that each individual Redcoat promised he would not fight again at any time for the duration of the war. Officers would be permitted to keep their swords, the ceremonial sword of the garrison commander not included, but the soldiers would be required to surrender their arms. Officers would be allowed to keep their personal horses and property they could "prove" to be personal, but all cannon, shot, powder, and supplies were to be surrendered.

The Redcoat courier went off with the reply, then returned

within a half-hour to say that his commanding officer wanted to speak privately to a representative of the enemy high command. Harry sent Armstrong off to Fort Cornwallis, but was still afraid of possible trickery, and all units of the assault force remained on the alert.

Captain Armstrong returned a short time later, laughing. The day, June 4, happened to be the birthday of King George III, and if Browne was forced to surrender on that date, the humiliation would spell the end of his military career. Unwilling to put a request for personal clemency into writing, he nevertheless begged the victors for the privilege of delaying his surrender until midnight.

Harry had learned to respect the foe whom he had threatened to chastise, and was willing to help Browne avoid a deeply embarrassing situation. He hit on the scheme of exchanging further notes relative to the surrender, and a stream of these communications kept couriers on both sides busy through the rest of the day and evening. The assault troops held their positions and rested on their arms.

It was far better to let the Redcoats surrender like gentlemen rather than shepherd them out of the fort in the dark, so the actual ceremony did not take place until mid-morning on June 5. Legion drummers and buglers broke the silence as the gates of Fort Cornwallis opened, and were answered by their British counterparts, who were the first to appear.

Then came Colonel Browne, riding alone. He dismounted, as did Captain Armstrong, who rode out from the American lines to meet him. The colonel surrendered his ceremonial sword, the Union Jack flying over the fort was hauled down, and the rest of the garrison marched out. The professionals on both sides were silent, and only a few of the militiamen cheered.

Armstrong rode to Harry and presented Colonel Browne's sword to him; that was the end of the ceremony. Legion infantry moved up to take the Redcoats' weapons, and a Legion detachment occupied Fort Cornwallis and ran up the American flag. It was time now for everyone to eat, so the troops of both armies built fires and started cooking their noon meal in iron pots.

Harry, taking no chances, kept a Legion guard posted in a circle around the members of the British garrison. At this point he was not worried about possible enemy trickery, but was afraid that some units of the South Carolina militia might not honor the surrender. He had no intention of allowing his own reputation to be sullied by another massacre like the slaughter that had taken place at Fort Grierson.

He invited Colonel Browne and General Pickens to dine with him at his headquarters, and for safety's sake posted a cavalry detachment around the house. He and Browne had learned to respect each other, and Captain Eggleston, who was present, wrote of their conversation as "animated."

Browne confessed that the sergeant who had appeared at the American camp was not a deserter. He had been a volunteer who had accepted the extremely hazardous assignment of setting fire to the logs of the ingenious American artillery tower. He had not been able to carry out his mission only because Americans had been at his elbow at all times. Harry would have been within his rights to keep the sergeant a prisoner, try him before a court-martial board and sentence him to a long prison term.

But the victor could afford to be generous. He had just achieved his greatest triumph, and as a man of courage he admired the sergeant's valor. So he ordered the man released, and the officers toasted each other before the defeated Redcoats marched off, a detachment of Legion cavalry accompanying them on the first leg of their journey to make certain they weren't attacked by vengeance-seeking militiamen.

Stores of powder, shot, and food were loaded onto wagons, and Harry formally turned over Fort Cornwallis to General Pickens. Then, several hours of daylight remaining, he ordered the Legion to prepare for an immediate march. His men knew he wasn't one to waste a moment, and were neither surprised nor dismayed. Even though they had been up since very early morning, they packed their gear and made ready for the next stage of their campaign.

XI

THE LAST VICTORIES

"Lee's Legion," Captain Joe Eggleston wrote, *"always marched as though the Hounds of Hell were nipping at our heels. There was no sedate pace for us, no pleasantries, no lazy dawdling after dinner under the trees. The colonel was an impatient man who goaded us again and again, until, unable to tolerate the verbal lashing any longer, we responded by marching until ready to drop in our tracks."*

Lee's Legion, encumbered though it was by the stores taken from Fort Cornwallis, marched due north from Augusta and reached General Greene's siege headquarters before Ninety-Six in a little more than forty-eight hours. The weary assault troops of the Army of the South greeted them with an enthusiasm that verged on hysteria.

Ninety-Six, so named because it was ninety-six miles from the principal town of the Cherokee, the largest Indian nation in the area, was undoubtedly the strongest British fort on American soil. The main defense consisted of a military town, complete with blockhouses, towers, and high walls. A deep ditch had been dug around the walls, which were "Z-shaped," angling first one way, then another, which made an assault hazardous. Directly in front of the stockade was a smaller, star-shaped fort, self-sufficient in case of need, with its own communications trench connecting it with the main fortress. Surrounding the entire complex was a fence of saplings sharpened to fine points, with still another deep ditch outside it.

By the time Harry Lee and his men arrived there, Ninety-Six had been standing off Nathanael Greene's attacks for almost three weeks. The results to date had been negligible. The British garrison had enough ammunition, powder, and food to withstand a long siege, and a small creek that flowed directly into Ninety-Six on the American left gave the defenders ample water.

Siege trenches and ramparts crisscrossed the entire area in front of the star-shaped fort, and still more were being erected by one of the most remarkable of Europeans to serve the American cause, a noble Pole and professional soldier, Thaddeus Kosciusko, who had arrived in the New World in 1776, and had been given a commission as a colonel on General Washington's personal recommendation. He was now acting as Chief Engineer for the Army of the South, and had his hands full, as the British defenders expected relief from Lord Rawdon, and refused to consider surrender.

Twice General Greene had sent messengers to the commandant under a flag of truce to explain that resistance was useless because Rawdon had retired eastward to await the arrival of reinforcements from England that Sir Henry Clinton had promised him. The Redcoat high command at Ninety-Six refused to accept Greene's word, instead believing he was trying to take the post by a trick.

Siege conditions were somewhat similar to those Lee's Legion had endured at Fort Cornwallis. Ordered to take up a position on the right flank, Harry moved up his battery of artillery, and on his first night in the line had to use his infantry to repel two savage attacks by the defenders.

On June 11 General Greene received a message from Brigadier General Thomas Sumter to the effect that three full regiments of British infantry had just landed at Charleston. Lord Rawdon now had more than two thousand men under his command, and the Americans felt certain he would make a determined effort to drive them off.

Kosciusko redoubled his efforts to take Ninety-Six, and construction was begun on a new line of trenches closer to the fort. The task promised to be long and arduous, and no one believed it could be completed before Rawdon marched to the aid of the defenders. So picket lines were tightened, and Greene issued an order requesting all units to be on the alert and prevent the

Redcoats at Ninety-Six from learning that help would soon be on the way.

Harry Lee asked for permission to cut off the fort's water supply, if he could, an operation similar to that which had resulted in the fall of Fort Watson. Kosciusko was dubious, but Greene believed there was little to lose, and authorized the effort.

Harry's plan was a simple one. The creek was guarded by one section of the fort, and if the Redcoats could be driven out of their tower there, the creek could be diverted. He asked for volunteers to set fire to the tower, and nine of his men responded, eight of them privates and one a sergeant.

The Army's artillery laid down a heavy barrage in other sectors to divert the enemy's attention, and the nine Legionnaires crept forward. But they were discovered when no more than fifty feet from the wall, and the British opened fire on them. Five men, including the sergeant, were killed, while the other four escaped by crawling back to the American line of trenches and breastworks. Harry had not only failed, but had lost five courageous men.

That same day a British courier disguised as a farmer managed to work his way to the most forward American position by posing as a Patriot sympathizer who lived in the neighborhood. He made a sudden, wild dash for the gates, and the men who fired at him were unable to cut him down. He reached Ninety-Six safely, and the blaring of bugles inside the fort served notice on the attackers that the Redcoats now knew that a relief column was on the march. The garrison would be more difficult to dislodge or discourage, and the Army prepared for a major battle.

General Greene, in desperation, requested South Carolina's three brigadiers, Marion, Pickens, and Sumter, to delay Rawdon by every means possible, and sent Colonel Washington's cavalry to help them in their attempt. But his effort was little more than a gesture, and Nathanael Greene knew it. Militia were not strong enough or disciplined enough to halt British professionals.

Rawdon soon proved what his enemies feared, and by a ruse left the South Carolina militia far behind him as he advanced toward Ninety-Six.

Greene was forced to make a choice he had preferred to avoid. He was not strong enough to face the defenders at Ninety-Six and Rawdon's column simultaneously, and knew he would be crushed if he tried. Therefore he had two painful alternatives: he could either abandon his siege in order to meet Rawdon, or could storm Ninety-Six before the relief column arrived. He favored the latter course, and his senior officers unanimously supported his decision.

The assault was made on the morning of June 18, Lee's Legion on the right flank. The attack was preceded by the heaviest artillery bombardment yet made, and then the infantry rushed forward with muskets, bayonets, and scaling ladders. Both sides fought desperately, and the encounter was the bloodiest fought in the entire campaign.

The Legion fulfilled its battle mission, and after a bitter struggle broke into the star-shaped fort, driving its surviving defenders back into the main town. Harry ordered the American flag hoisted, and waited for other units to join him before proceeding to the main defense line.

But other American units had been less successful. The enemy had held them off, and in every sector except the Legion's, the drive had been halted. General Greene sent a message to Harry, telling him to consolidate his position and wait for the rest of the army. The Legion waited all day, its commander fuming, and by sundown it became obvious that the American attack had been contained.

Harry was now in an exposed position, vulnerable to British attacks from all sides in the dark, but he still refused to retire until Greene again sent a messenger to him, ordering him to pull back. The Legion was compelled to abandon the star-shaped fort, and the unhappy Nathanael Greene had to make another major decision. With Lord Rawdon on the march toward him with a superior force and the British garrison under Lieutenant Colonel John Cruger still intact, he concluded that he had run out of options.

The Army of the South retreated once more into North Carolina, with the Legion, augmented by Oldham's Marylanders and a half-battalion of Continental light infantry from Delaware, acting as the rear-guard screen. Rarely, if ever, had Harry Lee's pride suffered such a severe blow. After winning a series of glittering victories, he was once more covering a major American withdrawal.

Rawdon turned north to pursue the Americans, but after a

short march stopped to reconsider his own situation. He, like Greene, was short of supplies and lacked the strength to deliver a decisive blow that would end the campaign. It was a supreme irony that neither army was powerful enough to win a clear-cut victory. In fact, Rawdon decided that he couldn't afford the luxury of maintaining Ninety-Six, and withdrew Cruger's gallant force from the fort, adding it to his own corps.

Nathanael Greene had won a victory as strange as any in military history. By abandoning his siege, he had accomplished his objective of forcing the British to abandon Ninety-Six. There were now no major enemy strongholds in the interior of South Carolina and Georgia. Lord Rawdon was ever-conscious of his own weaknesses when too far removed by seacoast bases that afforded him the support of the British fleet, and sensibly concluded that he could keep his corps intact only in Charleston.

Greene promptly and courageously decided to move closer to his foe, even though the Army of the South was dangerously short of munitions—and boots. The corps wearily went back into South Carolina, and the Legion was given a mission of the sort that had first won Harry Lee fame. He was ordered to raid British supply columns and send back everything he could capture.

From late June until the end of July 1781, the elite cavalry-infantry force acted as raiders and foragers, often venturing close to Charleston and swooping down on wagon trains sent out from the city to outposts in the vicinity. For weeks the Legionnaires ate fish, rice, and frogs' legs, but managed to send considerable quantities of beef and corn back to the main body.

Harry was so adept at this type of work that it afforded him no challenge. He was bored, his men were physically uncomfortable, and the Legion, which had thought of itself as the finest offensive team in the entire Continental Army, was miserable. Harry replaced some of his sick and wounded with Marylanders in order to bring the Legion up to its full authorized strength again, but he craved action more exciting than taking donkey carts from British quartermasters, and he inundated Greene with letters that begged the general to launch another major drive.

Soon after he rejoined the Army of the South at the end of July, a series of unexpected developments strengthened Harry's hand. The largest and most powerful French fleet in New World waters was expected to sail north momentarily from West Indian waters, intending to blockade British-held ports. As a result, according to a letter that Washington sent to Greene, Cornwallis was preparing to evacuate his base of operations at Wilmington, North Carolina, and move into Virginia.

There Cornwallis would be Washington's concern, not Greene's, and the Army of the South would be free to concentrate its complete attention on the corps at Charleston. There, too, unexpected changes had altered the situation. Lord Rawdon, who had been ill most of the summer, had sailed for a holiday in the West Indies. The officer he had left in charge was Colonel Alexander Stuart, an exceptionally able if somewhat reckless officer. Himself worried about the French fleet, Stuart had left only a small garrison at Charleston, and had moved inland and north to a pleasant spot called Eutaw Springs.

For a time the Americans were unaware of Stuart's new deployment, but some of the Legion cavalry that Harry happened to be leading in person on a scouting mission came across a large British reconnaissance party. There was a sharp skirmish in which most of the Redcoats were killed. Harry sent the survivors to the rear for questioning, pushed forward rapidly and learned of Stuart's presence at Eutaw Springs. He immediately notified his general of his discovery.

This seemed to be Nathanael Greene's best chance yet to force a showdown. Circumstances would never be more favorable for a battle, he believed, and he immediately marched with his entire Army toward Eutaw Springs. The Legion was given its usual assignment of acting as the vanguard.

Apparently the Redcoats had no idea that a major American force was in the area. The Legion came across two companies of British dragoons that had been sent out on a foraging expedition, and Harry immediately divided his cavalry into two sections, one under Rudolph and the other under Eggleston, who had just been promoted to the rank of major. The American horsemen advanced on the flanks of the enemy, and the Legion infantry, which Harry commanded himself, held the center.

The British dragoons fled, and most escaped, carrying word to Colonel Stuart that the Americans were in the vicinity. Harry reunited the Legion and continued toward Eutaw Springs. By the time he drew close to the place, Stuart was ready for him, and

British cannon halted the advance. Instead of pulling back and rejoining the main body, however, Harry elected to hold his ground and sent back an emergency request to Greene for guns.

The general obliged by sending forward all his light artillery. The Legion had dug into positions in the hills, and Harry employed his cannon so effectively that he pinned down Stuart, making it impossible for the enemy to advance. The artillery duel continued while Greene came forward with his entire army, and both sides drew up battle lines for the major engagement that had so long been inevitable.

The Legion was assigned the key place on the right flank, and Harry was ordered to act as an anchor. He was instructed to advance if possible, but not to withdraw under any circumstances. He was providing stability in a key sector, as the rest of the American right was held by militia units. That closest to the Legion was Francis Marion's brigade, the Swamp Fox having allowed himself to be persuaded by Greene, although with deep misgivings, to let his men participate for the first time in a formal battle.

Stuart held a strong position in the hills, and his force was perhaps the best the British had put into the field in a long time. Stuart's own regiment had seen service against the enemy for years, and was proud of its record. Cruger's hard-bitten garrison troops from Ninety-Six had already demonstrated their valor. And the cavalry, commanded by Loyalist Major John Coffin of Boston was as expert as Tarleton's dragoons, although less well known. The Americans would have their hands full before the day ended.

Cautiously, very slowly, Armstrong's troop of Legionnaires and Coffin's dragoons approached each other. Coffin made a mistake and, thinking he faced the entire Legion, decided to strike a swift blow that could shatter the best unit in the American Army. He ordered a general advance of his entire cavalry, and Harry was quick to exploit the development.

He ordered Armstrong to fall back toward the Legion infantry, and meanwhile sent Rudolph and Eggleston on a wide sweep around the enemy. The Legion cavalry executed its tactics perfectly, and struck with such force into the rear of Coffin's dragoons that the British dropped back in confusion.

The entire American right advanced, Harry timing his pace to suit the less certain gait of Marion's militiamen. Meanwhile Stuart moved up rapidly to support Coffin, and Greene countered by sending his center and left forward. The two armies met in violent collision.

Most of the American units faltered, but the Legion continued to push the enemy back, and Greene's men rallied. To their astonishment, the entire British line seemed to fall apart simultaneously, and the Redcoats fled along a road that ran parallel to the Santee River. For the first time in its history, the Army of the South was on the verge of sending its foes flying from the field.

The Americans drove straight into what had been the British camp, and there found a profusion of riches. The Americans gaped at barrels of beef and flour, at smoked hams and loaves of the first wheat bread that many of the back country men had ever seen. There were wagons laden with spare clothing, boots, and ammunition. Most tempting of all were barrels of rum and brandywine.

The troops of a dozen militia units were unable to resist the joy of looting. They fell over themselves and each other as they seized the enemy stores, and many began to drink the liquor on the spot. Harry, Colonel Otho Williams, and other Continental commanders were as helpless as the militia's own officers to halt the idiocy. Nathanael Greene rode forward himself, and in a loud voice pleaded with the men to reform their lines for a final thrust that could drive the enemy from the field. But the militia, starved for the good things of life they had been denied through all the long, lean years of the war, were deaf to his voice.

Colonel Stuart had the breathing spell he needed to rally his disorganized men and force them back onto the field. The Redcoats came forward again, and the Legion, aided by Colonel William Washington's dragoons, charged them while the American infantry officers tried to restore order. The disciplined Legionnaires held their own, but Washington's cavalry met Coffin's in a head-on clash, and Colonel Washington, who was wounded, was captured.

The fighting that followed in the next two hours was wild, confused, and savage. The two opposing forces surged back and forth across the field of battle, with one side gaining the initiative for a short time, only to lose it again. The British tried to erase the stain of their disgraceful fight, and at times only the Continentals held firm. On three different occasions the Legion drove forward with such force that it swept aside all opposition—but had to withdraw again when other American units were unable to maintain the same pace.

The carnage on both sides was so great that General Greene sent a courier to the enemy under a flag of truce to suggest a breathing spell so that both sides could remove their wounded from the field and bury their dead. Colonel Stuart, mistakenly believing that victory was in sight, was afraid he would lose whatever initiative he had gained, and refused. The slaughter went on.

After another hour, both sides were exhausted, bled white. Both withdrew from the field, although Stuart lingered just long enough to claim a hollow victory. Actually, both sides had suffered severely, with the Americans losing more than four hundred dead and wounded, the British seven hundred. Most of the senior American commanders had been hurt or killed, and among the Continentals, only Harry Lee and Otho Williams had escaped unharmed.

Nathanael Greene grieved over what he believed had been a stalemate. Not until the passage of time and subsequent developments gave him a better perspective was he able to see that he had completely broken the offensive power of the enemy in his theatre of operations. The British no longer had the mobility to roam at will through the Carolinas and Georgia or to engage in a major battle. Stuart was forced to retire to Charleston, and there licked his wounds.

The American Army of the South retired to regroup and rest, and Greene glumly considered his own position. He, too, had been weakened, and saw no prospect of victory without substantial help from the commander-in-chief. Washington, he knew, was in an excellent position at the moment. The largest and best-equipped American force ever to take the field had Lord Cornwallis under siege at Yorktown, Virginia, and the French fleet had arrived to cut off a British evacuation by sea.

Perhaps, he thought, Washington might soon be in a position to send him the reinforcements he needed so badly in order to win a decisive campaign. He wrote a long, unusually frank letter to the commander-in-chief, explaining his situation in detail and laying particular stress on his unwillingness to rely on militia. He begged for men, arms and equipment, cannon and cavalry and Continentals.

But the letter, in and of itself, was not enough, General Greene believed. He decided to send his message by special courier, and wanted someone who could give Washington a strong verbal report that would substantiate his own account of conditions in the theatre. Lieutenant Colonel Harry Lee, who enjoyed the personal friendship and favor of the commander-in-chief, seemed like the perfect choice for the mission. Greene called him in for a discussion, and Harry agreed to make the trip north, leaving Major Rudolph in temporary command of the Legion.

Harry rode north alone, arriving at the joint American-French camp outside Yorktown on September 10. Washington was busy supervising the siege, but received him warmly, read Greene's letter with care and spent two evenings questioning Harry in detail about operations against the enemy in the Carolinas. Until the Yorktown siege ended in either victory or defeat, however, the commander-in-chief was in no position to decide what help, if any, he could give Greene. The siege promised to be a long one, and he gave Harry a ten-day leave of absence, literally the first holiday the young cavalryman had enjoyed in a year.

The first stop was Leesylvania, where Harry found his family in a patriotic ferment. In fact, his father was so excited over the siege on Virginia soil that he spoke of leading the county militia to Yorktown. Harry, still filled with bitter memories of unreliable militia that allowed themselves to be butchered, gently and discreetly dissuaded him.

The greatest pleasures to be enjoyed at Leesylvania were those of bathing regularly, changing one's personal linen and eating three meals daily at a table laid with a white cloth. For seventy-two hours Harry did nothing but revel in the practices of civilization that had been denied him for a year.

Then he went to Stratford, on the Potomac, to see Matilda Lee. Virtually nothing is known of this visit in detail other than that Harry found his cousin to be a lovely adult of nineteen years, a girl accomplished in the playing of the harpsichord, at dancing and in other pursuits common to gentlewomen. There can be little doubt that he paid serious court to her, and that she accepted his proposal. By the time he returned to Yorktown at the end of his short leave, they had agreed to marry, and although no public announcement of their betrothal was made, the news was quietly circulated in the Lee family. It is unlikely, however, that a date had as yet been set. Harry was unable to make personal plans until the fate of Cornwallis was determined at Yorktown and the decision made regarding reinforcements for General Greene.

The young cavalryman was deeply impressed by the sumptuous mode of living he found at the American-French camp outside Yorktown, and after the hardships he and the other members of the Army of the South had suffered in the past year, he found the spectacle depressing. Senior officers entertained one another nightly at feasts, and everyone seemed well supplied with good wines and hard spirits. The larger tents were pavilions, each furnished with a comfortable bed, and it disturbed Harry to see such comfort when Greene and his officers were forced to endure the most primitive field conditions.

Harry's welcome at the headquarters of the mighty could not have contributed to his distress. On the contrary, he was accepted as an equal, as a distinguished comrade-in-arms by virtually all of the more important men in the Allied camp. He dined several nights with Major General the Marquis de Lafayette, and he renewed his friendship with Colonel Alexander Hamilton. He discussed literature, philosophy, and bookbinding with General Henry Knox on several occasions, after the Chief of Artillery had spent a busy day bombarding the Redcoats in Yorktown, and on at least one memorable evening he drank to excess with General Anthony Wayne.

The causes of Harry's strange, restless mood are difficult to determine. One of the simplest explanations of his unhappiness was his own physical exhaustion. After so many years in service, capped by his strenuous campaigning in the Carolinas and Georgia, he was bone-weary. Matilda was on his mind, too, and certainly he resented the plenty he saw in the camp. Mere lieutenants in the Army of the North were enjoying luxuries denied to Major General Nathanael Greene.

Another, none too subtle reason for Harry's malaise was that he had nothing to do. Loving and needing action, he was con-demned to play the role of an observer. It galled him when his old foe, Colonel Tarleton, led the British dragoons on raids in-tended to disrupt the American siege—and he had to watch other, less competent men repel the assaults. Everyone else was busy, everyone else was earning fresh laurels, but he was a mere spectator at the most lavish military banquet American troops had known since the beginning of the war.

On several occasions he applied for a more active role, but his requests were denied. He was still the commander of Lee's Legion and Chief of Cavalry in the Southern Department. Washington, a stickler for military etiquette, believed that even a temporary duty assignment would have been an insult to Nathanael Greene. So Harry glumly spent his days in idleness with the commander-in-chief's personal staff as the drama of Yorktown unfolded.

The noose around Cornwallis was tightened, several sharp engagements were fought, and finally, on October 19, the British reached the end of their endurance. Cornwallis sent Washington a note asking for an armistice so that terms of surrender could be arranged. The fighting ceased abruptly, and Harry attended a festive dinner given jointly by Generals Friedrich von Steuben and Benjamin Lincoln, both of them his admirers and friends.

He attended the formal surrender ceremonies with Washington's staff, again as an observer, and watched the tragi-comedy as Brigadier General Charles O'Hara of the Guards, Cornwallis' deputy, almost spoiled the solemnity of the occasion by repeatedly offering his sword to officers not authorized to accept it.

The defeat of Cornwallis was a decisive blow that signaled the end of major military operations and guaranteed America's independence. Sir Henry Clinton remained bottled up in New York Town and the survivors of Eutaw Springs huddled in Charleston, but for all practical purposes the war was ended. At the many victory celebrations that were held nightly, scores of officers began to think seriously of a return to civilian life.

Among them was Harry Lee, who now was troubled by still another thorn of discontent. The official report on the Battle of Eutaw Springs had just been published, and his name was not included among the list of officers who received special praise. He, who had accomplished more than anyone else, had been either deliberately or accidentally ignored. He found it difficult to believe that Greene had slighted him, but even harder to accept the omission as inadvertent.

With nothing better to occupy him until Washington decided what help to send the Army of the South, he brooded. The commander-in-chief was exceptionally busy, which gave Harry too much time to himself, and in his frustration he spoke openly of resigning his commission.

Late in October he received a fresh dispatch from General Greene, urging him to persuade Washington to send a force south by sea, via the French fleet. If such a corps were to land at Charleston, Greene argued, the war in the Carolinas could be terminated overnight, too.

Harry dutifully presented the case to Washington, who saw the advantages of such action. But the commander-in-chief was not free to dispose of the French warships as he saw fit. On the contrary, they had been sent to his assistance for a limited period only. America's war was only one phase of a much larger struggle between France and Great Britain, and the fleet was needed at once in the Caribbean.

Deprived of naval aid, Washington did the best he could and sent Greene two of his best brigades, Anthony Wayne's and Arthur St. Clair's. The two units started on the march south, and Harry preceded them, reaching Greene's headquarters several days earlier. His relations with his General were rather strained now, but he did not complain when Greene announced he would make another push against Charleston and the smaller posts on the seacoast—and assigned Lee's Legion to its accustomed place, that of the vanguard.

All through the long weeks of November and December the Legion marched and countermarched, launching attacks, capturing enemy stores and doing its share in bringing the war in the Carolinas closer to the conclusion universally regarded as inevitable. Men who had spent years fighting for their country were reluctant to expose themselves to hardships and dangers now, and the virus of peace, which had also infected the British in the area, reduced maneuvers on both sides to little more than shadow-boxing.

Lee's Legion reflected the spirit of its commander, and the officers, sergeants and men began to talk in terms of going home. Nathanael Greene, himself ill and weary, tried hard to live up to his responsibilities and keep his corps intact. But it was a battle he was destined to lose.

On January 26, 1782, three days before his twenty-sixth birthday, Harry sent a letter to his General, requesting permission to submit his resignation. His reasons, he said, were "*disquietude of mind and infirmity of body. The first arises from the indifference with which my efforts to advance the cause of my country is considered by my friends, the persecution of my foes & my consciousness that it is not in my power to efface the disagreeable impression. The second owes its birth to the fidelity with which I served & is nourished by my continuance in the same line of conduct. However disgusted I am with human nature, I wish, from motives of self, to make my way easy and comfortable. This, if ever obtainable, is to be got only in some obscure retreat.*

"*I have nothing more to say, & will but add my prayers for the honor and prosperity of your arms.*"

Nathanael Greene was deeply shocked by the blunt communication. He had not meant to exclude Harry's name from those commended at Eutaw Springs, and tried hard in a very long reply, that ran many pages and took two days to compose, to make amends. "*There is no inconvenience I would not submit to, to oblige you,*" he wrote, "*no length I would not go to serve you in the line of truth and honor. But I wish you not think of leaving the service. Everybody knows I have the highest opinion of you as an officer, and you know I love you as a friend. Whatever may be your determination, to retire or continue in service, my affection will accompany you, and as far as my influence with mankind has any operation, I shall take pleasure in paying a just tribute to your merit.*"

He continued in the same vein for hundreds of words, finally adding, "*I owe you the greatest obligations, obligations which I can never cancel, and if in this situation I should be unwilling to do justice to your exertions I should not only be guilty of the basest ingratitude, but a strange contradiction in my own conduct.*"

The general concluded on a firm note, saying, "*I believe few officers in America or Europe are held in higher esteem.*"

His candor and protestations of affection healed the breach, and from that time until the end of their days, he and Harry remained close friends. But the young cavalryman had made up his mind to return to civilian life, and would not be persuaded to remain in service. He and Greene continued to exchange letters at a furious rate, and in one of his franker notes Greene said he knew the reason Harry wanted to leave the Army was because of his desire to be married.

Harry acknowledged the truth of his superior's observation.

Greene finally granted his permission for the resignation, if Harry would agree to return for a few months in the event that military developments produced a need for services that he alone could perform.

To refuse such a request would have been a denial of all that Harry had done throughout his military career, and he promised to heed a call from the general if he was needed.

That settled the matter, but the Legion insisted on the final word. A group of volunteers, acting secretly, without Harry's knowledge, made a surprise raid on a small British outpost located only three miles from Charleston. Both cavalry and infantry took part, and the assault, made on February 13, 1782, was conducted for the sole purpose of gaining possession of the British commandant's dress sword.

On the evening of February 15 the entire Legion gathered at sundown to stage a review for its commander, and the saber was presented to Harry. All of his officers and sergeants had scratched their names on the blade, and he was so overcome he wept. So did his veterans, and then, with rank forgotten, everyone sat down to a meal of beefsteak and wheat bread, the raiders having shown the presence of mind to steal several head of cattle and sacks of wheat from the British, too.

The following morning, at dawn, Harry took the salute from the Legion's sentry outposts and rode north to Virginia, wearing his frayed, once-elegant green tunic and dirt-smeared white breeches for the last time.

XII

THE COUNTRY SQUIRE

Matilda Lee happened to be the heiress to a considerable fortune as well as being an enchantingly beautiful young woman. Her father had died in the year the war had started, her mother had recently remarried, and she was now the sole owner of a ten-thousand acre estate that produced tobacco and vegetables in abundance, a large stable and one of the most handsome great-houses in Virginia. She was also a minor, and Harry was required by law to post a bond with the executors of her estate before he could marry her.

His father loaned him the vast sum of twenty thousand pounds, which he posted with Richard Henry Lee, the president of the board of executors, and Matilda posted another twenty thousand. The law and the honor of the Lee family having been satisfied, Matilda and Light-Horse Harry Lee were married in March 1782 in the main hall of the bride's home, where the young couple intended to live.

Richard Henry Lee gave away the bride, and General George Washington, who headed the distinguished guest list, contributed several pipes of his best Madeira wine to help insure the festivity of the occasion. Matilda looked lovelier than ever, in the best tradition. Similarly, according to Cousin George Lee, never one to let any trifling detail escape his eye, Harry—who had never quailed before the enemy in battle—looked very pale and made his responses in a voice so faint that only those relatives who stood nearest to the couple could hear him.

The wedding reception was held at the new home of Matilda's mother, a few miles away, and the foods that tempted the palates of the guests was not only an indication of the grandeur of an occasion when a Lee married a Lee, but also, more significantly, demonstrated that the new nation was already beginning to enjoy the fruits of the peace that would be incorporated into a formal treaty with Great Britain in the following year.

Huge platters of roasted beef, mutton, venison, and oxen stood on tables, as did great bowls of oysters and plates of a delicacy virtually unobtainable since the start of the war, smoked trout. The ladies enjoyed dishes of "Italian salat greens," while the men preferred heartier fare, beef tongue and crocks of locally made cheeses, spiced with chopped spring onions.

The ladies toyed with glasses of a light sack, and in addition to Washington's Madeira there were seven other kinds of wine. Serious drinkers were able to concentrate on whisky, rum, and brandywine, washed down with ale, porter, or small beer. The reception was the first major social event of its kind held in northern Virginia since 1775, and was attended by more than four hundred hungry, thirsty guests.

The bride and groom accepted a number of toasts, and eagle-eyed Cousin George observed that Harry drank sparingly. Then, as the decibel count rose steadily, Harry and Matilda slipped off to Stratford, and the bridegroom carried the bride over the threshold of the house that had always been hers and that, as the result of a marriage ceremony and the posting of bonds, had now become his, too.

Harry surprised the relatives and friends who had thought of him only as a soldier by settling down at once to the life of a country squire. The management of Stratford was a time-consuming job, as Matilda owned a mill, four fisheries, and a small quarry as well as the plantation. The new squire made himself familiar with the operations of the estate. He had learned from several pre-war disasters suffered by his father that it was risky to put all his eggs in the tobacco basket, as tobacco prices fluctuated unpredictably from year to year. He wanted a diversification of crops, and within a few weeks of his marriage was planting both corn and wheat. At the same time he made arrangements with Colonel John Fitzgerald, once Washington's aide and now establishing himself as a grain broker in Alexandria, to handle the sale of Stratford's produce.

The young newlyweds lived very quietly on their estate, and much to the disappointment of those hungry for splendid entertainment after so many years of privation, gave no large parties. Their social relations were confined to quiet evenings with relatives and neighbors, which was tantamount to the same thing, as most property in the area was owned by one or another Lee.

Not unexpectedly, Harry also kept in close touch with his former officers. Lieutenant Colonel Henry Laurens, an efficient and courageous officer with a good combat record, had been made commander of the Legion after Harry's resignation, but men loyal to Lee didn't like their new superior's ways, and submitted their resignations at so rapid a rate that it appeared for a time that the Legion would fall apart.

Among the first to resign were Captain Armstrong of the cavalry and Captain Pat Carnes of the infantry, who paid a visit to Stratford en route to his own home and brought Harry up to date on the latest gossip.

Former Legionnaires who were encountering difficulty in adjusting to civilian life almost invariably wrote to Harry for advice and help, and he kept up a lively correspondence with them, intervening with General Washington in one instance, when a former lieutenant was arrested for an act he had committed while still in the service, an act—the requisitioning of a horse—performed on the order of higher authority.

The Virginia House of Burgesses voted a bill to pay bounties to all militiamen who had been in the state's service throughout the war, and Harry wanted to make certain that his Legionnaires, who had transferred to the Continentals, would receive their full share and not be penalized because they had shifted from the state's armed forces to the nation's. Thanks to his correspondence with various state officials, Legion members from Virginia were duly protected.

For three quiet years Harry concerned himself only with personal and domestic matters. Matilda gave birth to their first child, a boy, and he was named Nathanael Greene Lee, a gesture that pleased General Greene and tightened the bonds of friendship between the former comrades. Unfortunately, the baby died when only a few months old.

Matilda's second child, also a boy, was born soon thereafter, and was named Philip, after his maternal grandfather. General Washington, whom Harry frequently visited at Mount Vernon, accepted the honor of becoming the baby's godfather.

By 1785 Harry was becoming a trifle bored with a life devoted only to the management of an estate, and, in the true Lee tradition, decided to enter politics. He ran for a seat in the Congress of the Confederation, and being a Lee, won handily, with only a token show of opposition from two other candidates.

In the autumn of that year he went off to New York for the meeting of the Congress, and formed a personal friendship with a close associate of Thomas Jefferson's, James Monroe, even though their political views differed in most matters. Harry also revived his friendship with James Madison, with whom he'd had little or no contact since their college days in Princeton.

One of the most pressing questions of the day was that of navigation rights for Americans on the Spanish-controlled Mississippi River. The majority of Virginians, among them Patrick Henry, the most powerful political force in the state, were insisting that residents of the Kentucky District, which was cut off by mountains from the seaboard, be granted unrestricted rights to send furs and agricultural produce down the Mississippi to New Orleans.

The Burgesses had instructed its representatives in the Congress to vote in favor of legislation demanding such rights, and Harry obeyed orders, like a good soldier, but privately disagreed. His own views on the matter were parochial, and dictated by self-interest. If western products flooded the new markets opening in Europe, he feared, his own crops would bring far smaller prices. He made no secret of his opinions, which caused considerable distress in his constituency and paved the way for the first serious defeat of his life.

The months he spent in New York were an education of a new kind. The Confederation, Harry observed, was unwieldy, and it annoyed him to see each of the states zealously guarding its own rights. As an officer who had commanded men from many states and had fought in many, he thought of himself first as an American and second as a Virginian. Again he let his views become known.

In 1786 the voters in his district expressed their displeasure by refusing to re-elect him, and instead sent Madison to the Congress. James Madison actually held views even firmer than Harry's on the need for a strong federal government that would stop the petty bickering between the individual states, but he was far more discreet in his manner of expressing himself.

The victorious Madison wrote a gracious letter to his old friend, but Harry was furiously angry. Believing that Madison had worked behind his back for his defeat while professing friendship, Harry sent him an intemperate reply. Madison defended himself in a letter that was coldly correct, and the two men corresponded at length, their relationship growing more strained with each communication.

By the time Harry returned to Stratford late in December 1786, Matilda had given birth to a third child, a daughter who was named Lucy, after Harry's mother. The young father devoted himself to his family and estate, but needed more to occupy him. He had tasted political blood, and the old thirst for glory seized him again. His only public duty, which men of the Lee family accepted as a part of their heritage, was to act as a justice of the peace, and he fulfilled the few minor obligations of his office, but continued to think in terms of playing a role in larger, more important arenas.

All America was stirring in 1787, and Harry's restlessness was typical of intelligent men everywhere. The Confederation had proved so cumbersome and weak that plans were being made for the preparation of a new Constitution that would establish a strong federal government. Harry realized he had no right to a place in the Virginia delegation to the Constitutional Convention, but saw no reason why he shouldn't sit in the Virginia convention that would pass judgment on the efforts of the men who would draw up the new Constitution.

It was easy for a Lee to gain support from other Lees, and Harry went to Cousin Richard Henry, the most powerful member of the tribe, who promised to help him. Unfortunately, the seating of Harry would mean the displacing of another Lee, Richard, who liked his visits with fellow legislators so much that he saw no reason why he should retire in favor of his nephew.

There were personal joys and sorrows that occupied Harry in 1787. Late in the spring Matilda gave birth to another son, who was called Henry, the fourth in a direct line of descent to bear the name. A few weeks later Harry's father died, leaving the bulk of his estate to his four younger sons.

His reasoning, as explained in his will, was that his eldest possessed enough in the way of worldly goods to give him financial security for the rest of his days. However, as a token of his deep affection, he left Harry vast tracts of land in the wilderness of the Kentucky District.

Family concerns did not interfere with the fascination Harry felt for the activities of the Constitutional Convention, which met in Philadelphia under the Presidency of General Washington. Every literate man in Virginia held firm views on the subject, and only in Massachusetts were the state's leaders as violently divided. Washington, ably supported by Madison, believed America would perish unless a strong federal government was established.

Most of the other prominent political figures in the state disagreed. Richard Henry Lee and Patrick Henry were afraid that the government set up under the proposed Constitution would lead to a dictatorship that would destroy personal liberties, and two of the Virginia delegates to the Convention, Governor Edmund Randolph and Harry's next-door neighbor, George Mason, had refused to sign their names to the document.

Harry Lee unequivocally supported the adherents of a strong federal government. His experience as an Army officer had convinced him that the states worked against one another, and that only a greater power could govern the nation. The Continentals had been fine soldiers, but state militia, in the main, had been useless. The war would have been won at least a year earlier, he believed, had there been a federal government.

After Washington's return home from Philadelphia, Harry spent several evenings at Mount Vernon discussing the Constitution with the general, and then began to campaign on its behalf. The thirty-one-year-old embryo politician worked as hard and as enthusiastically as he had ten years earlier in raiding British supply trains. He made speeches everywhere. He went to taverns and addressed men who had gone there for a quiet drink. And he wrote scores of letters, some to friends and acquaintances, some to total strangers.

He announced his candidacy for the Virginia convention, but there were so many others who wanted the seat that he believed his chances of being elected slight. The most positive aspect of his zeal was the end of his feud with Madison. They stood on the same side in what both believed a great cause, and they corresponded at length. In fact, Harry was worried that Madison, who was spending much of his time in New York and Philadelphia, might not be elected to the state convention, and repeatedly urged his friend to come home. In the meantime, Harry made repeated visits to Madison's district and made impassioned speeches on his behalf.

Harry Lee was an articulate public speaker, and was so intense that he proved capable of arousing the emotions of his audiences. Experienced politicians were impressed by his ability to sway men's minds, although there was little in his thinking that was original.

Madison was elected to the convention as a delegate from Orange County. Westmoreland County, which favored ratification, surprised Harry by sending him to Richmond as one of its representatives. There he found the opposition formidable, and the convention dominated by Patrick Henry, Richard Henry Lee, George Mason, and Edmund Randolph. Madison was gloomy, and Washington, who had remained at Mount Vernon, was apprehensive—and with good cause.

If Virginia, one of the pivotal states, refused to ratify the Constitution, it seemed probable that New York and Pennsylvania, which had not yet voted, would reject the new form of government, too. And without these three states it would be impossible to set up a new system, even though every other state in the Union expressed its approval of the federal government.

Patrick Henry appeared invincible—as always. The most brilliant orator in the United States, many times Governor of Virginia and a man to whom many delegates were indebted for political favors, he made several speeches on the first day of the convention and even more on the second. He used every weapon in his potent arsenal, from logic to bitter ridicule, to smash his opposition. He was applauded violently every time he stood and demanded the floor.

The supporters of the proposed Constitution had not spoken a word by the time the third day's session was half-completed. James Madison coolly awaited his opportunity, marshaling his arguments. But Harry Lee lacked his friend's patience. A cavalryman always struck hard and, if possible, directed his attack at the enemy's core. So, on the afternoon of the third day, Harry managed to get the floor, and stunned even his friends by directing his assault at the semi-sacred person of Patrick Henry.

"Is it proper," he demanded, "to appeal to the fears of this House? The question before us belongs to the judgment of this House. I trust Governor Henry has come to judge and not to alarm. I trust that he and every other gentleman in this House comes with a firm resolution, coolly and calmly to examine, and fairly and impartially to determine.

"He was pleased to pass an eulogem on that character who is the pride of peace and support of war; and declared that even from him he would require the reason of proposing such a system. I cannot see the propriety of mentioning that illustrious character on this occasion; we must all be fully impressed with the conviction of his extreme rectitude of conduct.

"But this system is to be examined by its own merits.

"Governor Henry adverted to the style of government and asked what authority they had to use the expression, 'we, the people,' and not, 'we, the states.' This expression was introduced into that paper with great propriety. This system is submitted to the people for their consideration because on them it is to operate if adopted. It is not binding on the people unless it becomes their act.

"It is now submitted to the people of Virginia; by what style could it be done? Suppose it was found proper for our adoption and becoming the government of the people of Virginia, by what style could it be done? Ought we not to make use of the name of the people? No other style would be proper.

"Governor Henry then spoke of the character of the gentlemen who framed it. This was inapplicable, strange, and unexpected. It was a more proper inquiry whether such evils existed as rendered necessary a change of government.

"This necessity is evident by the concurrent testimony of almost all America. The legislative acts of different states avow it. It is acknowledged by the acts of this state; under such an act we are here now assembled. If reference to the act of Assembly will not convince Governor Henry of this necessity, let him go to our seaports. Let him see our commerce languishing—not an American bottom to be seen. Let him ask the price of land, and of produce, in different parts of the country: To what cause shall we ascribe the very low price of these? To what cause are we to attribute the decrease of population and industry and the impossibility of employing our tradesmen and mechanics? To what cause will the gentleman impute these and a thousand other misfortunes our people labor under?

"These are owing to the imbecility of the Confederation, to that defective system which can never make us happy at home or respectable abroad. Let us abolish it, now and forever. Let us, as Governor Henry himself has said in a memorable address that will forever enshrine him in the hearts of his countrymen, let us remember we are Americans all, and Virginians afterward!"

The cavalry brilliantly performed its mission of placing the opposition on the defensive. Harry's courage in striking direct at Patrick Henry startled the delegates, as did his insistence on keeping the figure of General Washington beyond reach. In one brief, pungent address, Harry Lee came of age politically, and immediately was regarded as a force of consequence.

In fact, Governor Henry paid him the compliment of exposing him to ridicule in an address that "lamented" the judgment of Westmoreland County's voters, who, he said, should have sent someone versed in statecraft and the law to Richmond rather than one whose sole claim to fame was his ability to sit a horse.

Harry had the good sense not to reply, but a later speech by the wily old politician infuriated him. The former Governor attacked the idea of a federal army as unsound, and Harry delivered an impassioned reply lasting more than two hours. Citing example after example, he recounted in detail the record of professional Continental soldiers and the feeble efforts of state militia. Among the opponents of ratification were a number of former officers, but they forgot politics and gave him a standing ovation when he sat down, still indignant.

In the days that followed there were maneuvers and countermaneuvers behind the scenes, with Washington quietly using his influence from Mount Vernon to further the cause of the Constitution's proponents, while Patrick Henry, devoting his days to endless speechmaking, used his nights to hold private meetings at which he tried to win converts to the opponents of the Constitution. Madison and Mason utilized logic on behalf of their respective causes, and each day's informal tally indicated that the vote would be very close.

Harry Lee remained in the thick of the fight, and although he was in no sense a leader of the Constitutionalists, he found himself so regarded by a large number of delegates. His two speeches, combined with his strong personality and military reputation, made him one of the best-known men in Richmond. Scores of visitors who were drawn to the town by the stirring debate sought him out, and it was not unusual for a crowd to gather outside his lodgings and applaud him as he left for the convention's morning session. Ironically, many of the visitors seemed unaware of James Madison's identity.

When the formal count was taken, the Constitutionalists won by a slim margin of ten votes. Harry was hailed by many of his colleagues as a worthy successor to Cousin Richard Henry Lee, a claim he had the good sense to recognize as nonsense. Harry was a man who always wanted—and may have needed—the good opinion of the world in which he lived, but he had sufficient insight to recognize his own inner strengths and did not allow himself to be swept away by the tides of his own vanity. His character weaknesses, which were subtle, had not yet manifested themselves.

Virginia's ratification made it certain that the new form of government would come into being, and as soon as Harry returned to Stratford he planned to take Matilda to New York to watch the birth of the federal government in which he believed. Like Madison and many others, he believed the nation's worst trials were at an end.

The concept of a strong executive branch of government was new to Americans, and in every state there were leaders whose friends began to promote them for the high office of President of the United States. Perhaps the most prominent of those mentioned in the late summer and autumn of 1788 was John Hancock of Massachusetts, the wealthy Patriot who had devoted most of his fortune to the cause of liberty, had served with distinction as President of the Continental Congress and was now Governor of Massachusetts. His associates, in no way discouraged by Hancock himself, began an active campaign on his behalf elsewhere.

Harry Lee was one of the first to take active steps on behalf of General Washington. Certainly there were men in every state who looked to Washington for leadership, but the general's austerity made them hesitate to urge that he consider the presidency. Harry felt no inhibitions on this score, however. With his own father in his grave for only a short time, he had already turned to the general as a substitute father-figure, and a letter he sent to Washington at Mount Vernon from nearby Stratford on September 13 was an honest expression of his sentiments.

He wrote, in part, "*Solicitous for our common happiness as a people, & convinced as I continue to be that our peace & prosperity depend on the proper improvement of the present period, my anxiety is extreme that the new govt. may have an auspicious beginning.*

"*To effect this & to perpetuate a nation formed under your auspices, it is certain that again you will be called forth.*

"*The same principles of devotion to the good of mankind which has invariably governed your conduct, will no doubt continue to rule your mind however opposite their consequences may be to your repose & happiness. It may be wrong, but I cannot suppress in my wishes for national felicity, a due regard for your personal fame & content.*

"*If the same success should attend your efforts on this important occasion, which has distinguished you hitherto, then to be sure you will have spent a life which Providence rarely if ever before gave to the lot of one man.*

"*Without you the govt. can have but little chance of success, & the people of that happiness which its prosperity must yield.*"

General Washington, true to his nature, refused to seek the presidency, believing that the office should seek the man, a natural attitude in one of his rectitude—which thereafter established a pattern copied by every candidate for the post.

In spite of his own modesty, however, his bandwagon began to move. Officers who had served under him and regarded him with a mixture of awe and wonder were now gentlemen of consequence in all thirteen states, and they began to clamor insistently for his election. None of his former subordinates worked more diligently or enthusiastically for this end than Harry Lee.

The anti-Constitutionalists in Virginia, men of high character like Patrick Henry and George Mason excepted, were still bitter over their defeat, but could not take out their wrath on Washington, in whom they could find little fault. The upstart politician,

Harry Lee, who had leaped into prominence overnight, was a natural target, and they attacked him venomously.

A whispering campaign was instituted, and it was said throughout the state that Harry was advocating the general's cause in the hope that he would be given a high position on the President's staff if his candidate should be elected.

Pat Carnes, Joe Eggleston, and other former Legion officers who knew Harry well expected him to deny the charge. He was neither a hypocrite nor greedy, they believed, and were confident he would squash the rumor with a ringing declaration of principles. When he said nothing, they were disturbed, and Carnes, rather uneasily, wondered on paper in a letter to Eggleston whether the incorruptible commander of Lee's Legion had changed.

The truth of the matter was that the story didn't reach Harry's ears until the active campaign for various candidates was well under way. Then a letter from James Madison, who was running for a seat in the Senate and whom he was also supporting, enlightened him. He was stunned and, as he declared in a lengthy reply, "sickened" by the charge. What bothered him most was not his own situation but the thought that anyone might believe Washington capable of "perpetrating political knavery."

In order to set the record straight, Harry prepared a long "Statement of Fact," which he had printed at his own expense, and to make certain that no one misunderstood, sent a copy to General Washington. The better part of the handbill was devoted to a spirited defense of the general. All who knew him, the indignant Harry declared, realized he would make no deals with any man for his own or mutual profit. "His purity shines in all his deeds, and there is no blemish or stain on any act committed by him in all the years the fate of this nation was in his hands."

As for himself, the budding politician declared flatly, he would not seek office from Washington, nor would he accept one if it should be offered to him. "*My experience in the conduct of civilian affairs of state is negligible, and I am not qualified to hold an office in which the national trust depends on the wisdom of a govt. official. I do not flatter myself that I would be entrusted with such a post; there are good staff officers in every state, & their counsel is of inestimably greater value than would be mine. I am content with my present lot, and do not desire that it be changed."*

Whether Washington might have asked him to accept a place in the federal establishment after his election as President is an unanswerable question. The general took him at his word.

XIII

TURMOIL, TROUBLE AND TRAGEDY:

THE ACHILLES HEEL

Gentlemen who had demonstrated their faith in the future of the United States by buying bonds during Confederation days breathed more easily when the new system of government was adopted. Their investments were sound now, they believed, and it was probable they would earn a profit.

That optimism was reflected everywhere, by men of every class. Hard times were past, and refusing to make allowances for the growing pains the federal government was almost certain to endure, they were convinced that America would overnight live up to the potential of her natural resources. The nation would expand, and soon everyone would become wealthy.

Land was a commodity men knew, or thought they knew, and there were millions of virgin acres waiting to be settled. Men by the thousands, including immigrants from Great Britain and, to a lesser extent, France and the German states, traveled across the mountains with their families to settle in Kentucky and Tennessee. The richness of the soil in the Ohio Valley became a topic of conversation in taverns, inns, and private dwellings from the sparsely populated Maine District of Massachusetts to rural Georgia.

In all thirteen states, men with cash in their pockets and strongboxes had the same idea. Settlers needed land, and those who owned large parcels of it could make a killing. Land speculation became a national mania.

Harry Lee was not immune to the disease, and his appetite was whetted by the sale of one of the Kentucky properties he had inherited from his father. He emerged from the transaction with a handsome profit, and looked for fresh fields to conquer. One of the most spectacular land development projects was being managed close at hand, so he didn't have far to search.

Virginia had always been conscious of the West's potentials, and the Burgesses had authorized the formation of a private organization known as the Potomac Company to carry out what was universally regarded as a farsighted project. A series of canals would be dug to link the waterways of Virginia with those of its Kentucky District, and then the great riches of the West could be carried to Atlantic seaports for transportation to Europe. Both East and West would profit, and the nation would no longer need to depend on an agreement with Spain permitting Westerners to send their boats and barges down the Mississippi River.

The directors of the Potomac Company were men of integrity, standing and personal wealth. The president was General Washington himself. And the organization was doing more than talk. Canals were already being dug, one at the Great Falls of the Potomac, which would become a key spot in the pipeline.

Colonel John Fitzgerald heard his former commander-in-chief discuss the canal with a rare display of enthusiasm, and passed along the word to his friend, Harry Lee. The two men decided to see for themselves what was happening, and rode westward to inspect the Great Falls. Harry was immediately struck by the potential of the site, and as promptly bought five hundred acres adjoining the place where the locks would be built, with an option to buy still more. Warehouses would be needed there for produce, furs, and lumber being shipped east; there was ample water power for mills, and the traffic would be heavy enough for the construction of two inns, one for the comfortably situated and one for bargemen, each with its own taprooms.

Harry conceived the idea of building a town there. He outlined his thoughts to Washington, who had just been elected President of the United States. The squire of Mount Vernon approved, and soon thereafter sent a glowing letter to Madison, who, as a potential investor, sought his advice concerning the future of the project. Unfortunately, Harry and Washington weren't businessmen, but Madison was canny enough not to sink a penny into the venture.

The engineers in charge of the canal digging were new to that sort of work, and made several errors that rendered their ditches inoperable. Harry's town remained a dream. Even worse, the people who had sold him the five hundred acres had not obtained clear title to the property, and he became involved in complicated and expensive litigation.

Had he been far-seeing, he would have dropped his project, accepted his relatively small losses and forgotten the matter. But he was fooled by an insistent clamor from merchants, innkeepers, and mill owners anxious to buy land from him. Even Madison was beguiled and, although he put no money of his own into Great Falls, tried to obtain major financial backing from friends in New York and Philadelphia, and even went so far as to write a letter to Thomas Jefferson, United States Minister to France, suggesting that wealthy nobles there might want to invest.

Jefferson, who knew more about land than either of the younger men, gently refused to associate himself with the project. Harry was caught in a dilemma. In order to sell parcels of land to eager, waiting buyers, he needed clear title to his five hundred acres. In order to get it, he would have to put up a strong legal battle that would cost him a considerable sum. But he had almost no cash in hand, having spent four thousand pounds in sterling for his purchase. All his other money was tied up in various expansion projects at Stratford.

There were numerous distractions in 1789 and 1790, too. The most serious of them was Matilda's physical condition. She had complained of dizziness and a lack of appetite before Harry took her off to New York to see Washington inaugurated as the first President of the United States, and the journey did nothing to improve her health. She went into a steady decline after their return, and required so much attention that she spent most of her time at the home of her mother, in Alexandria.

Physicians advised that she visit the hill country, where the air was sweeter and less steamy, but she rallied there for only a short time. Her loss of weight was alarming, and she failed to respond to a variety of elixirs prescribed for her.

Harry's old friend, Alexander Hamilton, now Secretary of the Treasury, did nothing to ease the Virginia squire's mind, either. Struggling desperately to put the finances of the young nation on a sound basis after thirteen years of budget juggling by thirteen separate states, he wanted the new federal government to assume the legitimate debts of the states—and pay for the operations of the government by taxing landowners. Harry, with Stratford's thousands of acres, property in Kentucky and the Great Falls land, became so perturbed that he lost much of his enthusiasm for the new system of government.

By early spring of 1790 he was so upset that he decided to run for a seat in the Burgesses, hoping that if Richmond led the way, other states would follow Virginia's example and prevent Hamilton from driving estate owners into bankruptcy. He opened a brisk correspondence with the Secretary, believing his friend misunderstood the situation and didn't realize what he was doing to men in Harry's position. The replies were cautious, and held out no promise of relief. Alexander Hamilton knew precisely what he was doing.

Matilda began to suffer from mysterious fevers that attacked her suddenly, and left her limp and exhausted when they subsided several hours later. The unexpected death of her mother put her into a melancholy frame of mind, and she was finding it difficult to breathe.

To top Harry's woes, the winter of 1789–90 was particularly severe, and the cold was followed by a period of heavy rains that lasted well into May and ruined spring planting. Cattle caught a mysterious disease attributed by most estate owners to the incessant dampness, and Harry lost about one-third of his herd.

There were only a few bright spots in that gloomy spring. He was elected to the Burgesses, and the new governor, Beverly Randolph, honored him by making him lieutenant for Westmoreland County. He was now the official commander of the county militia, with the rank of full colonel, and was the presiding justice of the peace. Unfortunately, the honor was an empty one, and he was given no additional salary for his increased responsibilities.

He went off to Richmond in a sour frame of mind, and found himself in agreement with other members of the Assembly who believed that the industrial states of the North intended to finance the government at the expense of the Southern landowner. Bills incorporating Hamilton's ideas had been introduced in Congress, and the whole South was alarmed. No one was more up in arms than Harry Lee, and although his faith in Washington never wavered, he suspected that the President, the most honorable of

men, was unaware of the knavery around him and was the un-
witting captive of cunning Senators, Congressmen—and Cabinet
members.

On the opening day of the session Harry relieved his mind by
making a fiery speech that covered a variety of subjects. He
protested at length against a tax on landowners, pointing out
that a factory or mill in Massachusetts or New York or Pennsylvania might occupy only a fraction of an acre, and hence its
proprietor, who might make an enormous annual profit, would
pay a tax infinitely smaller than that required of an unfortunate
squire whose thousands of acres were—in that very year—a
financial liability and drain.

He was applauded wildly.

Harry was just starting, however, and continued to let out his
frustrations. There had been a plan, approved by all Virginians, to
build a new capital for the United States on the banks of the
Potomac across from Alexandria. Now, however, it had come to
his attention that Senators and Congressmen from the North
were conniving to find a site located in their part of the country.

Virginians, Harry declared, believed in fair play. They favored
a site in the center of the country, equidistant from the northern-
most and southernmost tips. As it happened, a capital on the
Potomac would, through sheer chance, be convenient to Virginia.
But other states were jealous of Virginia's prestige, and wanted
to cheat her. "Their evil designs shall not prevail!" he shouted.

There was such tumult in the House that sergeants-at-arms
were required to restore order. And before the day's session
ended, Harry found himself elected to the post of floor leader
by his fellow Assemblymen. He was, after the Speaker, the most
important member of the lower chamber of the Burgesses. A
position that other men had worked for years to attain had almost
literally fallen into his lap, with no effort on his part.

As another direct consequence of his address he was offered the
chairmanship of the Committee on Propositions and Grievances.
It was this group that instructed—or tried to instruct—the state's
federal Senators and Congressmen how to vote on various issues
of the day, and consequently was considered by many to be the
most important of the Burgesses' committees. Overnight he was
catapulted into a position that led his colleagues to think of him

for the Governorship, and throughout the session he was a marked man, courted by every faction and group.

Perhaps the most remarkable aspect of Harry Lee's political career is that he achieved success so easily. His climb from obscurity to high places was proof of Washington's theory that the office sought the man.

Harry enjoyed the spring session of the Burgesses, just as he would relish the autumn meeting a few months later. But his own concerns remained pressing, and as soon as the Assembly adjourned he made another journey to the Great Falls. Work on the locks was progressing, even though some engineers were saying that water would not flow into them. And a warehouse had been built on the one lot he had sold before litigation had forced him into inactivity.

He returned to Stratford so fired with enthusiasm for his real estate development that he wanted to mortgage as much of the property he and Matilda owned as was necessary to finance the operation that had become his obsession. Matilda, who had always deferred to him in all things, stubbornly refused to give him a free hand. She believed she was dying, she had no faith in the Great Falls scheme, and she was afraid that her three children—who had no inheritance other than the Stratford estate—would become penniless orphans.

She understood her husband, but there were others in the family who knew him, too, and Matilda enlisted their help. Her sister's husband, Ludwell Lee, was one, and Harry's own brother, Richard, was another. Both were hard-headed lawyers with considerable experience in dealing with business matters, and both tried to dissuade him from squandering his children's future.

When Harry would not be budged, Matilda took another tack, and begged him—for her sake—to grant her wishes. A husband who loved his invalided wife and could not bear to see her in torment was unable to oppose her. Harry agreed to put the Stratford estate and several other valuable properties he and Matilda jointly owned in trust for the children. Under its terms, carefully drawn by Richard and Ludwell, he could not borrow on the estates or dispose of them; after his death and Matilda's, these lands—and everything on them—would go to their children.

Harry returned to Richmond for the autumn session of the Burgesses still searching for ways to finance his project. Meanwhile the state's business inundated him, and his popularity continued to soar. He was still popular with the Constitutionalists, whose cause he had espoused so vigorously at the Virginia convention. And their opponents, whose ranks were increasing, held views on most matters identical to his own.

James Madison, who had failed in his bid for a Senate seat and was now a member of the House of Representatives, had also suffered strong changes of heart. Strongly opposed to most of Secretary Hamilton's ideas, he had already become an articulate leader of the anti-Administration forces in Congress, and was applauded by most Virginians for his stand. He corresponded regularly with Harry and with others in the legislature, and it may have been he who first openly advocated that his old friend be elected governor the following year.

Whether he was the first is, in a sense, irrelevant. What matters is that he became Harry's champion. Other young men, among them James Monroe, who would follow Madison as President, and John Marshall, who would become the nation's most distinguished Chief Justice, were also enthusiastic. The older, most powerful Virginians kept their hands off, for one reason or another. President Washington didn't believe it appropriate for the dignity of his office to interfere, but everyone knew Harry had long been his protégé. Secretary of State Thomas Jefferson was preoccupied. Patrick Henry had retired from politics to support his large family by practicing law. Only United States Senator Richard Henry Lee was still concerned with state politics, and of course he favored the election of the cousin he had always helped.

The political pot bubbled furiously, but while the ferment was at its peak, Harry lost interest in the governorship, in Great Falls, even in life itself. He received a message from Stratford telling him that Matilda had died suddenly and unexpectedly in her sleep.

Harry left Richmond at once, and did not return to the state capital after her funeral. His devotion to his wife had been deep for the more than eight years of their marriage, and although her illness should have prepared him for what was to come, he was stunned.

He spent the winter at Stratford, and for days on end did nothing but sit in his library and stare out of the window. One day he conceived the idea of building a stone mausoleum in the rose garden Matilda had loved since childhood, and he spent weeks closely supervising the project, sometimes stepping in to cement a stone into place.

His many relatives and loyal friends could not console him, and Harry literally refused to leave the estate until the mausoleum was completed and Matilda's remains moved there. Spring came, and he stirred sufficiently to oversee the planting, but did little other than go through empty motions.

Great Falls no longer meant anything to him, either. For a time, at least, he was able to see he had been pursuing a dream, and on the infrequent occasions he bothered to answer friends' letters, he confessed he had been mad to think he could acquire a fortune in land speculation.

He stayed close to his children through the spring, and others in the family engaged in a conspiracy for his good. Philip and Henry urged him to take them riding, to teach them how to handle sword and pistol while in the saddle, and they were so insistent that he obliged them, and thus spent several hours each day exercising in the open.

He tried to be both father and mother to the children, and supervised their studies, read to them daily and told stories to his daughter every evening. No one, his own mother and brothers included, could induce him to leave Stratford long enough to dine with them.

But the world continued to come to him. Visitors dropped in to see him frequently, and men spoke of little but the "enslavement" of Virginia and the other states of the South by Alexander Hamilton. Already deeply depressed, Harry became gloomy almost beyond endurance. He heard nothing but bad news, and wished he had stood with Patrick Henry at the Virginia convention.

If he had, he told Madison in a brooding letter, the state would not have ratified the Constitution, and without Virginia's support the new system of government would not have been adopted. Therefore, he concluded in a burst of specious, guilt-ridden reasoning, he was responsible for the nation's catastrophe.

By summer Harry became active enough to start returning the condolence calls of relatives, in itself a full-time occupation. He took the children with him everywhere, and although more active physically, he had not yet recovered from the shock of Matilda's death and remained emotionally empty and drained. Occasionally he spent an evening with some of his leather-covered books, but engaged in no other intellectual pastimes.

Others continued to think of him as the best candidate for governor, however, and Madison wrote to ask whether he would accept the position.

"I wish to be done with government," Harry replied. "On the score of tranquility & peace I am also desirous to be quiet, for every day adds new testimony of the growing ill will of the people here to the government."

Some of his other comments in the letter were equally vehement. In one place he wrote, "How do you feel, what do you think, is your love for the Constitution so ardent as to induce you to adhere to it though it should produce ruin to your native country?" His views had swung from one extreme to the other since 1789.

Some men believed Harry would refuse the governorship even if elected, but Madison was not one of them. The very intensity of the feelings expressed in the letters he had received indicated to Madison that his friend was coming to life again. He quietly advised the legislature to elect Harry, saying he felt certain that "Colonel Lee will deem it his obligation as a citizen to accept."

Attempts to interest the grieving widower in a social life met with virtually no success. Attractive widows and unmarried young ladies were often included at the quiet dinner parties of relatives, but Harry had retreated into the shell from which he had emerged only to woo and win Matilda. Now, as in his early bachelor days, he was courteous but remote, and scarcely seemed aware of the existence of women.

Harry's brother, Charles, who had attended the College of New Jersey with him and was closer to him than other members of the family, finally decided to have a frank talk with him. It wasn't natural, he said, for a virile, adult man to spend all his time alone, and he suggested that Harry would recover sooner from his melancholy if he visited one of the brothels in Alexandria. If, because of the dignity of his position, he didn't want to be seen entering or leaving such a place, Charles felt certain that arrangements could be made to bring an amenable young woman to Stratford for an evening.

"Sir," Harry replied, according to a letter Charles wrote to Thomas L. Lee, another concerned relative, "were you anyone

*but the son of my parents I would take the flat of my sword to
your backside. Never would I sully the memory of the wife I
cherish by bringing a harlot under her roof. Nor,"* he added
gratuitously, *"will another lady ever replace her in my affections.
I died with her, sir, and now live only to serve our orphaned
children and my fellow citizens."*

Charles promptly let it be known that Harry was speaking in
terms of his duty to Virginia. His supporters throughout the state
were pleased, but no one dared approach him directly on the
subject. Again Madison's advice was asked, and the reply was
succinct: "Elect Colonel Lee Governor."

By the end of summer Harry was once again keenly concerned
with affairs of state. Hamilton remained his close personal
friend, he protested frequently—and truthfully, although he de-
spised Hamiltonian policies. This aspect of his nature remained
unchanged to the end of his life. He was destined to become
Hamilton's bitter opponent for a time, but his friendship never
wavered. Within a few years he would believe that Henry Knox
had cheated him out of a post of high honor he desperately
wanted, yet he retained a deep personal regard for Knox, too.
And although the Chief Executive of the government he reviled
was George Washington, he revered his former commander-in-
chief as he did no one else, dead or alive.

This curious quirk sometimes baffled Harry's political allies, who
believed him either insincere or shallow. He was neither, but
instead was naïve. A man's political views, he felt, or even the
acts he performed in line of duty, were irrelevant to his personal
relationships. One entertained a friend or was entertained by
him, and one confided matters of an intimate nature to him if
one wished. But one dismissed that man from office the next day
if one felt he had due cause. Holding these unalterable views
himself, Harry refused to allow differences of opinion or even
acts hostile to him to sway his regard for others.

Perhaps his greatest contribution to Robert E. Lee's character
was this lofty sense of duty. He had acquired it, at least in part,
from his own lifelong association with George Washington, and
handed down the concept to his son, whose high-minded idealism
as an officer, a gentleman, and a human being was often reminiscent of Washington's attitudes.

Harry's sense of friendship did not prevent him from striking out at policies he loathed, however, and in a letter he wrote to Madison in the autumn of 1791, he indicated that, after almost a year of mourning and inactivity, he was ready for action again. "*I had rather myself submit to all the hazards of war & risk the loss of everything dear to me in life,*" he said, "*than to live under the rule of a fixed, insolent majority. At present this is the case, nor do I see any prospect of alteration or alleviation. Something must be done to relieve a situation that has become intolerable! Our peril is great, and we can not afford delay.*"

On November 1, 1791, the Virginia Burgesses gave Harry Lee an opportunity to enter the lists against those he considered responsible for an intolerable situation. By an overwhelming majority the Assembly elected him governor, and a committee was sent to call on him at Stratford to notify him of his election and ask whether he would accept.

Harry's reply was brief: "I receive with humility and with gratitude the distinguished honor conferred upon me; to my mind invaluable because it conveys the strongest testimony of affection and confidence of the country."

He, like Patrick Henry before him, had been elected without lifting a finger on his own behalf.

Suddenly there was a great deal to be done, and very little time in which to do it. In less than three weeks the greathouse at Stratford was closed, and the estate left under the care of a general overseer recommended by Senator Lee. Harry, accompanied by his three children, a staff of servants and a housekeeper, set out for Richmond. The children and servants traveled in carriages, but Harry, as in the past, rode in the van on his horse.

XIV

THE FIRST CITIZEN OF VIRGINIA

On December 1, 1791, Light-Horse Harry Lee took the oath of office and began the first of three consecutive, turbulent one-year terms as Governor of Virginia, the maximum allowed any citizen under the state's law. The ceremony was so quiet that few legislators or private citizens even knew it was taking place. A justice of the peace administered the oath, and aside from Harry's three children the only guests present were a few wartime comrades, among them John Marshall, a Richmond resident who was engaged in the private practice of law at the moment.

Harry was still in a depressed frame of mind, and the appearance of Richmond, a raw, ugly town, could not have improved his spirits. A new community where construction work had just begun during the war years, it had been burned to the ground by Benedict Arnold, making it necessary to start again. Its atmosphere was that of a sleepy, rural village, and it lacked the urbanity of Alexandria and the charm of the former capital, Williamsburg.

The Governor's Palace, now called the Governor's Mansion by some, had been built just a few years earlier, previous governors having found it more pleasant and convenient to rent estates in the vicinity. Located only a stone's throw from the new Capitol, which was distinguished only by a portico with Greek columns, it was a two-story clapboard structure badly in need of paint. The rooms were cramped, the official furniture provided by the state was uncomfortable and several of the fireplaces smoked. And the kitchen outbuilding was so small that the governor could not ask more than a few guests to a meal.

Harry was not inconvenienced, however, as he had no interest in entertaining, and dined only with those officials with whom he found it essential to discuss the state's business. On some nights he ate alone, on others he brought the children to the table, and occasionally, when he grew tired of his cook's dishes, he went to a primitive inn at The Market House, where farmers of the area sold their produce. In his first six months of office, he accepted invitations only from the Marshalls and a very few others. On these occasions his hosts were invariably men who had served with him during the war.

But he more than compensated for his lack of sociability by giving Virginia the most energetic, controversial leadership the state had known since Patrick Henry had been its chief executive. In fact, his first official act brought him into immediate, sharp conflict with the federal government.

A month before Harry had taken office, Major General Arthur St. Clair had led the nation's Army to battle against a large force of Indians in the Ohio Valley. The savages had driven St. Clair from the field, inflicting heavy casualties on his corps, and the entire frontier was in a state of near-panic. Settlers, including thousands in Kentucky, which was soon to be admitted to the Union as a state but was still under the jurisdiction of Virginia, were certain the Indians intended to raid the wilderness settlements.

Harry was never one to wait in military matters. The War Department had not yet taken appropriate measures to safeguard the lives and property of the people, so Virginia's new governor called up three battalions of militia to strengthen the frontier outposts. The citizens of Virginia and Kentucky would be safe, no matter what might happen elsewhere.

However, inasmuch as the protection of Americans was a federal rather than a state responsibility, Harry promptly sent the War Department a bill for more than six thousand dollars to cover the payment of wages to the militia. Secretary of War Henry Knox protested, saying he had no authorization from the Treasury to pay such bills.

Harry, who had been spoiling for a fight, requested the state's Congressional delegation to take up the cudgels. Senator Richard

Henry Lee and his colleagues obliged, and threw themselves into the project with such enthusiasm that the harassed Knox paid the bill, but made it clear that a matter of principle was at stake. He had honored a request from the governor of a state because of the "respect" due him, even though the payment ran contrary to Treasury Department regulations.

For whatever the reason, federal troops did not replace the militia. Perhaps townsmen Knox and Hamilton failed to appreciate the danger to frontier dwellers, or it may be they thought enough federal units were in the area. Harry felt otherwise, and kept the militia on duty for another year, at the end of which time he sent Knox a bill for more than fifteen thousand dollars.

Again the Secretary capitulated, but wrote a formal letter stating that thereafter he would lack the authority to request the Treasury to honor such debts. Governor Lee cannily made no reply, and Henry Knox, aware that the stubborn Virginian would keep his men on duty until relieved, finally sent federal troops to replace the militia.

The Indian problems on the frontier created new personal anguish in Harry. He had never thought very highly of St. Clair, and in talks with Marshall, Major Thomas Gibbon, and some of his other old comrades, he discussed at length how he would end the raids if he were the military commander of the Northwest Territory. It was obvious, he declared, that only a force like his Legion, made up of superb horsemen and sharpshooting infantry, could bring the savages under control.

He spent many of his lonely evenings brooding, and wished he had applied to President Washington for a commission rather than accept the governorship. Even the highest civilian office in the state bored him. France was engulfed in a revolution, and word had reached the United States that the Marquis de Lafayette was commanding a large corps of troops on the side of those struggling to break the shackles of tyranny.

"*War suits me as well as peace*," Harry wrote to Cousin Richard Henry, and suggested that he was considering applying to Lafayette for a commission. After all, the gallant young Frenchman had helped the United States in a time of need, and it would be only fitting to "*repay the debt*."

By early 1792 the War Department had reason to feel that St. Clair was proving less than efficient, and Secretary Knox held several private conferences with President Washington on the possibility of replacing him. These talks were theoretically confidential, but all Philadelphia, now the seat of the federal government, buzzed with rumors. Madison and Cousin Richard Henry wrote to Harry that he was one of the leading candidates for the post, but warned him that several officers with rank far greater than his were also being considered.

Harry could hear the blare of bugles and feel the thrill of riding across a field at the head of his troops. He could visualize the gold epaulets of a major general of the line on his shoulders, and his excitement was intense.

Then, in April, Madison sent him a short, sympathetic note telling him the appointment had gone to General Anthony Wayne.

Harry felt deeply disappointed, and shot off an angry letter to Henry Knox, in which he stated repeatedly that he had been "cheated." He remained consistent in his approach to personal relations, however, and concluded by assuring Knox of his warm attachment to an old friend.

A few days later Harry was told that he had been rejected on Knox's recommendation to the President. The Secretary of War had felt that his relatively junior wartime rank would have created an awkward situation and made it impossible for many officers senior to him, who were still on active duty, to serve under him. Washington had agreed.

Harry went to great pains to confirm the story, and then sent an even angrier letter to the President. "Sir," he wrote, "*you have been deceived by those in whom you place the highest confidence, and consequently your own character as well as the public interest may be submitted to derogation and injury.*" Again, however, he closed on a note of personal warmth.

His feeling of frustration had become intolerable, and Harry finally sent off the letter to Lafayette that had been on his mind for months. To be on the safe side, he also dispatched another communication to a less well-known Frenchman who had fought in the American Revolution and was now a person of some consequence in Paris. Would he be welcome as a volunteer, he asked, and what rank might be offered him?

Lafayette's reply was sent from Cologne. The Marquis had been a victim of one of the many purges that characterized the French Revolution, and had been forced to flee for his life. He was now a refugee, waiting for another swing of the pendulum to return home.

Another letter, which arrived a few days later, was an official communication from the Adjutant General of the French Army. His Excellency, Colonel-Governor Lee, had acquired world renown as a soldier, and there were many in France who recalled his gallantry and leadership. He was indeed welcome in Paris, and would be given command of a division, with the rank of major general, the day he arrived.

Harry literally didn't know what to do. He loved his own country passionately, and had accepted the highest office that his beloved Virginia could bestow on him. But the temptation to accept the French offer was virtually irresistible. He needed to talk to someone about the problem, and instinctively sought the advice of the man he respected above all others, President Washington.

Learning that the President was paying a short visit to Mount Vernon, Harry made a hurried ride there, and was bitterly disappointed when he heard that the President had already gone back to Philadelphia. Aware that it would be both brash and improper to follow him, Harry wrote him a long letter in which he spoke of his loneliness since Matilda's death, his love of his "real profession" and his desire to return to it. Should he or should he not accept the French offer?

The President replied almost as quickly as he had done when Harry had sought his help during the war. But there was a difference now. George Washington was President of the United States, and was trying to prevent the spreading military upheaval in Europe from spilling across the Atlantic onto American shores. His letter was unsigned, but was written in the same dignified scrawl that Harry had known since childhood.

It was characteristic of George Washington to state, with some severity, that he could not give advice either in his capacity as President or as a friend. Then, having created the gulf that he always placed between himself and others, Washington expressed himself emphatically: "If the case which you have suggested were mine, I should ponder well before I resolved, not only for private considerations but on public grounds. The latter because, being the First Magistrate of a respectable State, much speculation would be excited by such a measure."

He went on to discuss the situation in France, and made it

apparent that he neither liked nor trusted the Revolutionary high command. Men in high places there were jealous of one another and jockeyed incessantly for position. They would "tear each other to pieces" before the Revolution ended, and in the process the principles for which they were fighting would be lost. The French would achieve neither the liberty nor the equality they sought, and in the end might find themselves saddled with a political system more tyrannical than the monarchy they had overthrown. The President proved himself an astute political prophet.

He also had a few words of advice from one soldier to another. As affairs became more chaotic, rations for the troops in the field would become increasingly scarce. There was already a shortage of bread, and it would grow worse. Hungry troops needed a cause as a substitute for food, but in the growing confusion that prevailed in France, he was afraid causes would be forgotten, and starving men would become deserters. Anyone who sought to command a division under such conditions was asking for trouble.

Washington's advice made so much sense to Harry that he abandoned his idea of going to France, and never again revived the scheme. In the meantime, a great many other things had been happening.

Harry led Virginia's fight against Hamilton-inspired legislation imposing a tax on all liquor distilled in the country, and when Hamilton's bill became law, he wrote an official protest which the Assembly supported by an almost unanimous vote. Paradoxically, although in keeping with his concept of friendship, this official opposition to the policies of Secretary of the Treasury Alexander Hamilton did not interfere with a private correspondence he maintained with Colonel Alexander Hamilton, his old friend.

It was an intimate correspondence, indeed, and it may be that he was inspired to confide in someone who was, with justification, known as a ladies' man. A few months after taking office, Harry suddenly became aware of the opposite sex again, and confessed to Hamilton that he was fascinated by attractive ladies everywhere.

A governor of Virginia was not free to pursue romance indiscriminately, however, and Harry began to wonder about girls he had met in various places during the war. One in particular, a "beautiful Miss Allen" of Philadelphia, still intrigued him, he confessed to Hamilton, and he wondered if she might still be unmarried. He asked his friend to pass along any available information on her. Hamilton was unable to oblige him.

Friends and relatives who became aware of the change in his attitude were relieved, but made no open reference to the subject in Harry's hearing. For his own peace of mind he continued to protest that there would never be anyone else in his life, and that he had buried his heart with Matilda. Cousin George predicted to others in the family that he would remarry within a year.

Harry may or may not have realized that he was beginning to look for another wife. Then, at a dinner at the house of John Marshall, he met Anne Hill Carter, the daughter of a plantation owner who lived at Shirley, on the James River. She appeared to Harry as a "lovely statue, carved in stone," and he devoted the better part of the evening to her. Not until he came to know her better would he discover that behind her solemn façade was a deliciously subtle and sensitive sense of humor that would perplex him to the end of his days.

Anne, although young, was wise beyond her years. Nevertheless she had done little traveling, and was lacking in sophisticated polish. She was flattered by the attentions of Virginia's first citizen, a debonair man in his mid-thirties still known throughout the country for his wartime exploits. Other girls had flirted with him in vain, but he made several trips to Shirley for the express purpose of seeing her, and whenever she came to Richmond he was very attentive to her.

The pace of correspondence in the Lee family quickened, and Richmond hostesses who hoped to snare the governor for an evening learned that the best way to insure his acceptance was to invite Anne as his partner for the evening.

It was during this period, however, that Harry, having just suffered the disappointment of losing command of the federal Army, was giving his most serious consideration to accepting a commission from the government of France. Not yet truly in love with Anne and lacking the deep-grained interest in politics that might impel him to use the governorship as a steppingstone to still higher office, he was still restless, still trying to establish permanent, comfortable roots.

In mid-July of 1792 he decided to make a personal tour of the militia outposts. The Assembly was not in session, Richmond was dull—except for the evenings he spent with Anne—and he found the urge to taste military life again overpowering. He left almost immediately on his tour, accompanied only by two aides, and spent a relaxing eight weeks in the field. This was the life he enjoyed most, and he felt refreshed and invigorated when he returned to his capital.

There one of the worst shocks of his life awaited him. His elder son, Philip, had died one night several weeks earlier.

Couriers sent to intercept the governor had not been able to catch up with him. He had traveled at such a rapid cavalryman's pace that not one of the messengers sent by staff members and relatives had found him. Philip's illness had been brief; he had complained of a headache one evening, and had gone to bed without his supper. A few hours later, before a physician could be summoned, he had expired.

The cause of his death had not been determined, but it was the general opinion that he had been carried away by "early swamp fever," which often attacked children. He had been given a temporary burial on the grounds of the Governor's Palace, but Harry immediately made the melancholy journey to Stratford in order to place his son's coffin in the mausoleum he had built for Matilda.

The fresh blow, coming at a time when Harry had just regained his equilibrium, almost unhinged his mind. But he was alert to the danger, and managed to overcome it in spite of his grief. More than ever before he looked forward to a military career—and forgetfulness—in far distant France.

Two influences saved his reason. One was Anne Carter, who gave him the tender sympathy he so desperately craved. At a time when he badly needed help, she was beside him, wise and sweet and strong.

The other factor was a change in his own nature that he began to recognize. In a later age men would explain such a balanced —almost philosophical—acceptance of tragedy as a process of emotional maturation. For the first time in his life he was able to examine himself objectively.

Only a few months later, while continuing to attack the policies of the Secretary of the Treasury, he said in one of his many personal letters to Hamilton, "I *wonder why men cannot differ in politics as they differ in other matters and yet hold established regard. I see no insurmountable difficulty in the way, & see its*

*practicability. I believe you are in some degree right in your
conjecture with respect to my friends.*

"*Generally speaking, those in the political line will be found
arranged with you, but in the opposition are some, too, loved by
me & attached to me. Why do not these violent parties coalesce?
Is there no middle ground on which a union might be formed—?
The public harmony as well as individual comfort would be promoted by such an event.*"

Harry's attempts to convert others to his way of thinking were
interrupted by public business, major and minor, that were an
integral part of his duty. A sensational murder case and the star-
tling complications that grew out of it attracted the attention of
the whole country for a time, and made even cabinet members
and senators forget politics.

A young woman named Angelica Barnett won dubious immortality by hacking her lover to death with an ax. Her case offered no legal complications; Angelica freely admitted the crime,
was sentenced to be hanged and was lodged in the small, cramped
two-cell log jail in Richmond. For a time Angelica was the only
prisoner, but eventually she was joined by one Jacob Valentine,
a merchant sentenced to imprisonment because of an inability to
pay his business debts.

Theoretically Angelica and Jacob should have occupied separate
cells. But the jailer was careless, and the locks were on the outer
doors of the building, not the cell doors. Angelica was a very attractive young murderess with elastic morals and, of course, as she
was under a sentence of death, she had nothing to lose. Time
weighed heavily on Jacob's hands, and he had nothing to occupy
him. Inevitably he found his way into Angelica's cell, they became
much friendlier, and before the death sentence could be carried
out, Angelica discovered she was pregnant.

Jacob was something of an amateur lawyer, and advised her to
submit a formal plea to the courts, asking for a stay of execution
until the baby was born. The news was splashed happily in newspapers throughout the country, and everywhere people formed
violent opinions. Some insisted that Angelica should be hanged
on schedule, while others declared she should not be hanged at all.
She was so notorious that in Boston and Charleston, cities that
were proud of their virtue, ladies did not mention the murderess-
harlot-mother-to-be by name, but called her only by her initials.

To refer to another woman as "an A.B." was considered a vicious insult.

The members of the Virginia bench had no desire to kill an unborn baby, and the Supreme Court of the state granted Angelica her reprieve. That, however, was only the beginning. A more or less spontaneous movement started in a dozen places, and large numbers of busy, sympathetic ladies signed petitions asking Governor Harry Lee to grant the admittedly criminal mother a pardon "so that her child will not be orphaned and be made to live on crumbs of charity."

Other ladies—and their husbands—were horrified by the prospect of a pardon. It would be a mockery of justice to let a wanton murderess escape unpunished, they believed, and they started counterpetitions. Harry was inundated, and even at dinners could get no peace, as Richmond itself was divided into pro-Angelica and anti-Angelica groups.

Relatives sent Harry long letters on the subject, and members of the Burgesses delivered speeches and debated the matter on the floor of the Burgesses. So many curiosity-seekers gathered outside the little Henrico County jail that a detachment of militia had to be stationed there to send the good people on their way.

Harry refused to discuss the case with anyone. The issues were clear, and he neither wanted nor would accept advice. He waited, hoping the furor would die down, but when it did not, he decided to cut it short and issued a very brief proclamation. "*Under the powers vested in me,*" he wrote, "*I hereby grant to Angelica Barnett, spinster, a full pardon for her crime of murder in the first degree. This I do in the name of humanity and the people of Virginia.*"

Harry's decision appeared to meet with strong public approval, and the Assembly promptly elected him to his second term as governor. Again he had not sought the office, and had done no campaigning on his own behalf.

He was involved, too, in a venture of far greater importance, which was destined to have a greater effect than that of seeing his name in print. It was directly related, however, to the power of the press, which Harry thoroughly understood. Soon after the beginning of his first term as governor, he and Madison sought some way to counteract the influence of the newspapers that supported the positions taken by Alexander Hamilton.

It was natural that both should think of their fellow Princetonian, Philip Freneau, who held views similar to their own. They privately petitioned Jefferson to find a position for him, and the Secretary of State obliged by giving Freneau the post of translating clerk in the State Department that would pay for his food and a roof over his head, if little else. A short time later *Freneau's Gazette* appeared, and Harry worked hard to enlist subscribers, as did Madison.

The *Gazette* was a success before its second edition was published, and its name was soon changed to *The National Gazette*. Freneau preached the doctrines of liberty, equality and fraternity, and attacked the attempts of the Hamiltonians to increase the powers of the federal government. Although expressing his own views, Freneau was regarded by the Hamiltonians as a mouthpiece for James Madison and Harry Lee. Inevitably, because he wrote opinions similar to those of Jefferson, his superior in the State Department, and because the anti-Hamilton groups were beginning to cluster around Jefferson, there were some who regarded the *Gazette* as Thomas Jefferson's newspaper.

These interlocking alliances worked to Harry's disadvantage. Freneau became increasingly caustic in his attacks on the administration, and his vitriol eventually aroused the ire of President Washington himself. Jefferson, who saw the President daily, was able to defend his own opinions and position.

But Harry Lee, in far-off Richmond, came to be regarded by both Washington and Hamilton as the mischief-maker behind Freneau. The President even went so far as to write Harry a letter in which he called the *Gazette* a scurrilous newspaper.

Harry had never openly disagreed with Washington in any matter, and did not do so now. But he found himself politically isolated. He had never been on friendly terms with Jefferson, and although both Washington and Hamilton still liked him as a person, neither was willing to take him into the cabinet when Henry Knox thought of resigning. Instead, Knox was persuaded to remain as Secretary of War, and Madison, who had been supporting Harry for the post, fell discreetly silent.

In short, Harry had no political support except that of Madison, who had limited influence. Enough time had passed for the vow not to accept an administration post to have been forgotten, and the governorship of one of the most important states in the

Union should have been a steppingstone to a place in the cabinet or some other high federal office.

But Hamilton, with the President's approval, wouldn't consider a man who had been one of Freneau's sponsors, and Jefferson wanted no part of someone who was Alexander Hamilton's close personal friend. Harry was out in the political cold, although he didn't yet know it. In all justice to him, he probably wanted no political position, although he hinted otherwise in correspondence with Cousin Richard Henry and others in the family.

Perhaps the truth of the matter is that Light-Horse Harry Lee was just beginning to find himself again after mourning so long for Matilda. And in finding himself, he found Anne Carter. They had been seeing a great deal of each other, and Anne had indicated that she would be willing to marry him.

But a young eighteenth-century lady was not free to do as she herself pleased, and Anne's parents were strongly opposed to her marriage with the mercurial governor. Harry had made no secret, in his talks with her, of his desire to accept a commission from the French. She had passed along the word to her parents, and Charles Carter didn't want his daughter to become the wife—and perhaps the widow—of a man who planned to go to war in an alien land across the Atlantic.

Occasional rumors were heard in Richmond and elsewhere during this period that Harry had taken a mistress. According to various accounts, this woman was a barmaid, a shopkeeper's assistant or the daughter of a farmer who lived near Richmond. The story was never substantiated, and may have grown out of Harry's celibate way of life. There might have been many who found it impossible to believe he was sexually abstinent, and therefore invented a mistress. If such an affair was fact rather than fancy, Harry managed to keep the details secret. There are no records, almost two hundred years later, to indicate that the woman was a real person.

Inasmuch as he was falling in love with Anne during these months, it is far more likely that the mistress was a figment of gossips' imagination. An idealist who tried to live according to high principles was not the sort to propose marriage to one woman while living with another.

In any event, Charles Carter withdrew his objections to the marriage when Harry abandoned his idea of going to France. For the sake of romance it would be pleasant to record that his growing attachment to Anne was responsible for his change of mind, but evidence indicates that the only important factor was President Washington's letter. Then, but not until then, did Charles Carter relent.

Anne told her suitor that her father was in a more receptive frame of mind, and Harry rode to Shirley, a few miles from Richmond, to ask for the girl's hand. Carter agreed, and once again Harry Lee was betrothed to an heiress who would inherit a large plantation and exceptionally handsome greathouse.

Harry paid his visit to Shirley in May, and thereafter lost no time. He and Anne were married a few weeks later, on June 18, 1793. Henry, Jr. and Lucy acquired a stepmother, there was now a hostess in the drab Governor's Mansion and Virginia had a gracious, very pretty first lady. The ceremony at Shirley was a quiet one, as befitted a second marriage for the bridegroom.

The Lee family welcomed Anne, and all of Harry's friends and relatives sent gifts and their congratulations. There was one notable exception: Thomas Jefferson took no note of the marriage. Perhaps he felt he didn't know either the bride or groom sufficiently well, or it may have been that he was preoccupied with President Washington's Proclamation of Neutrality pledging that the United States would remain aloof from Europe's troubles.

No matter what the cause of his silence, Harry was annoyed. People could slight him, if they wished, but he considered Jefferson's aloofness as an insult to his bride. It seems unlikely that the courtly Jefferson deliberately snubbed Anne Carter Lee, even if he disliked her husband. But Harry interpreted the matter as he wished, and quietly seethed.

The year 1793 was one of the busiest in Harry's life. He revised the tax structure of Virginia on a more equitable basis, using an individual's prosperity rather than his mere ownership of land as a standard for determining the taxes that a man owed. This gentle rebuke to Hamilton was a crude form of the income tax that was later to become the Treasury Department's greatest single source of revenue.

Virginia obeyed the Proclamation of Neutrality to the letter. Washington's word was final to Harry in all things, and he called out units of the state militia again and again to seize incoming or outbound ships that were trying to do business with the French.

Relations within England were deteriorating, too, in part because of Jefferson's sympathy with France and the goals of the Revolution there.

Harry indiscreetly concluded a private letter to Hamilton with a condemnation of Jefferson's stand on international matters, and the Secretary of the Treasury "happened" to let others see the communication. Word soon got back to Jefferson that Governor Lee was criticizing him and, although the Secretary of State made no direct reply, he reacted coolly whenever the governor's name was mentioned in his presence. All of the elements of a feud were in the making.

In November 1793 Harry was elected to his third one-year term as governor. There were no other candidates, and although several of Jefferson's friends abstained, the actual vote was unanimous.

Meanwhile the Governor's Mansion had come to life. Guests were entertained several nights each week at dinner, receptions, and levees, and on at least three occasions, when the house was deemed too small for the size of the party Anne was planning, she transferred the festivities to Shirley.

She was a good hostess, and her charm was one of her husband's greatest assets. Harry obviously was much in love with her, and his children worshiped her. Henry, Jr. and Lucy remained devoted to her all their lives, and were close to her long after their father's death.

Early in 1794 Harry made what was to prove the greatest political error of his life. He learned of a small dinner that Thomas Jefferson had given at his Monticello estate, and was told that the usually tactful Jefferson had been critically bitter in comments directed at the President.

Harry exploded. He thought of George Washington as godlike, and all his accumulated resentments boiled to the surface. The President, he believed, should be made aware of such treachery, so he sat down and wrote a long, furious letter to Washington.

Whether by accident or design, the letter—or a copy of it, also in Harry's own hand—was sent via Monticello. Harry Lee was not one to strike at a man behind his back.

Jefferson, who was renowned for his own temper, promptly lost it. He, too, sent a letter to Washington, in which—among other names—he called Harry a "miserable tergiversator," a "malicious intriguer," and "a purveyor of falsehoods, half-truths and exaggerations."

It is doubtful that Harry ever saw the communication or learned of its contents. Washington was the great master of the art of stifling feuds among his subordinates, and was at his best when snuffing the flames of controversy.

But, whether Harry did or didn't hear of Jefferson's reaction, the fact remains that he had made a bitter enemy. Governor Harry Lee had made a mistake that Colonel Harry Lee would not have tolerated or forgiven: he had underestimated the strength and striking power of a foe.

For the moment, however, he didn't care what Thomas Jefferson thought of him. He was unprecedentedly popular in Virginia, he was happy in his private life with a lovely young wife and he had learned to handle his duties as governor so well that he had ample time to spare.

When Harry Lee wasn't busy, he became restless, and restlessness always caused him to think in terms of resuming his military career. He wrote a short letter to Henry Knox, indicating that he wouldn't be averse to accepting an appropriate commission. And he had become sufficiently sophisticated in political matters to realize that Knox wasn't the real decision-maker. To insure he got his point across, he also sent a similar communication to Secretary Hamilton, the most powerful man in the government, after the President, and the man to whom Washington left innumerable details of policy-making.

Hamilton surprised and delighted his old friend by replying that it was possible, even probable, that there would be a military assignment of great importance for his old friend in the immediate future, but it would entail rather considerable personal sacrifice.

Harry's reply was typical, as Hamilton must have known it would be. There was no sacrifice too great for him to make if the safety and honor of his country were at stake, Light-Horse Harry declared. The stage was set for a new and strange adventure.

XV

THE WHISKY REBELLION

The Whisky Rebellion of 1794 meant many different things to many different people. Its instigators regarded themselves as martyrs and, with some cause, believed themselves the victims of unjust tyranny. The controversy, the most violent in the United States since the foundation of the Republic, had its roots in one of Secretary Hamilton's pet financial policies.

Farmers west of the mountains were cut off from the markets of the seaboard because of the difficulty of transporting their grain to the cities. Similarly, they were not allowed to send their produce off to Europe by way of the Mississippi River because of President Washington's Proclamation of Neutrality. Consequently they did the next best thing and converted their solid assets into liquid ones, distilling their grain.

Hamilton's excise tax on American-made liquor robbed them of nearly all their profits. Meantime the seaboard dwellers, who drank Western whisky and who still managed to get their rum by way of the West Indies and their other imported spirits by virtue of dubious smuggling operations, remained untouched by the tax. Westerners seethed, and claimed they were being subjected to discrimination identical to that which the American Colonies had been forced to endure in the days prior to the Revolution.

In some places men merely grumbled, but in southwestern Pennsylvania the farmer-distillers, who were led by Harry Lee's college friend, Hugh H. Brackenridge, decided to take action. The majority refused to pay the federal tax, and the more violent used intimidation to threaten those law-abiding citizens who tried to comply with the tax law. Eventually and inevitably, stills and barns were burned, there were raids and counterraids, and several men were killed. Reports to the federal government from Pittsburgh, the nerve center of the insurrection, indicated a state of near-anarchy there.

President Washington took his usual dispassionate, farsighted view of the situation. In his view the national government represented all the people of the United States, and therefore that government could not tolerate a refusal to obey its laws, either on the part of the states or individuals. However, he hoped that the passage of time would bring the Westerners to their senses.

Alexander Hamilton shared a portion of the President's opinion, but his own was far more partisan. His personal authority had been flouted, and the rebellion, if successful, would seriously hamper his efforts to increase the power of the central government. A man of great political sensitivity, he realized that the issue was delicate, and that any attempt to coerce the rebels to submit would be unpopular not only in the West, but in the South as well.

Thomas Jefferson sat squarely on the opposite side of the fence. Hamilton's excise tax law, he wrote to James Madison, was "the instrument of dismembering the Union," and he referred to it again and again as "infernal legislation." He was in favor of repealing the law, but did not—at that juncture—make his views public, as he did not want to antagonize the President.

While officialdom talked, pondered, and observed, the situation in the "field" grew steadily worse. The rebels were carrying arms, weapons were being distributed to other malcontents, and it became evident that unless punitive measures were undertaken, the federal establishment, which had just begun to create prestige for itself, would lose the respect of citizens everywhere. The President was reluctant to meet force with force, but at last Hamilton persuaded him to act, and he made the challenge his own, declaring that his reputation and that of the national government were inseparable.

Hamilton and Knox made secret plans to call a total of fifteen thousand militiamen, the majority of them from Virginia, Maryland, and Pennsylvania, into federal service. These troops would march toward Pittsburgh and use "whatever force was required of them" to put down the disturbances and arrest the ringleaders.

The touchiest question before the President and his advisers was that of naming a military commander. Hamilton knew that the show of force would be deeply resented in the West and South, so he conceived a brilliant idea to soften the blow. At a private meeting with the President he suggested that Governor Harry Lee of Virginia, the South's most prominent citizen and a known opponent of the excise tax law, be given the post. Washington, thinking in terms of Harry's loyalty and often-demonstrated military abilities, approved heartily.

Secretary Hamilton wrote Harry the first official letter on the subject, and said that if the governor would take the assignment, he would be given the rank of major general by the Secretary of War. The President himself would ride with the army for some days, he said, and he would accompany the expedition, too, but would consider himself no more than an "aide" to General Lee. What Hamilton did not mention was that, by remaining in relative obscurity in the background, he would escape at least a measure of public disapproval.

Harry was overwhelmed by the proposal, and found it irresistible. He knew of no other officer who had jumped, in a single leap, from the rank of lieutenant colonel to that of major general. The Virginia Assembly was in recess, the state faced no serious problems and Lieutenant Governor James Wood was capable of handling routine business. Harry called the Virginia militia to active service, and even persuaded Brigadier General Dan Morgan to come out of retirement to lead the state's troops. Morgan, eager to don a uniform again, too, was not reluctant to serve under a man who had been two ranks his junior during the war.

Anne Lee agreed with her husband that it would be inappropriate for her to continue living in the Governor's Mansion while Harry was on federal duty, so she and her stepchildren moved to Shirley, taking all the family's personal belongings with her. Then, after Harry returned from a whirlwind tour of mustering centers, she accompanied him to Philadelphia and watched as Secretary Knox administered the oath and gave Harry his commission as a major general. After paying brief calls on the Washingtons and Hamiltons, General and Mrs. Lee returned to Virginia early in August.

For the first time in his life, Harry was wearing the blue-and-buff of the old Continental Line. He had been tempted, he wrote Morgan, to don the green of the Lee's Legion, now the uniform of his cavalry, but he could not, as he was the head of the entire expedition.

No matter how strong Harry's personal convictions may have been on the issues at stake, he put them aside. In a message to the Assembly written only a few weeks before his appointment he had thundered against the further usurpation of power by the federal government, but he felt he was no longer in a position to express his own opinions. He had been given a military mission by the commander-in-chief of the United States Army, and it was his duty to fulfill that mission.

Whether he realized he was committing political suicide is debatable. In letters to officers he asked to join his staff he indicated an awareness that the expedition was unpopular in some sections of Virginia. But, deliberately or otherwise, he made light of their numbers. "*There are some among us,*" he said in one letter, "*from the influence of party spirit and from their own ambitious views, who rejoice in national adversity, and gladden when they hear of governmental embarrassment.*"

Madison and some of Harry's other friends expressed the belief in later years that he had been too naïve to realize that he was digging his own political grave by taking the command of an army that most Virginians regarded with either loathing or alarm. But a letter that Harry wrote to the President during this period indicates that he had a firmer grasp on the principles at stake than many of his contemporaries realized.

He himself had been opposed to much the federal government had done, he wrote, but he believed that opposition should be confined to "*such methods as are provided under the Constitution.*" He expressed his determination to "*maintain inviolate our government at the risk of our lives and fortunes,*" and he ended the letter by saying, "*The awful occasion demands united efforts.*"

Hamilton wanted a show of force so great that there would be no other, similar insurrections in the future, and certainly an army of fifteen thousand, the largest ever mustered since the war, was more than enough to disperse a small number of surly, cantankerous farmers in the hills of western Pennsylvania. The

President, always one to extend the olive branch with the sword, sent a number of personally appointed commissioners into the area ahead of the troops. It was the mission of these men to use persuasion in the hope that a peaceful capitulation could be achieved.

While the President thought in terms of peace, Major General Harry Lee prepared for war, and was busier—and probably happier—than he had been in years. Early in September, however, shortly before he was scheduled to leave Richmond and take command of his army in the field, Anne and Henry, Jr. fell ill. Both ran high fevers, and neither of the physicians called in to attend them could diagnose their ailment.

Harry was reluctant to leave them. The memory of his elder son's sudden, unexplained death was still fresh in his memory, and knowing he would never forgive himself if anything happened to wife and child during his absence, he thought of resigning his commission. But Anne, knowing how much the expedition meant to him, wouldn't hear of it, and insisted that he go. He delayed as long as he could, and finally left, nervous and apprehensive.

The Virginia militia convened from all parts of the state, and marched together to Pennsylvania, where the other militia divisions were waiting. Washington and Hamilton were there, too, both in civilian clothes, and Harry stood beside the commander-in-chief while the corps marched in review before him. Colonel Hamilton found it preferable for his own purposes to remain in the background.

Washington returned to Philadelphia almost immediately, leaving Harry a long letter, which regimental adjutants copied and read to the troops. The President thanked the men for the sacrifices they were making, and referred repeatedly to the "hardships and privations of a military life."

In the next two weeks the army had ample cause to remember that letter. A cold October rain fell day and night as the long columns struggled across the Appalachian Mountains, many of the tents were made of inferior canvas and the men were soaked. Plodding day after day in ankle-deep mud, chilly and hungry, the veterans in the expedition were reminded of their wartime service.

The corps divided into several units, which fanned out over several counties, and Harry continued to march toward Pittsburgh, the seat of the insurrection. Accompanying him were Secretary Hamilton and Federal Judge Richard Peters of Philadelphia, who was prepared to bring the rebel leaders to immediate trial when they were captured.

None of the columns saw much action, but Dan Morgan's men were, characteristically, busier than any others. A letter sent by General Morgan to General Lee summarizes the campaign— and gives some idea of Morgan's still-fiery temper. He wrote from the little village of Washington, Pennsylvania:

We arrived here at half past one o'clock this day; the arrangement in getting across the river was a good one; I had the infantry over by eleven, took the two boats to Parkerson's, I went in one myself, found another on the way, took that.

Boarded a Kentucky-man on the way loaded with apples and cider, and only twelve barrels of flour—let him pass—got to Parkerson's in time to get the waggons over, which got to camp last night—but was obliged to give the tavern-keeper where we lodged, a knock in the mouth, for selling whisky to the soldiers at a dollar a gallon—these sales he kept up nearly all night, and when I told him of his fault, he began to treat me with indignity, and I broke his mouth, which closed the business.

I received a line from General Freelinghauson last evening— I don't expect he will be here before tomorrow evening; however, that will be time enough, as I shall get in train by that time.

The people look very sour at us, but I will bring them to by good treatment; the rebuff I gave the tavern-keeper will assist me, as it will show them that they must not be too impertinent. There is no forage or any thing laid in here, nor do I know what has become of the forage-master; however, we must provide for ourselves till these people come on. We have brought all the troops and waggons up, without any sickness or accident.

I shall be ready to execute your orders in two or three days . . .
I have the honor to be,

Your obt., humble servant,
DANL. MORGAN

P.S. General Biggs will hand you this, to whom I refer you for further intelligence. I saw our friends from Ohio, on their way to you yesterday—God blast them, do handle these fellows very

*roughly—they are shocking fellows. Fulton is now in this town,
I intend to tame him, when I can lay my hands upon him. Nor
do I think Bradford is far off. I will thank you to send me the
rates of sales and purchases that you have established.*

The Fulton and Bradford to whom tough old Dan Morgan
referred were two insurrectionist leaders. Harry had ordered his
subordinate commanders to let none escape, and they were
obeying him diligently. Nowhere had there been organized
resistance to the army, and it appeared that the Whisky Rebellion
might collapse. But Harry knew—and privately admired—the independent, stubborn men of the West. He had to make certain
the insurrection did not flare up again after he marched his
troops back to the seaboard.

The main column arrived in Pittsburgh at sundown one evening, and the quartermaster took Harry to a large, comfortable
house that had been requisitioned for his use. He made himself
comfortable, and not until he and his staff had dined at his absent
host's table did he ask the identity of the fugitive. He was
mortified to learn that the house belonged to his friend, Hugh
Brackenridge, who had been a close associate at the College
of New Jersey. It was bad enough to be forced to hunt down
Brackenridge like a common criminal, but insult was being added
to injury, and the following morning Harry insisted on being
moved to another house.

Virtually all of the insurrectionist leaders were rounded up
within a few days and were lodged in a hastily built stockade
outside Pittsburgh. They had no roof over their heads and were
forced to sleep in the open, the meager food brought to them
by their guards was inedible slop, and they were subjected to
mental torture by the sentries, who told them they would be
hanged for treason.

When Harry learned of the treatment being accorded the
prisoners, he lost his temper. The rebel leaders, most of them men
of substance, were moved to more comfortable quarters at Fort
Pitt, and strict orders were given to treat them as gentlemen.
Then the officers and men responsible for their mistreatment were
made to appear before Harry, who gave them a tongue-lashing
and directed that official reprimands be lodged in their permanent
military records.

At last, early in November, a special courier reached Pittsburgh from Shirley. Anne had written to her husband that she and little Henry were completely recovered and that he need not fear for their health. Harry was able to put his gnawing worry out of his mind and concentrate on the business at hand.

Unfortunately, he had very little to do. Judge Peters had established a court at Fort Pitt, and the leaders of the Rebellion were put on trial. Secretary Hamilton attended every session, but Harry thought it inappropriate for a military commander to appear in the courtroom, and he deliberately stayed away. It was bad enough that the people of the area regarded him as the symbol of tyranny, and that his provost had an almost impossible task trying to prevent daily fights between bored soldiers of the occupation force and surly river bargemen and farmers.

It was not easy to act as a representative of the federal government in a business that was so repugnant to the citizens of the West, Harry was learning. He struggled hard, but in vain, to establish cordial relations with the community. Only once did he and Secretary Hamilton clash. The evidence against Hugh Brackenridge was hazy and circumstantial, and it soon became evident from the testimony of other prisoners that he had counseled moderation rather than open rebellion.

No formal charges had been placed against him, and Harry thought it a miscarriage of justice for him to be held at Fort Pitt with the other prisoners. Hamilton thought him too dangerous to be released, but Harry stubbornly insisted that he be given his parole, and held his ground so firmly that the usually strong-minded Secretary of the Treasury was compelled to back down. "General Lee," Hamilton said when Judge Peters signed the order for Brackenridge's release, "represents the Executive here."

Soon thereafter Brackenridge was given a clean slate, and even Hamilton, who sought the maximum penalty against everyone connected with the Rebellion, was forced to admit that Brackenridge had been loyal to the United States and that his role had been misunderstood. Harry's victory in the affair was minor, and failed to compensate for the long hours of boredom he was forced to endure.

Late in November he received some mail from Virginia that included a number of documents requiring his signature as governor. He had not resigned his office when he had accepted his commission, and Wood had acted in his stead. By now, however, a new governor had been elected, so Harry thought it appropriate to return the papers for his successor's signature. He extended his best wishes to the new governor for a happy and successful term, and commented lightly that he was so far removed from state politics that he literally didn't know the new governor's identity.

By December 10 the last of the trials had been completed. Several of the ringleaders in the conspiracy had been found guilty of treason, and were sentenced to be hanged, but President Washington, whose chief concern was national unity, granted them pardons.

The army was recalled, and the troops marched back across the mountains, now snow-covered, hoping to reach their homes by Christmas. They did not arrive until early January 1795, and Harry was given the power to release them from federal service. His own term of active duty expired, too, and he went off to Shirley as a private citizen.

On his arrival there he was astonished to find himself the object of a furious campaign being waged by the Jeffersonians. Inasmuch as he had been Governor of Virginia, they claimed, his appointment as a major general had been illegal, and he himself had violated his oath to serve the people of Virginia when he had accepted the commission.

Harry realized that he was a convenient instrument for attacks by Thomas Jefferson and his adherents on Hamilton, and believed himself on insecure legal ground. He wrote a private letter to Secretary Hamilton in which he admitted his vulnerability. What he did not include was his shock at discovering that he had lost the support of most Assembly members—and of the people of Virginia.

On the long march through Virginia at the head of the state's contingent of troops, he had been dismayed to find that the citizens of the state were either apathetic to him—or openly hostile. In every village and town people had lined the roads to watch the militia march through, and everywhere the regiments had been greeted by that most devastating of welcomes, silence. Not one cheer had been raised for General Lee, and even the tavernkeepers at whose inns he had slept had treated him with indifference.

For a time it appeared that he would become involved in

a legal fight, but the Jeffersonians were not certain of their Constitutional grounds, and decided to wait for another occasion. Had President Washington not been personally involved in the matter, it is likely that Harry would have been charged with violating his oath of office as governor. But no one, not even the most ardent anti-Federalist, wanted a direct confrontation with the one man who stood above politics and had kept the affections of a vast majority of the people.

Harry, deeply confused by the subtleties of the situation, took his wife and children home to the estate at Stratford, and was glad to escape, for a time, from the political arena at Richmond. He had done his duty, accepting a high military command at the request of the President of the United States. And no matter how unpopular the cause he had represented, he had fulfilled his mission: all Americans had learned to respect the authority and power of the federal government.

Harry could see that far more than his own reputation was at stake, but couldn't rid himself of the feeling that Jefferson was only too happy to use him for purposes of personal vengeance.

Regardless of his previous opinions of the federal government, he was being pushed closer to the Hamiltonians—because he had nowhere else to go. But the advocates of a strong central government regarded him with jaundiced eyes and would not make him welcome. There was a significant difference between a purely military federal appointment and a civilian political association. After all, he had been one of Freneau's sponsors, and at no time had he completely disavowed his attacks on the federal system. Most important, perhaps, was that he had no political following of consequence, having used up his credit with the people. A political leader without troops was no asset.

Harry had become that lowest of creatures, a discredited politician.

XVI

THE PART-TIME STATESMAN

With less than two years still to serve, President Washington was counting the months until his retirement and return to his peaceful acres in Virginia. Under no circumstances would he consider accepting a third term, in part because he believed that no man should serve for more than two terms as President, in part because he was heartily sick of the backbiting of associates who put personal ambition before public welfare.

In 1795 a new storm broke that widened the cleavage between the Hamiltonian Federalists and the Jeffersonian anti-Federalists. John Jay, perhaps the ablest of American diplomats, had negotiated a new treaty with Great Britain that settled—at least on paper—a number of issues that had remained unresolved twelve years earlier. The Federalists claimed the treaty a triumph of international diplomacy, and Harry Lee, who believed that friendly relations with England were essential to American security, heartily agreed with them, both in his private correspondence and in the Virginia Assembly, to which he returned as a lowly delegate from Westmoreland County.

The anti-Federalists, following the lead of the strongly pro-French Jefferson, roundly condemned the treaty. Edmund Randolph, who had succeeded Jefferson as Secretary of State, was the only member of the cabinet to vote against its acceptance. Soon thereafter he was the victim of a cruel political hoax, and was accused of having accepted bribes from the French government.

Although he was innocent, as he subsequently proved, he immediately resigned.

Therefore the post of Secretary of State was vacant at a critical time. Washington, trying to steer the nation on a neutral course as more and more nations in Europe were becoming embroiled in the expanding war there, refused all partisan suggestions in an attempt to select a new Secretary who would help him heal the breaches in an increasingly divided nation.

Meanwhile political paradox piled on paradox. Madison, one of the Constitution's "fathers," had become so disillusioned over the way the new system of government was working out that he had cast off all his former allegiances and had joined the Jeffersonians. John Marshall was one of the few Virginians of consequence who unequivocally approved of the federal government in both theory and practice. And Patrick Henry, who had been devoting himself to his private law business since his almost successful attempt to prevent the ratification of the Constitution by the Virginia convention, had undergone a complete change of heart.

He told John Marshall, who in turn passed along word in a letter to Harry Lee, that he was astonished and gratified to discover that the system was effective and that, thanks to the Bill of Rights incorporated in the first ten Amendments, the personal liberties he deemed so important were being safeguarded. With Madison and Henry changing places, it was small wonder that other men, from the highest official to the humblest private citizen, were confused.

Early in 1795 President Washington paid a brief visit to his home at Mount Vernon, and a day or two after his arrival there, General Harry Lee rode over from Stratford to pay his respects to his mentor and friend. Anne accompanied him, and the call was a purely social one. Certainly there was nothing in Harry's previous relationship with Washington that indicated their relationship was about to enter a new phase.

When the ladies left the table at the end of dinner, however, and the President took his guest on the inevitable stroll that ended on the veranda overlooking the Potomac, the tired Washington began to speak freely of his problems. Harry was a man who had no political ax to grind, wanted nothing for himself and for almost twenty years had unfailingly demonstrated personal loyalty and friendship.

Washington discussed the complicated international situation and his own efforts to find a Secretary of State who might help pull America's warring factions closer together. After talking candidly at some length, he posed a question: Did his guest have any possible candidates to suggest?

As it happened, Harry did. Patrick Henry, who had demonstrated his executive talents as Governor of Virginia, would be perfect. More than any other one man, perhaps, he had inspired the Revolution, and was enormously popular everywhere. New England revered him for the fiery stand he had taken before and during the war. The South loved him because he had so long been her champion. And the West admired him because he had lived for long periods on the Virginia frontier and because he had authorized and promoted the George Rogers Clark expedition that had made so much of the West safe for the United States during the war.

Beyond all these factors was another that made the suggestion worthy of a Machiavelli—or an Alexander Hamilton. If the one-time champion of the anti-Federalist cause accepted the appointment, the sting would be drawn from the fangs of those who criticized the government. Even if he refused, the Jeffersonians would be forced to curb themselves for a time.

Washington not only agreed to the idea, but accepted Harry's offer to carry a presidential letter to Henry and to use whatever powers of persuasion he possessed to insure acceptance. The following day Harry returned to Mount Vernon for the letter and, before setting out, Washington discussed other possible candidates for the office. Perhaps it was the crowning paradox that Harry Lee, whom neither of the opposing political factions wanted, had —perhaps in part for that very reason—become one of the few genuine advisers to whom Washington had ever listened.

Patrick Henry rejected the offer, but his reasons were personal rather than political. He had a very large family, two of his older daughters were widows and he had to support them and their children in addition to his own younger brood. But a coldness he had felt toward the President for several years evaporated, and he discussed the nation's affairs at length with Harry, who duly reported back to Washington.

The President was pleased that he found a selfless man he could trust, and took Harry even more into his confidence. There were two other openings in the cabinet, the places of Attorney General and Secretary of War. Washington discussed candidates with Harry, and approved of his suggestions, Governor John Howard of Maryland, who had been a colonel in Nathanael Greene's Army of the South, for the War Department opening, and John Marshall for the Attorney Generalship.

Harry rode up to Baltimore to see Governor Howard, and then privately reported to the President that he had changed his mind as Howard, in his opinion, was growing senile. John Marshall turned down a place in the Cabinet for complex personal reasons, and Harry had still another candidate to suggest, his own brother Charles—who accepted.

In the autumn of 1795 Harry returned to Richmond as a delegate to the Assembly. There he was regarded as a member of the hopelessly outnumbered Federalist minority, but the real Federalists—Marshall excepted—refused to find a place for him in their ranks. Nevertheless he voted with them, but in vain, as the Jeffersonians pushed through a resolution that condemned the Jay Treaty.

Virtually no one knew that Harry had become the President's confidential agent, and he himself kept his mouth shut. Much as he enjoyed glory and the limelight, he vastly preferred the intimate friendship of George Washington.

In the winter of 1795-96 the President called on him again, this time to inquire whether Patrick Henry would accept the Chief Justiceship of the United States. Again the old man refused, but by now he, too, had learned to appreciate Harry Lee's brand of forthright but quiet diplomacy, and to the end of his days, within the decade, Patrick Henry remained Harry's close friend.

Frequently called into conference by Washington during his last year in office, Harry was asked for assistance by Hamilton and the other Federalist leaders in the election campaign of 1796. He agreed, without enthusiasm, and did less for the Federalists' man, General Charles Pinckney, than he did against Thomas Jefferson. He showed no disappointment when the cold but able John Adams of Massachusetts, who was his own man, won the election.

At no time during this period did Harry show or express personal political ambitions of his own. He had won sufficient prominence as a three-term Governor of Virginia and commander of the largest peacetime military force in American history to take a more active role in politics had he been willing to play the game according to its rules. But he had no patience with such maneuvers, and his thirst for power was satiated by his confidential relationship with Washington.

Besides, other matters occupied his attention, not the least of them sparked by a rekindling of his desire to make a fortune in land speculation. But his years in the Governor's Mansion had not made him a more astute businessman, and he compounded some of his earlier errors.

The Great Falls project was still on his mind, even though the canal that would link East and West now seemed a far-distant dream. Harry and John Marshall, together with Marshall's brother, James, bought a vast parcel of more than one hundred and fifty thousand acres in northwestern Virginia. James Marshall's father-in-law was the venerable and distinguished Philadelphia banker, Robert Morris, who had been one of America's financial geniuses in the Revolution, and James confidently expected Morris to put up most of the money for the purchase.

Unfortunately, Morris was himself in debt because of the failure of several land speculation projects, and Harry found himself loaning a considerable sum to the embarrassed old aristocrat. According to some accounts Harry gave him ten thousand dollars, but in other letters he himself refers to as much as forty thousand. The simple truth of the matter may be that Harry was becoming so involved in so many financial affairs that he could no longer keep them straight.

Through General Benjamin Lincoln, one of his wartime commanders, Harry was one of several purchasers of a mammoth tract of nearly a quarter of a million acres in the Ohio Valley. His partners, Boston businessmen whom he had never met, had given him verbal promises to buy him out at any time.

Harry had been counting on his 1796 crop at Stratford to ease his difficulties, but the estate produced no more than usual, and he tried to obtain his release from the Ohio Valley venture. The gentlemen in Boston proved to be silently and stubbornly reluctant to part with cash. In deep water and unable to swim,

Harry borrowed twenty-seven thousand dollars on a short-term basis from President Washington. By selling several small properties he gathered enough cash in hand to repay at least a portion of his debt to Washington, and hoping to wipe out the obligation quickly, purchased some bank stock that, he was told, would soon triple its face value.

He gave the stock to Washington, who accepted his explanation that it would soon be worth three times the current price. To his mortification, the stock depreciated rapidly. Harry hurriedly sent seventy barrels of corn, all he had on hand, to Mount Vernon as a token of his good will, and sold other properties in order to repay the full debt.

The more he juggled his finances the more complicated they became, and the less cash he had for day-to-day expenses. Anne made no complaint, but the greathouse at Stratford began to look shabby. Anne, in fact, had her hands full. Her first child, born at Stratford in 1795, had died a few months later, and from that time on she hated the vast estate, so much larger and less intimate than the home she had known at Shirley.

The year 1798 was the happiest the family had known in years. Anne's second child, Charles Carter Lee, was born at Stratford, and was a plump, healthy baby. The infant came into the world at a critical time for the country—a war with France seemed imminent, and Light-Horse Harry, after years of relative obscurity, was suddenly thrust to the forefront of national affairs again.

President John Adams, almost totally unprepared for a fight with a major power, made frantic efforts to put the United States on a war footing. He conferred by letter and in person with former President Washington, and the country breathed a little more freely when Adams announced that Washington had accepted a new commission as the senior major general and would lead the Army if it became necessary to declare war. Militia units in every state began to drill in scenes reminiscent of the eve of the Revolution, and Congress authorized the appointment of four major generals to serve under Washington. Again the President and ex-President consulted.

Second on the list of seniority was Henry Knox, although most military men believed him too elderly, ailing, and obese to go into the field, despite his fiery declarations to the contrary. Next was Charles C. Pinckney of South Carolina, still vigorous in his fifties, but more a diplomat than a soldier. He won his appointment in part for political reasons, as he had been an unsuccessful candidate for the presidency in 1796, and partly because it had been he who had disclosed that France had threatened war unless the United States loaned her a large sum of money. Pinckney had served during the Revolution as a captain, and had spent more than two years as a British prisoner.

Only the two junior major generals were actually expected to lead troops in the field. Alexander Hamilton had served with great distinction in the Revolution, and even the Jeffersonians who hated him did no more than grumble quietly when they learned of his appointment. The officer at the bottom of the list won the greatest popular ovation. Major General Harry Lee, said newspapers everywhere, would teach the French a lesson they would never forget.

Hundreds of letters from every state and territory made the delivery of mail to Stratford a backbreaking chore. Officers who had served with Harry, officers who wanted to serve with him and scores who wanted commissions for themselves, their relatives or their friends wrote him at length. The nation was running a high war fever, and that spirit was reflected in the correspondence that filled the library at Stratford and overflowed in bushel-baskets piled high in an adjoining room.

Harry made a quick trip to Philadelphia, where he accepted his commission and took the oath. Then, returning home to await a call to active duty, he decided to answer every letter sent to him. The chore soon proved too great, however, and he had to give up when special couriers were sent from Alexandria with bags and baskets crammed with still more mail. Oddly, none of the other generals, Washington himself included, received so many requests. Harry and his friends concluded that if war should come, men wanted to fight under the command of an officer in whom they had confidence.

The domestic situation became more clouded and unpleasant as the war hysteria mounted. Several times President Adams was on the verge of declaring war, but refrained only because the country was not yet ready to fight. Hamilton openly suggested a scheme he had long favored, an alliance with Great Britain, which alarmed people who still regarded Redcoats as the enemy.

Jefferson, who still liked and respected France and the French, was convinced a sensible solution could be found, and gradually formed the opinion, which Freneau's *National Gazette* trumpeted to the nation, that the war scare was nothing more than an insidious "plot of the Generals" to abolish the democratic form of government and establish a monarchy under "King Alexander I."

These attacks by the Republican-Democrats, as the Jeffersonians were now calling themselves, were primarily directed at Hamilton, but as they increased in vindictiveness, Harry was smeared, and not even Washington went untouched. Harry was infuriated by the gibberish he read in the Jeffersonian newspapers, and became more staunchly and articulately Federalist in his views.

"The real enemies of the Republic," he declared in a single-sheet broadside that he published at his own expense, a gesture he could ill afford, "are Vice-President Jefferson and his henchmen. Like rodents they gnaw at the very foundations of our system of government at a time when our liberty itself is in peril."

He was not alone in his anger or in the intemperance of his language. Chief Justice Oliver Ellsworth, a sedate gentleman from Connecticut, called the Vice-President, his supporters in Congress and the leaders of the French government "apostles of Atheism and anarchy, bloodshed and plunder."

No adjectives were spared in the verbal war that split the United States, and the alarmed Federalists, who still controlled Congress, were afraid that the country might refuse to fight unless stern measures were taken. Four major bills were passed and signed by President Adams. Known as the Alien and Sedition Acts, they were the Federalists' worst blunder.

In brief, the Alien Acts extended residence in the United States from four to fourteen years before an alien could become a citizen, granted the President powers to deport or imprison aliens he deemed undesirable, and granted him even greater powers to deal with citizens of nations that might be at war with the United States. The Sedition Act gave the government power to punish any persons, citizens included, who "conspired together to impede the operation of Federal laws," and forbade anyone to write, publish or speak any "false, scandalous and malicious statement against the government of the United States."

The Republican-Democrats were appalled, and so were some

of the more moderate Federalists. These laws struck at the very core of human liberties on which the American democratic system was founded. Even Hamilton thought the Sedition Act so strong that it might lead to tyranny, and supported a Congressional amendment to the bill that would make it less obnoxious. But his mild protest was not heard as the Republican-Democrats thundered and fulminated.

Responsible officials and other men of standing in the South and West spoke seriously of breaking away from the Union, letting New England and the other industrial states struggle alone as best they could while the dissatisfied formed another new nation of their own. Vice-President Jefferson thought it unnecessary to go that far, although he tacitly admitted that a state had the right to secede. In his opinion the Federalists had made a monumental blunder that he and like-minded men could use to their advantage.

The voter was the ultimate source of power in a democracy, and he believed that an enlightened electorate would display a common-sense attitude at the polls that would end the Federalist reign. James Madison was pressed into service, and wrote a set of resolutions condemning the Alien and Sedition Acts that the Virginia Assembly passed by an overwhelming vote. Harry Lee was one of a small minority who voted in vain against the measure. A companion set of resolutions was prepared by Jefferson himself, but because of his position as Vice-President he deemed it unwise to admit his authorship. John Breckinridge, later to become a national figure of note, sponsored them in the Kentucky legislature, where they were adopted by a large majority.

The Virginia and Kentucky Resolutions were the clearest, most pungent critique of the Federalists yet to appear, and did incalculable damage to the men in power. Meanwhile the Republican-Democratic press continued to see—or profess to see—evidence of a "Generals' plot" that endangered the very foundations of the American system.

Washington was treated relatively gently, the editors knowing their efforts would boomerang if they lashed out too hard at the one man respected by nearly every American. Ailing, bankrupt Henry Knox made a poor target, and Pinckney, who was not well known, seemed to be a colorless personality. That left Alexander Hamilton and Harry Lee as targets, and they were on the receiving end of a prolonged campaign that alternately slashed at them and ridiculed them.

Harry, who had always been proud of his popularity, was still sensitive to his public image. The rational, calm arguments presented in the Virginia and Kentucky Resolutions might or might not have intrigued him under other circumstances. But he was under personal attack, and knew only one way to fight back —personally. He was the cavalryman who had been unfairly attacked by the enemy, and he wanted to charge at his foes, saber in hand.

The best way to deal with a malicious opposition that spread lies about him, he decided, was in the political arena. He hadn't yet been called to active duty in the Army, and there were rumors that there would be a quiet diplomatic settlement of the dispute with France, the Dutch having offered their services as intermediaries. Therefore he decided to run for a seat in the United States House of Representatives, even though friends warned him that the electoral tide everywhere was running strongly in favor of the Jeffersonians.

He ignored the pleas of the well-wishers. The mud of libel had spattered his reputation, his integrity had been questioned, and the more hopeless his cause appeared, the more convinced he became that his only response to his detractors would be to present his case to the voters. The war clouds were dissipating rapidly, but his own problem remained.

Early in 1799, acting against the pleas of everyone who knew him, he began a long campaign in the five counties that comprised his Congressional district, Westmoreland, Richmond, Lancaster, King George, and Northumberland. Reactions were mixed. Men who had served under him in the war and in the Whisky Rebellion—and there were many of them—had already dismissed the accusations of the Republican-Democratic press as nonsense. Ardent Jeffersonians had made up their minds that he was a potential tyrant, and jeered at him when he rode through the streets of small towns.

Harry waged his campaign with the same ferocity he had demonstrated in his fight against the British. He was tireless, refused to let himself become discouraged and struck two blows for every one aimed at him. Between early February and Election

Day, April 24, he spent no more than five or six nights under his own roof at Stratford.

John Marshall, who was also running for Congress as a Federalist, was having an equally difficult time. But his cause was helped immeasurably when old Patrick Henry, who was one of his constituents, wrote a public letter praising Marshall lavishly. Henry had lost none of his powers of analysis, and saw what others would not realize until many years later, that the Virginia and Kentucky Resolutions encouraged the states to defy the national government and, in Henry's words, "would, if logically applied, lead to the dissolution of the Union." Jefferson did not recognize his error until long after he had served two terms as President.

John Marshall's constituents were persuaded by the Henry logic—and by the still-potent force of his popularity. If he thought John Marshall should be elected, that settled the matter. The Republican-Democrats were willing to concede Marshall his seat in the House of Representatives.

Harry Lee's position was far different. A hard core of his supporters was balanced by an equally determined band of his foes, but most voters seemed undecided, and no one was willing to predict the outcome.

April 24 dawned clear and bright in Virginia, which was fortunate, as there was only one polling place in the entire district, and many men had to ride long distances in order to cast their open ballots. The electorate was composed of those who owned at least one hundred acres of land in the district and made their homes there.

By the standards of later times, the setting was bizarre. An election board composed of five judges sat in the open, each recording the returns, and each voter was required to state his preference aloud. As the day was long, the judges relieved their thirst from time to time with small beer or porter.

Men who had come to vote made a holiday of the occasion, and gathered in two groups, Harry's adherents on one side of the judges, and the followers of his opponent, a physician named Jones, on the other. They, too, developed a need to soothe their palates occasionally, particularly as they cheered each time a ballot was cast in favor of the candidate of their choice. Barrels of potent Virginia whisky had been provided by thoughtful friends of the candidates, along with sizzling short ribs of venison, sugar-cured ham, smoked eel, raw oysters, and other delicacies. Those who had not yet made up their minds were courted by both sides with persuasion, drink and food, and inevitably fist-fights broke out between the partisans of Lee and Jones. As there was a strict Virginia law prohibiting brawling, dueling or knife-play within sight of the polls, men who were either sober or fairly sober usually managed to separate the combatants before too much damage had been done.

By early afternoon the followers of both candidates, who had been keeping a close count, knew that neither had yet achieved a decisive advantage, although Jones held a slight lead. Most men who had reached the polling place had not yet voted. Harry's friends sent a messenger to Stratford to tell him the situation was far from promising.

A particularly unpleasant argument was stifled when an un-usually tall, lean gentleman wearing expensive clothes and a powdered wig rode alone to the polling place, dismounted and nodded absently at several acquaintances. Men fell silent and pressed forward to hear the choice of the district's most dis-tinguished citizen.

A verbatim account of what was said was recorded by several of those present, among them George Lee, who was slightly miffed because the elderly gentleman hadn't seen fit to raise his hat to him.

The chairman of the election board was required to pretend he didn't recognize the voter, and asked, "Your name, sir?"

"George Washington."

"Your occupation?" George Lee wrote that there was a silly expression on the chairman's face.

"Planter."

"Your home, sir?"

"Mount Vernon."

Most voters were required to show proof they owned at least one hundred acres in the district and lived on the property, but the chairman of the election board obviously felt he had done his duty, and had no desire to embarrass himself further. "Your vote, sir?"

Major General Washington, the nation's first President, replied in a parade-ground roar, "I cast my vote for Major General Henry Lee of Stratford."

Ignoring the roars of the Lee camp, he doffed his hat to the judges and walked back to his horse, ignoring several outstretched hands. A half-dozen men offered to help him, but he waved them away courteously, climbed into the saddle unaided and started off for home, looking neither to the right nor left.

Harry's friends were deliriously happy. It was obvious to all but the most rabid Republican-Democrats, who had voted earlier in the day, that Washington would not cast his ballot for someone he believed capable of conspiring against the Republic and establishing a monarchy in the United States.

The undecided, fortified by Washington's views and Harry's whisky, began to move forward in a long, steady line.

At sundown the election judges retired to the nearby courthouse to compare their tallies, and a short time later the chairman reappeared to notify the crowd that Harry had won. Some days would pass before it would become known that in all of the United States, Harry Lee and John Marshall were the only Federalists elected to Congress from districts previously held by the opposition. Harry and Marshall were destined to be marked men in the House of Representatives.

XVII

THE HON. GENTLEMAN FROM VIRGINIA

Anne Lee accompanied the Congressman-elect to Philadelphia, leaving the children at Stratford. She would have preferred to take them with her, although it was contrary to the custom of the time in well-bred families, but a lack of appropriate living quarters to accommodate two growing youngsters, a baby and the servants needed to look after them made it impossible for her to indulge her wishes.

The Lees were fortunate. They reached the capital on December 8, 1799, three days before the new Congress was scheduled to convene, and lodged at an inn. The first business at hand in the overcrowded city was that of finding appropriate, more permanent quarters, and after a search of only a few hours they were able to rent a small, tidy house that was, nevertheless, large enough to accommodate them and the John Marshalls.

The two freshmen members of the House presented their credentials on the opening day of the session, December 11, and took the oath of office. Harry, who had no intention of remaining silent and listening to his elders, made a point of speaking a few words that same day. On December 16 he made a speech on the need to overhaul the militia of the states, and even though the Federalists had lost their majority, he impressed his colleagues sufficiently to be made chairman of a committee to draw up uniform regulations for the militia of the various states. In less than a week he had established himself as a man of consequence in the House.

Two days later tragedy struck. Harry was walking from his rented house to the halls of Congress when he saw small groups of glum people gathering in the streets and muttering in low voices. He was stunned by their news: George Washington was dead. Unable to accept the shock, he verified it when he reached the House. Weeping openly and without shame, he returned home and spent the morning alone, grieving for his mentor and lifelong friend.

That afternoon he sprang into action. The Republican-Democrats now controlled Congress, and he was afraid they might be moved by partisan considerations to refuse America's greatest citizen the posthumous honors he deserved. First, Harry wrote a simple resolution for the consideration of Congress, and in his sorrow it is doubtful that he knew some of his words would achieve an immortality outlasting his own reputation. He wrote:

The House of Representatives of the United States, having received intelligence of the death of their highly-valued fellow-citizen, George Washington, General of the Armies of the United States, and sharing the universal grief this event must produce, unanimously resolve:

1. That this House will wait on the President of the United States, in condolence of this national calamity.

2. That the Speaker's chair be shrouded with black, and that the members and officers of the House wear mourning during the session.

3. That a joint committee of both houses be appointed to report measures suitable to the occasion, and expressive of the profound sorrow with which Congress is penetrated on the loss of a citizen, first in war, first in peace, and first in the hearts of his countrymen.

By the time Harry reached the House he found that Congress, acting on a motion of Marshall's, had already adjourned for the day. The two Virginians conferred briefly, Marshall readily agreeing to second Harry's resolution, and then they went home together. That night Harry, who had eaten nothing since breakfast, was unable to touch his dinner, and Anne was afraid he might become ill.

The next morning, when the House reconvened, Harry was

recognized by the Speaker and tried to present his resolution, but emotion overwhelmed him, and Marshall had to read it for him. His fears proved groundless, and Republican-Democrats as well as Federalists voted unanimously in its favor.

Later in the day Harry recovered sufficiently to present several other resolutions. In one he proposed a state funeral for the late President, and again the House voted unanimously in favor of the measure. The government had bought a large tract of land on the Potomac River, where it was planned to build a new national capital to be called Washington City, and Harry further proposed that a marble monument be erected there to "commemorate the great events of General Washington's military and political life." Before resuming his seat he begged his colleagues to cast aside all political prejudices so there would be no blemish cast by Congress on the memory of a great man.

The House obliged him by passing the resolution, and not one vote was recorded against it. This near-miracle was neither a tribute to Harry's skill as an orator nor a desire on the part of many Republican-Democrats to forget partisan considerations. They held Washington to blame for numerous Federalist "excesses," but didn't want to antagonize voters at home who might look with disfavor on their attempts to discredit the most renowned American of his era.

That evening a delegation from both Houses called on Harry at his rented home, its numbers including Speaker Theodore Sedgwick and two senators representing Vice-President Jefferson, who thought it indelicate to appear in person because of his strained relations with Congressman Lee. Everyone in the government recognized the special nature of the long friendship that had bound Harry to President Washington, and it was the unanimous wish of the legislative branch that he deliver the funeral oration.

The honor, Harry wrote to his brother Charles, was the greatest and most sorrowful ever conferred on him. He worked long and hard on the address, and the memorial service was held soon after Christmas in Philadelphia's German Lutheran Church, one of the largest auditoriums in the city. President Adams and his Cabinet attended, as did the Justices of the Supreme Court, the members of the Senate and House, a large number of high-ranking military officers and the ministers of foreign governments.

The eulogy was as long as most speeches made in an age when

men did not stint on words, and Harry spoke for more than two and one-half hours. At his climax he repeated the phrase he had composed in his initial grief, saying, "First in war, first in peace, and first in the hearts of his countrymen, he was second to none in the humble and endearing scenes of private life; uniform, dignified and commanding, his example was as edifying to all around him as were the effects of that example lasting."

Immediately after the service Harry and Anne made a trip home for the purpose of paying a condolence call on Mrs. Washington, who had not felt up to the ordeal of traveling to Philadelphia. There is no record of what was said in private, but Harry presented her with a gold-bound copy of the eulogy, written in his own hand.

After spending a few days at Stratford to see their children, the Lees returned to Philadelphia, and there Harry was gratified to learn that Congress had ordered his eulogy printed, at government expense, in pamphlet form. Citizens by the thousands in all parts of the country were requesting copies.

The bi-partisan spirit of mourning lasted only until mid-January, at which time the Republican-Democratic majority in the House refused to appropriate funds for the marble memorial to the late President. Harry was not surprised, and plunged into battle.

On the same day the Jeffersonians introduced a bill into the lower chamber to reduce the size of the standing Army, and Representative Albert Gallatin, who would later show a genius for handling the nation's finances as Secretary of the Treasury, but who knew very little about military affairs, argued that the militia of the various states were competent to replace the professional soldiers.

Harry, who still held his commission as a major general, was shocked, incredulous, and wildly angry. In speech after eloquent speech he led the fight for the maintenance of a strong Regular Army, citing his own experiences and those of other Continental officers with militia during the war.

It was obvious that he knew what he was talking about, and the House, including men too young to have fought in the Revolution, listened to him with respect and interest. But his arguments made no deep impression on the Republican-Democrats, who contended that the conclusion of a new treaty of understanding with France would make an Army unnecessary, as the United States would have no enemies. Harry believed otherwise, and declared that friendship with France would create new friction with Great Britain.

Others rallied to him, including Republican-Democrats with long memories of militia failures, and only a token cut was made in the military budget. Harry had won a major legislative battle, and Jefferson paid him the compliment of referring to him as "dangerous, too eloquent for his own or the nation's good."

In the main Harry voted with the Federalists, but was always his own master, and when he thought it in the best interests of the country he sided with the Republican-Democrats. Perhaps the most striking example of his independent attitude was exemplified by the position he took when the Administration worked out a new commercial treaty with France. The Federalists, trying to block the measure, submitted a bill prohibiting all trade with France, but Harry worked hard against them.

Trade, he declared in an impassioned speech on the floor of the House, was a necessary prelude to continuing friendly relations between any two countries, and honorable, peaceful commerce was always preferable to the destructive disasters of war. He influenced a number of fence-sitters, and in an odd coalition, the Adams moderates, supported by the Republican-Democrats, saved the commercial treaty.

Anne Lee went home to Stratford to have another baby, an experience she would repeat on three more occasions in the years to come, and Harry remained alone in Philadelphia. During this period he spent one of the most unsatisfactory and embarrassing evenings of his life. President Adams invited him to dinner, and one other guest was present, Vice-President Jefferson. Either the President didn't know that Harry or Jefferson weren't on more than the most distant speaking terms, or didn't care.

The two antagonists were civil to each other, but the atmosphere remained strained all evening. The principal subject of discussion was politics, and it dawned on Harry that Adams, who expected to be elected to a second term, didn't realize that Jefferson had his own eye on the nation's highest executive post. The Vice-President was the first to leave, and Harry, thinking he was doing the President a favor, mentioned what was common gossip in the halls of Congress.

John Adams was an efficient, coldly shy man incapable of making close friends or building a personal following. According to
a long letter Harry wrote to his brother Charles the following day,
the President was shocked by the disclosure, refused to believe
that Jefferson would not support him in his bid for a second term
and lectured his guest sternly. Their parting was formal, and Harry
did not again receive an invitation from Adams, who was to
discover within a few months that Jefferson had ambitions of his
own.

Congress adjourned for a few weeks in the late summer of
1800, and before reconvening in the raw, uncompleted buildings
that were being erected in Washington City, the coming presidential campaign took shape. The Federalists made Aaron Burr
their candidate, the Republican-Democrats supported Jefferson,
and the high-minded John Adams found himself a President
without a party.

The electoral vote produced confusion of the worst kind. Burr
and Jefferson were tied, New England gave some support to
Adams and parts of the South, in a wait-and-see attitude, stood for
the moment with General Charles Pinckney.

In the meantime the battle lines were being drawn tighter in
Congress, where both major parties were trying to shape the future
of the country through legislation reflecting their opposing philos-
ophies. In a three-month period, between mid-November 1800
and mid-February 1801, Harry Lee established a record in the
House that, even if he had done nothing else for his country,
would have won him a permanent place in history.

He was one of the prime movers of a bill to enlarge and
strengthen the federal judiciary, and led the fight for the measure
in the House with such skill and verve that the law was passed in
spite of bitter Republican-Democratic opposition. For the first
time the judicial branch became the equal of the executive
and legislative in fact as well as theory. And in January, when
Harry's good friend, John Marshall, was appointed Chief Justice,
the future of the judiciary was assured.

Harry introduced a bill establishing a national library, and
another that put the nation's main highways, the post roads, under
federal control. He supplemented this measure with another authorizing the extension of the post road system to all parts of
the country. Virginia and Maryland were both clamoring for

control of Washington City, but Harry, believing the federal government should not be subject to the whims of a state, was one of the movers of a bill keeping Washington City under federal jurisdiction. He was also the author of a bill, little noted at the time and subsequently defeated, which gave the federal establishment the power to tax individual citizens as it deemed fit, but provided that a portion of taxes collected should be turned over to the states for their own use.

Early in February legislative programs were pushed aside when it was officially reported that there had been a tie in the electoral vote for President, and that the decision, under the Constitution, was now referred to the House of Representatives.

Harry stood firmly in favor of his college friend, Aaron Burr, whom he probably would have supported even had they been total strangers. Any man, he believed, was preferable to Thomas Jefferson. But the situation was complicated by the fact that Alexander Hamilton, the arch-Federalist, could not tolerate Burr and urged every man in the House he knew to support his old foe, Jefferson.

Harry received a long, earnest plea from Hamilton asking him to switch to Jefferson's side. He refused, but saw the handwriting written large on the wall, and wrote a discouraged note to Anne, then at Stratford, saying that if Jefferson was elected he would retire permanently from the political arena.

Thirty-six ballots were taken over a three-day period, and Harry unwaveringly cast his vote for Burr on all thirty-six. Emissaries from Hamilton tried repeatedly to persuade him to change his mind, but his personal animosity to Jefferson was as great as Hamilton's hatred for Burr, and he would not budge.

From the start, Harry knew he was fighting a lost cause. In one letter, written to Hamilton and explaining at some length why he could not change his mind or vote, he declared, "Jefferson's friends are confident of success, and there is in my own mind little doubt that he will be victorious. For your sake I am pleased that you can await this outcome with a complacency of mind. For my own, however, and for that of the United States, I see the nation entering upon its darkest days.

"I admit that my views are colored by a rancor for Mr. J. that I cannot alter or control. We have opposed each other in too many matters for too many years for me to develop a fondness for him or his methods. There are others, you will say, who have also opposed the principles for which I stand. That is true.

"Madison comes first to mind in this regard, and before him, you yourself. Never once, however, did my affection for you falter, or yours for me, and this same is true of my friendship with Mr. M. But Mr. J. has been vindictive and petty, has denounced me in a manner unbefitting a gentleman and has, behind my back, sneered at the financial misfortunes that have befallen me. I cannot, therefore, give my confidence, my hand or my vote to one who allows himself to be ruled by petty considerations when he should be concerned only with the welfare, the good and the future of all our people.

"The perpetuation of our freedoms, in peace and equity, must be the first regard of every statesman. I pray that Burr would be such a statesman were he to receive the vote of the House. I fear that J. would not, and must oppose him to the end."

The end came on February 17 when, after some prolonged and delicate maneuvering behind the scenes, several state delegations of Federalists were persuaded to cast their ballots for Thomas Jefferson, who was elected the third President of the United States. Under the system then prevailing, Burr became Vice-President.

Harry Lee immediately became a lame-duck Congressman, announcing that he had no intention of seeking re-election. He was still a gentleman, however, and when the House waited on Jefferson to extend its congratulations, he accompanied the other Congressmen.

It was evident from the frigid greetings he and Jefferson exchanged that Harry was banished to a political wilderness. Both men bowed coldly, and neither extended a hand.

"I offer you my felicitations, sir," Harry said.

"I thank you, sir," Jefferson replied.

That was the end of the conversation and, for all practical purposes, Harry Lee's political career.

In the spring of 1801 he returned to Stratford, intending to resume his life as a planter and, if possible, recoup his financial losses of the past in land speculation. No matter how often he had been burned in the past, he still envisioned the pot of gold at the end of the rainbow. Others had done it, and so could he.

Unfortunately, he refused to profit by the lessons of some former military colleagues. Henry Knox had been forced to declare bankruptcy, and so had Anthony Wayne. Prowess in war was no guarantee that a man would live happily ever after in comfortable circumstances.

XVIII

THE WILDERNESS

There were two more children in the growing brood at Stratford by the summer of 1802, Anne, born two years earlier, and the new infant, Smith. Henry, Jr. was now old enough to be enrolled as a student at the College of William and Mary, annoying his father because he preferred it to Harry's alma mater at Princeton. Lucy was growing up, too, and discovered boys. She was considered a flirt, and according to family rumors, sometimes behaved in a manner unbecoming a lady and a Lee. Anne's young brother, Bernard M. Carter, was a frequent visitor to Stratford, and fell so completely under Lucy's spell that, a few years later, they were married and lived stormy lives, sometimes together, sometimes apart.

The head of the household was having more than his usual share of troubles, and there was no indication of daylight ahead. The distinguished Robert Morris of Philadelphia had been unable to repay the money Harry had so impetuously loaned him, and was now incarcerated in a debtors' prison, a situation that distressed the gentry everywhere. It upset Harry more than most, as he had been counting on the repayment of the debt to see him through his own difficulties.

He sold some property he owned in Richmond, and when that proved too little to satisfy his creditors, he disposed of a portion of the Stratford estate, much to the distress of the entire Lee clan. The ever-observant Cousin George now began to call the eldest son—and heir to Stratford, "Poor young Henry."

Harry was true to his word and took no active role in politics, but his hatred of Jefferson remained unabated. The War Department, acting quietly and without publicity, had retired him from the active list of generals, a move that did not cause him to think any more highly of the President.

In fact, as he wrote to Madison, now Secretary of State but still his friend, he felt certain that Jefferson and Albert Gallatin, the Secretary of the Treasury, had made a deliberate attempt to humiliate him. Madison tried to reassure him that, with the country at peace and no wars anticipated anywhere, there was no need for a reserve pool of generals. But Harry refused to be reconciled to the situation.

His only friends in the Administration were Madison and James Monroe, who became the American Minister to France in 1803 and to England in 1804. He corresponded with both, and although they remained warmly sympathetic, they found it diplomatically necessary to avoid commenting on his bitter observations and criticisms of Administration policy.

Harry also maintained a brisk correspondence with John Marshall, but the Chief Justice considered himself above party partisanship, confining his views on the government to Supreme Court decisions that would do so much to shape the America of the future. It was frustrating to Harry. No one, he complained, would admit to him that Jefferson was truly a rascal.

In the years that followed, Harry struggled incessantly but in vain to stay out of debt. Every financial venture was a fiasco, every investment a disappointment. Anne was ill for the better part of a year with a "bone fever" that forced her to spend much of her time in bed. Money for luxuries was scarce, and there were few servants at Stratford now. But husband and wife remained devoted to each other. And Harry, by any standards, was a good father.

He spent long hours augmenting the education of his children by teaching them Latin, philosophy, and French, and reading to them from the classics of literature. There were still horses in the Lee stable, of course—Harry would never become so poor that he could not afford to own a few horses—and his sons learned to ride like cavalrymen, wield sabers like cavalrymen and shoot like cavalrymen.

Harry was still Squire Lee to his neighbors, many of whom

brought their problems to him. According to one story that may be apocryphal, two residents of the area had a violent argument, decided their quarrel could be settled only by a duel and went to Harry soon after dinner one evening to ask him if he would referee the affair. He invited the combatants into his library, where he spent almost the whole night talking to them, and when they departed shortly before dawn they were fast friends.

In the spring of 1806 Anne became pregnant again, to her own dismay and her husband's. Neither wanted the expense and bother of still another child. Harry's financial mess was rapidly becoming insoluble, and relatives who tried to help him untangle his affairs soon gave up in despair.

Then Anne's father, who had been ill for several years, died very suddenly, and she had to travel to Shirley for the funeral. The few servants at Stratford were so unreliable that she traveled alone in the family's one remaining carriage, leaving Harry behind to take care of the children. The mighty had fallen, but were to fall still lower.

Charles Carter had been worried about his son-in-law's inability to handle money for years, and when Anne reached Shirley she discovered he had done everything possible in his will, which he had written in 1803, to protect her inheritance. He was afraid, he said, that Anne and her children might "be distressed and come to want." Therefore he charged the executors and trustees whom he named to "secure the said property for the use and benefit of my said daughter in such a way that she solely during her natural life may enjoy the rents, issues, profits, emoluments, interests and advantages of the said property both real and personal, free from the claim, demand, let, hindrance of molestation of her husband, General Henry Lee, or his creditors, directly or indirectly."

Anne was not comforted by the knowledge that she and her children would not starve. Never had she been so miserable. Her pregnancy was difficult, the first of her five that had caused her any trouble, and her discomfort was compounded by the ague, which she contracted on her journey. She was depressed by her father's death, and when she returned to Stratford she found her husband's gloom almost unbearable. For the first time in Harry's life his vision of the pot of gold had dimmed, and he was beginning to wonder whether his lot would ever improve. He had achieved so much early in life that he had expected continued success, but now, in his middle years, he knew nothing but futility and despair.

On January 19, 1807, precisely ten days before Harry Lee's fifty-first birthday, Anne gave birth to her fifth child, a boy. His disconsolate, brooding parents named him Robert Edward.

In spite of their many problems, Harry and Anne unexpectedly doted on their youngest child. To whatever extent environment shapes a man's character, Robert E. Lee benefited from the unstinting love of his father and mother. But Harry was destined to know the son whose fame would far eclipse his own for only a few years.

He would teach a very small boy to ride and to prize intellect, to seek a military career and to place a higher value on personal integrity and moral courage than on life itself. The son learned that honor was precious and, after his father's death, gained an appreciation of the glory that the most fearless, dashing officer in the American Revolution had won.

These things, ephemeral and intangible, would be Robert E. Lee's inheritance from his father. Yet it would be no accident that in 1867, two years after his own enforced retirement from a military life, General Robert E. Lee would, as his first task after laying down his arms, edit and publish a new edition of his father's *Memoirs*. The renowned son of a famous lion would be proud of his heritage.

There was little cause for pride or joy in the days that followed Robert E. Lee's birth. Anne's sister, Mildred, died, and following their father's example, left her estate to Anne in such a way that Harry could not touch or dissipate it.

Harry, who had enjoyed robust health nearly all of his life, went to bed with a bronchial disease that almost killed him. His creditors were pressing him, and he could not afford to rest, but had no choice. He was unable to leave his bedroom for three months, and never again completely recovered his health. To the end of his days he suffered from a racking cough, and lost so much weight that he looked and felt like an old man.

He enjoyed only one minor compensation. America's relations with England were deteriorating steadily, a situation that would not improve until the War of 1812 had been fought, and President Jefferson, who hated war, was forced to prepare for armed conflict. He requested the states to raise a force of one hundred and twenty-five thousand militiamen, he placed an embargo on all trade with Great Britain—and he reactivated the commission of Major General Harry Lee.

Bad health and worse finances notwithstanding, Harry instantly put the call to duty above family or self. He climbed into uniform, and once again made a familiar tour, traveling through Virginia from county to county, seeking, selecting, and supervising the training of volunteers.

War did not come in 1808, but Harry spent the better part of a year in the saddle and in the field, ignoring his own problems and his weakened condition. When it finally appeared that war had been averted and he returned home, he was exhausted. Anne had suffered a recurrence of the ague, too, and the family physicians suggested that the Lees seek another climate. Charleston was too warm, all of Georgia was too humid, and the water in New Orleans was "impure and unfit for invalids." Harry and Anne were advised to travel to South America, preferably to "the Brazils."

Jefferson's embargo blocked their departure, however, as American vessels lay at anchor, unable to move, and American ports were closed to British ships. Harry appealed to Madison for help, hoping that the Secretary of State, who appeared almost certain to succeed Jefferson as President, would find an embargo loophole.

But there were no loopholes, and Madison could do nothing for his old friend. The noose was tightening as Harry's creditors became more stridently demanding, and even Stratford would not shelter the family much longer as Henry, Jr., soon to be graduated from William and Mary, would inherit what was left of the estate when he came of age. Harry was reduced to the humiliation of sometimes leaving the house by one door when creditors came to another, and sometimes hiding in the vast greathouse while Anne, the most honest of women, was forced to lie on his behalf and tell creditors he wasn't at home.

The situation became intolerable; Harry had always faced danger without flinching, and the mortification was greater than he could bear. On April 11, 1809, one month and seven days after James Madison took office as the fourth President of the United

States, his college mate and lifelong friend, Light-Horse Harry Lee surrendered himself to the sheriff of Westmoreland County and was jailed as a debtor.

Never had a Lee sunk so low, and never before had a Lee failed to provide for his family. It was no help to Harry, pacing his cell—sixteen feet long and thirteen and one-half feet wide—to know he had joined the illustrious company of Revolutionary War bankrupts. His pride and conscience were shattered, even though he realized that, thanks to the farsightedness of two fathers-in-law who had put their estates beyond his reach, his wife and children would not starve.

The process of declaring bankruptcy and winning release from debtors' prison was long, tedious, and involved, so Harry labored under no false illusions. He would, he knew, be forced to remain in jail for a long time. Anne wanted to visit him frequently, but he preferred to spare her the indignity, and he requested other, sympathetic relatives to leave him in peace. On his strict orders, his children were forbidden to see him behind bars.

For a time prison life almost drove Harry mad. He, who had been active all his life, was confined to quarters smaller than his dressing room at Stratford. Fortunately he had no appetite, as the food provided by the county was at times inedible. He lived on the meat and bread that Anne brought him from home, although she took care not to visit him herself, letting him believe she sent a servant with the food parcels. Harry didn't know there were no more servants at Stratford.

With nothing better to occupy him, he began to write a personal history of his wartime experiences, and at first he was indifferent to the project, seeking only some way to kill time. Thirty-three years had passed since he had first answered his country's call to military duty, and he was surprised to find that, although he remembered some things clearly, there were details of incidents he no longer could recall.

Gradually he warmed to the book, and began to work with his old, unquenchable enthusiasm. At some point along the way he decided to devote the bulk of the *Memoirs* to his service in the South under Nathanael Greene. In order to obtain background and facts that escaped him he opened a lively, increasingly prolific correspondence with old comrades who were still alive and with the families of those now deceased.

Twice during his imprisonment he was moved to the jails of other counties in order to comply with the legalities necessary in bankruptcy petitions. But it didn't matter to him where he was held. He worked sixteen to eighteen hours each day on the book, and the days weren't long enough.

In April 1810 Harry was released from prison. He had duly declared himself bankrupt, his creditors had been forced to accept a few cents on each dollar he owed them, and he was now free of debt. The price—a year in jail—seemed a small one now.

He returned to Stratford, although he would live there for only a short time, as Henry, Jr. was scheduled to inherit the estate in his own name within a few months. There was still work to be done on the book, and Harry devoted much of his time to it, hoping it would earn him enough to provide his family with a few of the luxuries that were such rarities in the Lee household.

It would have been out of character for Harry to write a book that failed to express his frank opinions of men and their deeds. Because of his candor he planned to publish the *Memoirs* anonymously, but friends who submitted his partly completed manuscript to various publishers in New York and Philadelphia reported to him that editors showed no interest unless it appeared under his own name. He was afraid of libel suits, however, and was reluctant to agree. All the same, he continued his work.

He soon discovered that no stigma was attached to his imprisonment, and within a few weeks of his release he was again sitting as a justice of the peace in the Westmoreland County courts, a position he had held most of his life. After all, he was still Light-Horse Harry—and a Lee.

Late in the summer of 1810 Henry, Jr. legally took possession of Stratford. And soon thereafter his father, stepmother, and their four children moved out, although the young man repeatedly urged them to stay. But Anne had never liked the place, and Harry was too proud to live under the roof of anyone else, even that of his eldest son.

Anne had found a quiet, modestly priced house in Alexandria, across the Potomac from Washington City, and there was enough money left from the financial debacle to buy the place. Harry took with them two of his favorite horses, a cow to provide milk for the children and butter for the family table, a pony and cart for

Robert Edward, and a dog that was the favorite pet of the whole family. The rooms were small, but large enough for the family's needs, and—luxury of luxuries—the budget, which Anne super-vised, permitted the Lees two servants.

Harry ignored the social life of Washington City, much of which spilled over the river into Alexandria, and devoted his time to his family and the completion of his book. Parties had lost their savor, and he and Anne could not afford to return in-vitations. He had been out of the limelight so long that hostesses who competed for the privilege of seating the lions of the hour at their tables ignored the Lees in return.

There was one notable exception, however. President Madison and his lovely wife had not forgotten old friends, and on a num-ber of occasions Anne and Harry dined quietly at the Executive Mansion, which wouldn't be called the White House until it was repainted after the British tried to burn it down in the War of 1812.

Harry completed his *Memoirs* late in the summer of 1811, and finally faced reality. The book was worthless without his name, so he decided to run the risk of being sued for libel. A man who had taken so many daring chances was not one to hold back now. The staid and prosperous publishing firm of Bradford and Inskip of Philadelphia promptly agreed to publish the book, which they brought out early in 1812, in two volumes.

The threat of a new war with England loomed on the im-mediate horizon, so interest in the Revolution was revived, and the *Memoirs* enjoyed a brisk sale, larger than the publishers had anticipated. Harry Lee again became something of a celebrity, although he no longer wanted prominence. He was fifty-six years old, his bronchial condition continued to bother him, and now that he had a little money again, he began to think once more of moving to a warmer climate.

A chance remark made to him at dinner one day by Secretary of State James Monroe revived his hopes of settling elsewhere. A hurricane had devastated several small islands in the Caribbean, and although American ports had again been closed a precau-tionary measure prior to a declaration of war, the government was thinking of sending a small fleet of provision-laden ships to the West Indies on a humanitarian mission. The cooperation of the British would be necessary, however, as both President Madison and Secretary Monroe were unwilling to dispatch the ships unless given some assurance that they would not be attacked and captured by the Royal Navy, whose high-handed attitudes, including the impressment of American seamen, constituted one of the principal reasons the United States was preparing to defend herself.

Harry envisioned an opportunity to obtain transportation for his family to a warm place where he and Anne could recover their health. He returned to Alexandria from Washington City by ferry, suffering a slight case of indigestion caused by the rich foods and wines that Monroe had served, and sat down to write a long, formal letter to the President.

He and his family would occupy very little space on the voyage, he wrote. If necessary, they could travel on board two ships, with Anne taking the two younger children on one while he escorted the elder on another. For the first time a wistful, almost pleading note crept into Harry's plea. He offered his services to the Administration without charge, and said he would be glad to act as the President's emissary in presenting the food and other supplies to the stricken West Indians.

He reminded Madison—unnecessarily—of his previous desire to make a journey to "the Brazils." And he made an attempt to salvage his pride by declaring that he was asking no extraordinary favor, but merely sought passage on board vessels sailing to a destination hitherto inaccessible to him. If the President wished, he added with a touch of bravado, he would pay any fee that the government deemed appropriate.

Madison, who had been concerned over Harry's failing health, was sympathic, and would have given his approval had the voyage materialized. But the British refused to cooperate. Aware of their naval superiority and convinced that a sea blockade could force the United States into a quick surrender, they saw the projected mission as a trick, a way to send American merchantmen to sea before hostilities began.

The United States was forced to abandon the plan, and Harry once again was frustrated. But he soon forgot his disappointment. On June 18, 1812, the country formally declared war, and both the President and his Secretary of State, who would soon take over the War Department portfolio, too, privately told him that his services would be needed. In spite of his age and infirmities, Light-Horse Harry Lee was the logical choice to lead the American Army. The long years in the wilderness were ended—or so it seemed.

XIX

DON QUIXOTE, WHO TILTS AT WINDMILLS

The United States was woefully unprepared for war in 1812, and in many ways her defenses were in a sorrier state than in 1775. "Mr. Madison's War," as the conflict was called by newspapers in Hartford, New Haven, and Providence, was so unpopular in New England that a serious threat of secession developed in that part of the country. Most of the agitation in favor of the war came from the new Western states, where expansionist fever was strong and British-inspired Indian raids were frequent. Elsewhere, the great seaboard states that had been the mainstays of the Revolution, New York, Pennsylvania, New Jersey, Virginia, and Maryland, accepted the coming of the war with almost fatalistic calm.

Bonfires were burned, of course, and patriotic speeches were made and duly applauded, but nowhere east of the mountains did the people display enthusiasm for the war. The nation had been enjoying unprecedented prosperity, and there had been indications that her wealth would be quadrupled, at the very least, within a few years. Now a new era of bleak self-discipline had been inaugurated.

The Navy was pitifully small, although her officers and men were exceptionally efficient, thanks to years of serving together in the nation's "little war" against the Barbary pirate states of North Africa. It would be impossible, however, for a fleet consisting of only four frigates mounting more than forty guns and fifteen smaller ships to meet the great Royal Navy, with its vast armadas of ships-of-the-line, many of them seventy-fours.

The United States Army was in even worse shape, and there were many, Secretary Monroe among them, who considered it no more than a tiny military police force. The Regular Army consisted of 6483 officers and men, and except for a few who had taken part in frontier skirmishes against Indians, most had never fired a musket or cannon in earnest. The officer corps was in an especially deplorable state. There had been so little hope of professional advancement for so many years that few energetic, courageous men with a talent for leadership had been attracted to a military career.

Secretary of War William Eustis was an amiable politician with no qualifications for his post. At the outbreak of war his small corps was scattered from the Canadian border to the Floridas' frontier, and from the Atlantic seaboard to the Mississippi. A few weeks before the formal declaration signaling the outbreak of hostilities he had, at the President's instigation, begun a campaign for volunteers, but no one knew how successful it had been. In a Cabinet report destined to become famous for its inefficiency, Eustis guessed that five thousand recruits had answered the call to the colors, but he couldn't be sure.

In the early stages of the war the government had to fall back on the state militia, which were as unreliable as they had been a generation earlier. And the governors of the New England states compounded the Administration's problems by refusing to call up their militia.

The shortage of efficient commanders was critical. Soon after the start of the war, Congress accepted the War Department's recommendations and appointed five generals, two of them major generals, the rest brigadiers. The youngest was in his mid-fifties, and only two of the five had held commands of consequence in the Revolution. Former President Jefferson, sympathizing with his successor's predicament, wrote from his estate at Monticello, "*The Creator has not thought proper to mark those on the forehead who are of the stuff to make good Generals.*"

The situation seemed tailor-made for the re-emergence of Major General Light-Horse Harry Lee, and he had reason to hope, after brief conferences with the President and Monroe, that his commission would be reactivated and that he would be given command of the field forces. But James Madison was troubled. Harry's health was so frail that he was incapable of withstanding the rigors of campaigning. By temperament and training he was unsuited for a post as a desk soldier, or military adviser to the President, and would have to be given a place in the field—or none at all.

The busy Madison made a tactful attempt to sound out Anne, but she was of little help. She knew her husband's heart was set on returning to action, but she, too, wondered if he was strong enough for a hard life in the open. While Madison hesitated, Harry Lee brooded.

By the end of July Harry was thoroughly aroused. More than five weeks had passed since war had been declared, but he had not yet been asked to don his uniform. And the fact that Henry, Jr. had already been called to duty as a major and battalion commander of Virginia militia increased his sense of frustration.

Feeling out of sorts and impelled by motives never made clear in his own lifetime or later, Harry made a journey to Baltimore on July 26, traveling the short distance from Washington City by public coach. Whatever the reasons for Harry's visit, he immediately became involved in a complicated, dangerous situation.

Support for the war was strong in Baltimore, and so was opposition to the Administration's course. A young man named Alexander C. Hanson, whose late father had been a friend of Harry's, was the publisher of a newspaper called *The Federal Republican*. On June 19, the day after war had been declared, he wrote a long, angry editorial in its columns, claiming the people had not wanted war, but that it had been forced on them by a blundering, shortsighted Administration.

The following day a mob had gathered, and while the officials of the city administration had looked the other way, had torn down the newspaper office, forcing Hanson to flee for his life. Now he had returned, bringing with him copies of a new and vituperative edition of his paper, which he had printed elsewhere. Determined to make a stand, Hanson had rented a house on Charles Street, which he planned to use as a combination office and home. Rather than be driven out by another mob, he had made up his mind to protect himself, and a number of his friends had gathered at the house, armed with muskets, pistols, ancient rifles, and sabers that had become heirlooms.

Most of Hanson's "guards" were young men of good Baltimore

families, and had earnest convictions but little common sense. They had decided to make a "stand for life" if another mob tried to attack Hanson, and planned to emulate Light-Horse Harry Lee's farmhouse defense near Valley Forge in 1778.

Whether the arrival of the old hero in Baltimore was coincidental or planned has never been determined. And whether he called on Hanson, which he did, to remonstrate with him and urge him to support the war, or to offer him moral encouragement is also unknown.

Only a few facts can be gleaned from the hysterical reports that were printed thereafter in the nation's press. Harry arrived at the house at approximately 7:00 P.M., and found it crowded with Hanson's "guards" and well-wishers who were welcoming him home. After chatting briefly with his host, Harry took his leave, but was forced back into the house by a gang of boys and young men who threw stones at him.

He immediately sent two of the guests out by way of a back door to notify the city authorities that a mob was gathering, and he requested, in his own name, that steps be taken to disperse the throng. Meanwhile the mob continued to grow. Hanson and several of his friends opened windows and exchanged insults with the crowd, and Harry was alarmed when Hanson declared he intended to fire a volley over the heads of the mob. Such action, the old soldier said, would be certain to precipitate a real riot.

The police did not appear, but the crowd continued to grow rapidly, and became more menacing. An unending shower of stones rattled against the walls, and nearly every window in the house was broken. The rumble of the crowd became menacing, and Harry realized the besieged men in the house could be in for real trouble.

He set about organizing their defenses until either the police or a company of militia came to disperse the throng, and showed his usual skill in placing the defenders in strategic places. He insisted, however, that no shots be fired unless the mob rushed the house, and Hanson reluctantly agreed.

Meanwhile the men who had been sent for help were encountering time-consuming difficulties. The signatures of three magistrates were required to call out a force of sufficient size to disperse a throng of the size that had now gathered, and before the legal amenities had been satisfied, the crowd acted.

At 10:30, or thereabouts, the mob tried to break down a door, and its defenders fired through the panel, deliberately aiming high, in an attempt to scare them off. The attackers retreated, the mob grew still more unruly and the siege entered a new phase. Several men raced off, returning a half-hour later with a small cannon and some iron shot. It was later charged that the gun and ammunition had been stolen from a state militia armory, but the issue was not pressed.

By midnight the defenders were literally fighting for their lives. The cannon had made several holes in the walls of the house, but the mob was still being kept at a distance, thanks to the singlehanded efforts of Harry, who hurried from one post to another and himself fired an occasional shot, with deadly accuracy, that sent the throng scurrying back to safety.

A short time before dawn a small detachment of Maryland dragoons arrived at the scene, but the troops, themselves only half-trained, were not capable of coping with the crowd, which now numbered well into the hundreds. The commander was able to make his way to the house, where he held a short discussion with Harry, promising he would do what he could to restore order and, above all, to protect the person of General Lee.

Soon after daybreak a larger militia force appeared, and with them came the mayor and several other officials. To Harry's astonishment, they refused to disperse the mob, now more than one thousand strong, and declared that the only solution of the problem was to arrest those in the house for disturbing the peace and then take them off to jail. Harry agreed, reluctantly, and the entire party was marched to the jail.

The mob was restrained with difficulty, and the militiamen, who formed a double line on each side of the prisoners, sympathized with the majority. Three or four of Hanson's friends were roughly treated before officers, moving up and down the line, were able to rescue them.

The day passed quietly, too quietly, and although the prisoners enjoyed the illusion of safety, they were uneasy. No formal charges had been made against them, and they were not called before a magistrate. Twice Harry demanded that they be charged or set free, but the militia officers paid no attention. They, like the members of the mob, called him, of all people, a "Tory" and "Redcoat."

There was no sign of a crowd outside, and in the afternoon the militia was withdrawn. The sheriff, a conscientious man, vainly appealed to both the militia and the city authorities for help, saying he and his few deputies could not cope with the situation if another mob formed.

Shortly after nightfall the attackers who had laid siege to the house reappeared, completely surrounding the jail. They were raucous, very noisy and obviously thirsting for blood. It soon became evident they intended to storm the building, and the sheriff, accompanied by his deputies, went out to plead with them. The mob refused to listen, swept the few officials aside and poured into the jail.

Escape seemed impossible, but Harry saw one chance. At his suggestion Hanson and the others blew out the candles that lighted their cells, and when the crowd broke down the doors, they tried to slip away in the dark. But their efforts proved futile, and Light-Horse Harry Lee stepped forward, alone.

His fellow citizens accomplished what no foreign enemy had ever been able to do. Harry was knocked to the ground, clawed and kicked. He was beaten with clubs and staves until he was unconscious, and then dozens of men trampled on him. Not one of the unfortunate prisoners escaped unharmed, but as Harry lay alone, his fate was worse than that of most of his companions. The scores of men who ran into the prison saw his crumpled body, and new blows were rained on him.

The mob assumed its victims were dead, but one man conceived the idea of jabbing the faces of the unconscious to "test" them. Those who moved or groaned were subjected to still more beatings. There is no precise record of how long the senseless torture lasted, but by the time the mob finally withdrew, there were several deep, jagged cuts on Harry's face, one shoulder was dislocated and he was suffering from severe internal injuries.

Several physicians had arrived at the scene, and the sheriff led them into the slaughterhouse after the mob withdrew. Two of Hanson's friends were dead, and the rest—about thirty-five in all—were unconscious. The injured men were taken off to the various Baltimore hospitals before a new mob could be formed.

Harry had been battered beyond recognition, and the physician who was treating him, a man named Hall, is alleged to have said, after working over him for more than a half-hour, "My God, this is General Lee!"

Drunken mobs were still roaming the streets, terrorizing passers-by, and most citizens retired behind the locked doors of their homes. The militia remained at its barracks on the outskirts of the city, its commanders later offering the lame excuse that no one had notified them there had been any violence.

The authorities at the hospital where Harry was being treated held a hurried conference. They were horrified by the outrage, and were afraid that their patient, one of the nation's most distinguished citizens, might be murdered if the mob learned he was still alive. In the early hours of the morning a carriage drew up at the hospital door, and the unconscious body of Harry was placed inside, two physicians climbing in with him. A volunteer posse of Baltimore gentlemen who had been rounded up during the night surrounded the coach. All were heavily armed, but it was not necessary for them to use violence. They left the city without attracting notice, and rode for the town of Little York, across the Pennsylvania border, reaching it soon after daybreak.

There, in a tiny hospital, attended day and night, Harry Lee fought against death, and his battle was perhaps the greatest and most difficult of his life. For a week the physicians were afraid he would not recover. But, on the seventh day after the attack, when Anne arrived at Little York after making arrangements for Mrs. Richard B. Lee to take care of the children in Alexandria, Harry opened his eyes and recognized her.

Four more days passed before he recovered the powers of speech. Anne spent two weeks with him, and Harry remained at the hospital until mid-September, when the physicians finally pronounced him sufficiently well to travel. He was still unable to walk, however, and internal pains were so intense he could sleep only in short snatches. One of the slashes on his face had become infected, and his eyesight was imperiled. He went home to the house in Alexandria an invalid, with a crippled body that would never be completely healed.

Harry knew nothing of the sensation that the senseless attack had created throughout the country. The first news reports had declared him dead, and newspapers everywhere had printed his obituary, the majority praising him in glowing terms. Only a few of the more rapidly Republican-Democratic papers tried to excuse the riots and the vicious mistreatment of helpless men.

The news that Harry was still alive created still more headlines, and when his carriage rumbled through Washington City, large crowds gathered to stare in silence at the drawn curtains. Still another crowd assembled at the house in Alexandria, but no one spoke or moved as the invalid was carried inside.

President Madison, ordinarily the most cautious of men, left no one in doubt of his feelings. Less than twenty-four hours after Harry's arrival he paid a call on his old friend and issued a public statement denouncing the rioters as "barbarians and hypocrites who have done nothing to advance our national cause, but instead spent their wrath on a citizen whom this nation will forever honor."

The name of Robert E. Lee first appeared in print on the occasion of the President's visit. The boy, four months short of his sixth birthday, was told by Madison, "Let your father's honor and matchless gallantry set an example that you will never forget."

The next day Secretary Monroe came to see Harry, and the following week a select committee of senators and congressmen paid him a visit. Members of both political parties were in the group. Anne tried to insure her husband as much privacy as possible while he recovered what he could of his strength, but the task was not easy. She could not turn away Mrs. Madison, who came twice weekly, nor Mrs. Monroe, nor the President— who appeared unannounced on several occasions, nor the many members of the Lee clan. One of the most welcome of the callers was Chief Justice Marshall, who read aloud to Harry from the current newspapers when he discovered that the invalid was still troubled by poor eyesight.

It is unlikely that Harry knew his relatives, friends and old associates, many of them now the most important men in the land, were paying him a final tribute. He remained optimistic, in spite of his ceaseless pain, and assured everyone that he would soon be completely well again. Those who believed otherwise did not disillusion him.

Anne was not fooled. *Each day he is a little stronger,* she wrote to Mrs. Richard Lee, *but only a little. I weep for him, but my tears will not cure him.*

XX

"BRAVE DEATH, WHEN PRINCES DIE WITH US"

By January 1813 the United States was compelled to face the fact that her Army was being commanded by incompetents and blunderers. The officers and men of the little Navy were performing near-miracles against almost superhuman odds, but the military establishment, although growing rapidly, was an almost formless body without a head.

Official eyes in Washington City turned in speculative wonder across the Potomac, and men in high places asked each other whether Harry Lee might be strong enough to take command in the near future. A desperate James Madison decided to find out, and formally offered Harry a commission as senior Major General of the Line, the highest rank in the Army.

Had the offer been received before the riot in Baltimore, Harry would have accepted instantly, in spite of his delicate bronchial condition. Now, however, he had learned to live with incapacitating pain, and had finally reached the point where he doubted that his recovery would ever be complete. Injuries sustained in a mindless attack by a savage mob forced him to reject the position he had long coveted above all others—and deprived his country of the talents of her most competent living soldier.

"Should I get well," he replied to the President, "I will cheerfully give you my assistance in the war wherever it may be deemed useful."

Any help from Harry Lee was better than none, and Madison took him at his word. At his request Harry prepared a series of recommendations on the disposition and realignment of troops, all of which were adopted and subsequently proved that the daring strategist-tactician of the Revolution had not lost his cunning. Whether the Army would have made a better showing had he been in command during the earlier years of the war before Andrew Jackson and other new leaders emerged is an interesting but unanswerable question.

The help Harry was able to give his country was limited by his physical condition, however, and he suffered severely from the damp cold of Alexandria in winter. His bronchial condition became aggravated by his other ailments, and the physicians again urged him to seek a warmer climate where he could recuperate at leisure.

Harry and Anne discussed the problem at length, and it was decided that he should travel alone. All of their children with the exception of their youngest, a baby daughter, were in school, and Anne was reluctant to uproot the entire family. Harry had just enough money to live abroad fairly comfortably while he regained his health, and during that time Anne and the children could live on her inheritance from her father and sister. Again Harry asked President Madison and Secretary Monroe for help, and his appeal was extraordinary.

He knew no Spanish, he said, and had forgotten most of the French he had learned. Therefore, even though the United States was at war with England, he wanted to go to a British possession in the Caribbean. Neither Madison nor Monroe thought the request unusual, and at the President's direction the Secretary of State opened negotiations with the enemy through third parties.

As it happened, Admiral Sir John Warren, the commander of the Royal Navy's North American fleet, with headquarters in Jamaica, was a student of military affairs who had been an admirer of Harry Lee. He could see no harm in allowing a man broken in health to rest beneath the Caribbean sun, even if he was an "enemy alien." Sir John granted permission for Harry to visit any West Indian island he wished except Jamaica.

The question of transportation was another stumbling block, but Monroe and Sir John overcame that obstacle, too. A Portuguese schooner was sailing from Quebec for Barbados, and the United States allowed the ship to put into Baltimore. Instructions were sent to both American and British men-of-war not to molest the merchantman on the high seas.

Virtually nothing is known of Harry's farewell to his family except that he said goodbye to them in Alexandria. Anne remained at home, and so did Charles, who would be leaving soon for college. Harry's children by his first marriage did not go to Baltimore to see him off, either. And although no one realized it at the time, he would not see his wife and family again. If relations between husband and wife were strained, their later correspondence did not reveal it. What did happen was that they drifted farther and farther apart. Anne became increasingly immersed in her children—while Harry spent his last years as, almost literally, a lost soul.

Initially he found Barbados much to his liking. He arrived there in the early spring of 1813, and the warm weather was all he had hoped it would be. He wrote a letter to President Madison in which he insisted he would soon be completely recovered. And, as a token of his appreciation, he sent the President some Madeira, a gift he could ill afford, and the largest live turtle he could locate in Bridgetown, the capital of Barbados. "When you and your lady dine on turtle stew," he declared a trifle wistfully, "I hope you will think of me."

The British in Barbados treated the convalescing alien enemy with every consideration, and he became friendly with Sir George Beckwith, the governor, who often invited him to dine at Government House. They found themselves in agreement on most phases of the war. The British would not be able to subdue the United States, which, in turn, would find it impossible to conquer Canada. As a matter of national principle Great Britain would not give up her self-assumed right to stop the ships of neutral nations on the high seas to search for deserters, but in practice Royal Navy vessels would not halt American merchantmen once peace was achieved. Both men proved to be accurate prophets.

Harry, with little to occupy him except reading, kept in touch with the news of the world, and predicted the fall of Napoleon. The British had been gaining valuable experience in their war against the master of the Continent, he said, and would beat him once they understood the principles of containing his cavalry. Had Napoleon been able to read Harry's letters to Secretary

Monroe on the subject, the outcome of the Battle of Waterloo might have been different.

By January 1814 sleepy Bridgetown had nothing more to offer the bored invalid, who still clung fiercely to the belief that he would regain his health. "I am getting well, and will soon be able to come home," he declared in a letter that he wrote to Monroe a short time before beginning his own version of a later era's sport, island-hopping.

Sir George granted him a passport and gave him a personal letter of introduction to the Spanish Governor-General of Puerto Rico, Don Salvadore Malendez. So Harry sailed to San Juan, in spite of his inability to speak Spanish. In less than six months, however, he was ready to leave, and had become so homesick that he insisted he was healthy again, even though the two English-speaking physicians in the Puerto Rican capital advised him not to travel north.

He applied to the Royal Navy for a safe conduct permit to travel to the United States, but times had changed during his fifteen-month sojourn in the Caribbean. Warren had returned to England, and the Royal Navy's American command was now divided between two admirals who were making strenuous efforts to blockade the entire American coast. The request was refused.

He began to travel, almost aimlessly, from island to island, trying in vain to find some way to lessen his pains and to conquer his all-encompassing boredom. In April 1815 he learned that the United States and Great Britain had signed a peace treaty, and he wrote warm letters of congratulations to Madison and Monroe.

Often he wrote to his family of returning home in the near future, but his feeble health made a long voyage impossible. So he wandered from Santo Domingo to Turks Island, to New Providence and Caicos and Nassau, vainly searching for a still better climate. He had grown very frail and thin, and a long scar on his face was an ever-present reminder of the Baltimore riot. On cool evenings his bronchial condition bothered him, and he coughed incessantly until the heat of the morning sun enabled him to breathe more easily. Two pains in his back, one of them "low, on the right side," and the other "about mid-back on the left side" kept him in constant torment.

He lived in lodging houses in the various small towns of the islands, as he was unable to afford better quarters, and in a sense it was fortunate that he had so little appetite, as his limited funds forced him to eat cheaply. Everywhere he went he was received pleasantly, and was entertained by officials and permanent residents. But his life was lonely, far lonelier than he dreamed possible, and he lived for the letters he received from home.

Often he complained to Anne and to Henry, Jr. that they wrote infrequently. They tried to keep up a brisk correspondence with him, but their lives were as busy as his appetite for mail was insatiable. Anne was trying to rear a family alone, and Henry, Jr., who had served his country with distinction in the War of 1812, was now holding his father's former seat in the United States House of Representatives.

At last Harry found an outlet for his emotions in Charles Carter Lee, who was now a student at Harvard. In long letters, seldom answered, Harry poured out advice that expressed his own philosophy of life. *"Encourage your love & practice of virtue,"* he wrote. *"Pursue learning so that you will fit yourself to be useful to your country and an ornament to your friends."*

A love of truth was a theme in almost all of the innumerable letters Harry sent to his son. *"It is the essence of virtue." "You know my abhorrence of lying, which leads to every vice." "Abhor deception." "Disdain the mean & infamous practice of telling untruths."*

"Dwell on the virtues," he declared in one particularly long letter, *"and imitate, so far as lies in your power, the great & good men whom history presents to your view—Lycurgus, Solon, Numa, Hannibal."*

He also quoted George Washington to his son: *"A man ought not only to be virtuous in reality, but he must also appear so."*

Riding a horse at a wild canter and simultaneously striking a target with a pistol or carbine shot were *"agreeable, useful and manly pastimes, but secondary always to the pursuit of knowledge."*

In the realm of philosophy he repeatedly urged Charles to study the works of John Locke, the spiritual father of the American Revolution. *"Consult him,"* he said, *"as the Grecians did the Delphic oracle."*

The man who dispensed advice now resembled a heavily suntanned derelict. He, who had once been so conscious of his appearance, was still wearing the clothes he had brought to the Caribbean from Virginia. They were worn, and some were actually threadbare, but he could not afford a new wardrobe. He tried to pretend he no longer cared, but in a letter to Anne, written in the spring of 1817 when he was longing to return home and trying to find passage from Nassau on a ship bound for Virginia, he said, "*I am reduced to only one remaining hat, of cream-colored felt, which you gave me on my last birthday before my departure. I know the need of making a presentable appearance when I return home, which I pray shall be soon, so I go bareheaded here in order to preserve my hat.*"

Ships did put into Nassau that would have taken Harry to New York or Boston, the principal ports of commerce in the West Indian trade, but he was too ill to travel overland any considerable distance after landing, and therefore waited for a ship that would drop him at Baltimore, the closest major port of call to Alexandria. In February 1818 he met an American merchant master who intended to put into Norfolk, and he immediately bought passage on the ship. His ticket, plus the cask of Madeira wine he bought to bring home with him, virtually exhausted his funds.

The voyage was a quiet one, in calm seas, but Harry was so exhausted that he was unable to leave his bunk to see a squadron of American warships off the coast of the Floridas or to go ashore at Savannah, where some of the brig's cargo was landed. Fourteen miles north of the town was Mulberry Grove, where the widow of General Nathanael Greene and her family lived on an estate called Dungeness, Harry asked the master of the ship to put him ashore there, saying he could travel no farther and would surely die if forced to spend another night at sea.

The master obliged, Harry was lowered into the ship's boat and rowed to the Dungeness wharf, where two sailors carried him ashore. Word was sent to the greathouse of the unexpected arrival of General Greene's companion-in-arms, and Mrs. Greene immediately sent a carriage to the dock, as Harry was too weak to walk or ride a horse. The Greene family gave the dying Light-Horse Harry a hero's welcome, put him in a guest room and assigned a servant to take care of him.

Word spread through the area that General Harry Lee was at Dungeness, and the Army garrison at Savannah promptly set up a rotating schedule so that two officers were present at the greathouse at all times. A small ship from the squadron off the Florida coast carried the news to Commodore J. D. Henly, who sailed to Dungeness and also assigned two officers to duty at the estate.

A Naval surgeon attended Harry, but it was too late for medication. Mrs. Greene sent a letter to Anne, at Alexandria, but it did not arrive in time. Light-Horse Harry Lee died in his sleep late in the afternoon of March 25, 1818.

He was given a full military funeral at Dungeness, with Commodore Henly and two brigadier generals of the Army in attendance. The coffin was escorted by an honor guard of Marines from the frigate, *John Adams*, an Army band from the Savannah garrison played appropriate music and the pallbearers were Army officers in full-dress uniform. The service was performed by the local Anglican minister, the Reverend J. W. Taylor, and the Marines fired thirteen salvos, the correct salute to a major general. Then, as the cannon of the squadron boomed thirteen times, Harry's body was lowered into a grave beside that of Nathanael Greene.

No relatives attended the funeral, and none of Harry's old friends or Army associates were there, either. Anne, busy at home, postponed a visit to Georgia, then postponed it again—and again. Henry, Jr. was a very busy man, Lucy had a life of her own with her family in Philadelphia, and Charles was at school at Harvard.

Charles had saved the letters his father had sent him, and later they were devoured by the youngest of Harry's sons, Robert Edward, who memorized long passages and took every word to heart. He, who scarcely remembered his father, wanted most to emulate him.

Not until 1862 did any member of the immediate family visit Light-Horse Harry Lee's last resting place. In that year, General Robert E. Lee, commander of the Confederate Armies and standing on the climactic threshold of a career that would bring him greater glory and fame than his father had ever achieved, laid a wreath on the grave and stood for a long time staring down at it. Aides who waited for him as he left the cemetery said that the imperturbable general's cheeks were wet.

Bibliography

Manuscripts

Greene, Nathanael, Correspondence (New York Public Library)
Hamilton, Alexander, Correspondence (Library of Congress)
Knox, Henry, Papers (Massachusetts Historical Society)
Lee, Henry, Personal Papers (Library of Congress)
Lee, Robert E., Private Papers (Library of Congress)
Madison, James, Correspondence (Library of Congress)
Morgan, Daniel, Correspondence (New York Public Library)
Monroe, James, Papers (New York Public Library)
Washington, George, Correspondence (Library of Congress)

Books

Abernathy, T. P., *Western Lands and the American Revolution,* New York, 1930.
Adams, James Truslow, *The Living Jefferson,* New York, 1936.
Adams, John Quincy, *The Life and Character of James Madison,* Boston, 1816.

Bernardo, C. J., and Bacon, E. H., *American Military Policy and Its Development Since 1775,* Harrisburg, 1955.
Beveridge, Albert J., *The Life of John Marshall,* Boston, 1916 (2 vols.).
Beverley, Robert, *History and Present State of Virginia,* Chapel Hill, 1947.
Bowers, Claude J., *Jefferson and Hamilton,* Boston, 1925.
Boyd, Thomas, *Lighthorse Harry Lee,* New York, 1931.
Brackenridge, Hugh H., Jr., *Notes on the Whisky Insurrection,* Pittsburgh, 1857.
Bruce, P. A., History of Virginia, Chicago, 1924 (vols. 1–3).

Callahan, North, *Henry Knox,* New York, 1958.
Campbell, Charles, *History of the Colony and Ancient Dominion of Virginia,* Philadelphia, 1860.
Carr, Albert Z., *The Coming of War,* New York, 1960.
Clark, Allen C., *Life and Letters of Dolly Madison,* New York, 1914.
Coleman, R. V., *Liberty and Property,* New York, 1951.

Collins, Varnum L., *Princeton*, New York, 1924.
Custis, G. W. P., *Recollections and Private Memoirs of Washington*, New York, 1860.

Dos Passos, John, *The Men Who Made the Nation*, New York, 1957.
Drake, Francis S., *Henry Knox*, Boston, 1873.
Duckworth, Homer R., *Land! The Great American Dream*, New York, 1924.

Edwards, Howard, *Lee's Legion; a Military Analysis*, Boston, 1899.
Elliott, F. S., *Western Lands: the Gamblers and the Settlers*, New York, 1903.

Forney, John W., *Anecdotes of Public Men*, New York, 1873.
Freeman, Douglas S., *R. E. Lee*, New York, 1934 (4 vols.).
————, *George Washington*, New York, 1951 (8 vols.).

Gibbs, George, *Memoirs of the Administrations of Washington and John Adams*, New York, 1846 (2 vols.).
Greene, G. W., *Life of Major General Nathanael Greene*, New York, 1871.

Hartley, Cecil B., *Life of Major General Henry Lee*, Philadelphia, 1859.
Henry, William W., *Patrick Henry*, New York, 1891.
Hunt, Gaillard, *The Life of James Madison*, New York, 1902.

James, William, *Military Occurrences of the Late War Between Great Britain and the United States*, New York, 1820.
Jensen, Merrill, *The New Nation; a History of the United States During the Confederation, 1781–9*, New York, 1950.
Jernegan, Marcus W., *The American Colonies*, New York, 1930.
Johnson, William, *Sketches of the Life and Correspondence of Nathanael Greene*, Charleston, 1822 (2 vols.).

Koch, Adrienne, *Jefferson and Madison, the Great Collaboration*, New York, 1950.

Lancaster, Bruce, *From Lexington to Liberty*, New York, 1955.
Lee, Edmund J., *Lees of Virginia*, Philadelphia, 1895.
Lee, George, *The Lee Family of Virginia; a Notebook*, Richmond, 1827.

Lee, Henry, *A Correct Account of the Conduct of the Baltimore Mob*, Winchester, Va., 1814 (ostensibly written by Light-Horse Harry Lee himself, this short book was actually written by an anonymous author using information supplied by General Lee).

——, *Memoirs of the War in the Southern Department of the United States*, Philadelphia, 1812; later edition, edited by Robert E. Lee, New York, 1870.

Lee, Henry, Jr., *The Campaign of 1781 in the Carolinas*, Philadelphia, 1824.

Marshall, John, *The Life of George Washington*, Philadelphia, 1850.

Morgan, George, *The Life of James Monroe*, Boston, 1921.

Osgood, Herbert L., *The American Colonies in the Eighteenth Century*, New York, 1924.

Parton, James, *The Life and Times of Thomas Jefferson*, Boston, 1894.

Pratt, Julius W., *Expansionists of 1812*, New York, 1925.

Pyle, David F., *The Baltimore Riots; a Study of Mob Rule*, Boston, 1903.

Ramsey, David, *History of South Carolina*, Charleston, 1809.

Rivers, William J., *A Sketch of the History of South Carolina*, Charleston, 1856.

Roberts, E. E., *The Great Cavalry Duel: Lieutenant Colonel Lee and Lieutenant Colonel Tarleton*, Philadelphia, 1886.

——, *Nathanael Greene: a Study of Command*, Philadelphia, 1889.

Sargent, Nathan, *Public Men and Events*, New York, 1875.

Schachner, Nathan, *Alexander Hamilton*, 1946.

——, *Thomas Jefferson*, New York, 1951.

Smith, Mrs. S. H., *The First Forty Years of Washington Society*, New York, 1906.

Sparks, Jared, *Correspondence of the American Revolution*, Boston, 1853 (4 vols.).

Sullivan, William, *Familiar Letters on Public Characters and Public Events*, Philadelphia, 1834.

Sumner, William H., *An Inquiry into the Importance of the Militia*, Boston, 1823.

Tarleton, Banastre, *History of the Campaigns of 1780 and 1781 in the Southern Provinces*, Dublin, 1787.

Turner, F. J., *The Significance of Sections in American History*, New York, 1932.

Tyler, Moses C., *Patrick Henry*, Boston, 1887.

Umbreit, Kenneth B., *The Founding Fathers*, New York, 1931.

Washington, George, *Diaries*, Boston, 1925.

Winsor, Justin, A *Narrative and Critical History of America*, Boston, 1887 (8 vols.).

Newspapers

Alexandria Gazette
Baltimore Federal Republican
Boston Gazette
Boston Herald
Gazette of the United States
National Gazette
National Intelligencer
New England Chronicle
New York Advertiser
New York Gazette
Pennsylvania Gazette
Pennsylvania Ledger
Richmond Enquirer
Virginia Gazette
Washington Federalist

INDEX